No Gods
and Precious Few
Heroes

Scotland since 1914

No Gods
and Precious Few
Heroes

Scotland since 1914

Christopher Harvie

Edinburgh University Press

© Christopher Harvie, 1981

First published 1981 in The New History of Scotland by Edward Arnold
(Publishers) Ltd
and reprinted with corrections and additions 1987
New edition 1993 by
Edinburgh University Press
22 George Square, Edinburgh

Printed and bound in Great Britain by Bell & Bain Ltd, Glasgow.

A CIP record for this book is available from the British Library

ISBN 0 7486 0387 5

To Virginia

Contents

Introduction to the Edinburgh edition

I have taken advantage of the change of publisher of the New History of Scotland to update the text more generously than was possible in the 1987 reprint. While constrained by the need to retain the original plates, I have been able to revise the tables, correct errors and alter some interpretations, and add a longish final section covering the 1980s, an extended bibliography and an up-to-date chronology and index. On the whole, I think that most of the judgements that I made in 1981 still hold good, even where there was a hunch-like element about them. This wasn't the result of any sagacity on my part, but of keeping an ear open for the talk of my historian colleagues, and guessing where their enquiries might lead them. The fact that the rubric 'place of publication is London except where otherwise stated' has vanished from the post-1987 bibliography is a tribute to them and the renaissance in Scottish publishing. Among others who have helped as hosts and informants over the last decade, I'd like to thank in particular Kenneth Morgan, Tom Gallagher, Graham Walker, William Storrar, Jay Brown, Hamish Fraser, James Mitchell and Jim Treble. And not least those friends in Scotland, writers and artists, whose verve and originality has diffused much of the miasmatic pessimism which enveloped my original introduction. We may not have reached our Indies – yet – but there are absorbing places *en route*, and we now have the energy to see them.

Christopher Harvie
Tübingen, May 1992

Introduction

> I do not wish to discuss now if what was done was good or bad; for my part I believe much of it to have been bad; but I'd like to tell you at once what you'll only understand after spending a year among us.
>
> G. Tomasi di Lampedusa, *The Leopard* (1958).

From the other edge of the European periphery, Sicily, the Prince of Salina's words to the Piedmontese envoy, Chevalley, echo, oddly but appositely, at the beginning of a history of modern Scotland, both in their statement of intention and in their subject-matter. The writer of a textbook must of course exercise selectivity: principles for this are necessarily subjective ones. Yet the book ought not to be an exercise in intellectual autobiography; personality and opinions must not obtrude, concealing or distorting evidence to further a case. The reader, like Chevalley, must gain a picture that corresponds in its general contours as much as possible to the reality of 'life as lived', in which the features are noted and discussed commensurately with their importance. 'Reality' may be a question-begging phrase, but statistics of agricultural production, and sequences of political events are not. If the index does not yield a basic range of factual information about such matters, the book is not serving its proper purpose.

Yet any landscape is seen from a point of view, and subjectivity accentuates particular features. My standpoint, like that of Salina, is a sombre, critical one. I leave it to the reader to determine whether this pessimism is justified, as it has informed the structure of the book. In my chapter-divisions — the largely chronological treatment of World War I, and then four parallel chapters on economy, society, politics, and culture, covering 1922–64, ending with a further chronological account of 1964–80 — I have necessarily accentuated the theme of Scotland's industrial stagnation and eventual decline: from being by any standards a substantial world industrial power in 1914 to its present insecurity and insignificance. But ought I, perhaps, to have stressed the advance in living standards of the mass of Scots people that has, apparently paradoxically, accompanied this process?

I believe not. This advance has been common to all West European nations, and in most of them has been much more rapid than in Scotland, where until the late 1950s similarities to the pre-1914 era were probably greater than to Sweden or Switzerland. The expansion in well-being has been recent, and looks like being short-lived, while the industrial base remains in decay. It has, moreover, benefited only 77 per cent of those born in Scotland since 1911, the rest having emigrated. In 1911 Sweden's population was only 16 per cent greater than Scotland's; by 1970 this margin had widened to 55 per cent. Swedish gross domestic product per head was barely half that of Scotland in 1911: about £32 against about £62. By 1970 it was £1,812 against £709.

By such standards, Scotland's twentieth-century performance has been grim. If those excluded from the beanfeast of nineteenth-century capitalism — the working class, for example, and women — have been let into the restaurant at last, they have found a cleared table and a decrepit kitchen, and have lacked the organizational experience or cohesive ability to do much about this.

Lampedusa's Prince characterized his Sicily as punch-drunk, crippled by climate and recurrent invasions, a country that could only be a senile spectator of the nineteenth-century industrial world. It was the perceptive comment of a man — Lampedusa himself — drawn from an older stratum of society yet powerfully affected by the main current of twentieth-century thought, Marxism. But it was fundamentally pessimistic: modern industrialization and class-formation were too much for the ingrained traditions of the country; and qualities of consciousness, however perceptive, were not enough to combat this; the intellectuals solved their problems by moving out. If there can be little quarrel with this analysis of one type of decadence, then something analagous to it applies only too accurately to Scotland: two centuries of industrialization have done the work of 2,500 years of Sicilian subjugation. Perhaps now, when the motor of industrial change seems to have worn out, leaving a talented intelligentsia, footloose and ambitious, and otherwise a politics constricted by class-barriers and persistent economic and political failure, the same words are apt: 'In Sicily it doesn't matter about doing things well or badly; the sin which we Sicilians never forgive is simply that of "doing" at all'. In the seven years that have succeeded the anticlimax of devolution this reaction seems to have prevailed: stasis has united unionist and nationalist alike.

So, if I am to admit to a point of view — largely acquired during writing, not a previous conviction — it is this: that the strength of the nationalist case and the weakness of nationalist politics are facets of the same issue. Nationalists have, I think, been less wrong about the Scottish economy than anyone else; on the other hand their gloomy diagnosis of its problems has to include the failure of Scottish society to sustain credible alternatives to restrictive class-loyalties and mediocre personnel, and to a secretive bureaucracy. A structure of distinctive Scots corporations — church, education, law, local and devolved administration — has effectively transformed organic discontent into a sequence of manageable complaints. By contrast, nationalist political organization, without an identifiable 'foreign' presence to react against, and usually milked of its talent by UK institutions, has always proved inherently unstable. MacDiarmid's words:

> To prove my saul is Scots I maun begin
> Wi' what's still deemed Scots and the folk expect,
> And spire up syne by visible degrees
> To heichts whereo' the fules ha'e never recked

suggest incipient lack of control as well as enlightenment — something evident in the history of nationalist politics as well as in his own remarkable career. There is much here that resembles the condition of *anomie* diagnosed by Emile Durkheim — self-destructive violence which follows the collapse of accepted social norms — and it is all the more intense because the norms that are collapsing are those, not of pre-industrial society, as in Durkheim's day, but of industrial society itself.

European nationalism, at least of the liberal sort on which Scottish nationalism has modelled itself, was seen as an instrument that assisted economic development while preserving social cohesion. Scottish nationalists have attempted, almost uniquely, to use their politics and community-centred ideals as a means of mitigating economic decline. If they have so far failed in this task, they can at least console themselves with the fact that the institutions of the UK have been no more successful.

I may have offered my nationalist friends a backhanded compliment, but that is simply a necessary personal statement. As an

historian, my business is not to prescribe political solutions, nor to con-
vey reassurance about the past, but to 'tell it like it happened', and not
flinch from Thomas Hardy's injunction: 'If way to the better there be,
it exacts a full look at the worse'.

Acknowledgements

I would like to thank the staff of Edinburgh University Library, the
Open University Library, the Mitchell Library, Glasgow, and the
National Library of Scotland, the Public Record Office, Kew, and the
Scottish Record Office, Edinburgh, for their aid in securing access to
papers in their custody, and the *Scotsman*, in which sections of
chapter 1 originally appeared. My former colleagues David Englander
and Angus Calder at the Open University, and Hans-Werner Ludwig
of Tübingen commented on parts of the draft. Jenny Wormald and
Christopher Smout read through all of it. For their comments,
encouragement, and advice I am most grateful. Much of the research
for the book was done while I was Visiting Fellow at the School of
Advanced Studies, Edinburgh University, during the winter of
1978—9, and I am greatly indebted to Professor William Beattie and
Margaret Jardine for their hospitality. Tom Nairn, Neal Ascherson,
Gordon Brown, and Stephen Maxwell helped me kick ideas about, in
the interstices of the devolution campaign and Ian MacDougall's
splendid *Labour Records in Scotland* could not have been more
timely. My parents not only sustained me beyond the call of duty but
had to undergo frequent interrogations about their experience of
recent Scottish history; so too did my friends Chris and Bob
MacWhirter. My debt to their daughter, Julie Brotherstone, for her
friendship and enthusiasm, cannot now be repaid. Her death early in
1981, after a brave struggle with a crippling illness, leaves all who
knew her the poorer. Ethel Kriger and Birte Gräper of the University
of Tübingen typed much of the manuscript. My wife Virginia, besides
making a home for me in three countries, cast a helpful eye over the
proofs and organized the index. My gratitude to everyone. I hope the
result justifies their efforts.

Christopher Harvie
Tübingen

The title of this book, No Gods and Precious Few Heroes, *is taken from
Hamish Henderson's 'First Elegy', and is used by his kind permission.*

1

'When the Lamps Went Out'
1911 – 1922

I

In the summer of 1911 Glasgow hosted its third great exhibition. Elaborate Scottish vernacular buildings, in Kelvingrove Gardens, emphasized its 'patriotic and educational' aim of endowing a Chair of Scottish History at the University of Glasgow. Its predecessors of 1888 and 1901 had been cosmopolitan. Nationalism was now in the air. The Liberals, confirmed in power largely by the Scots in 1910, were about to legislate on Irish Home Rule; their Scottish Federation was committed to Scottish devolution. The 60-year schism in the Church was on the point of being healed; the land system was being reformed; Gaelic culture had been popularized by William Sharp, Marjory Kennedy Fraser, and Hugh Roberton's Orpheus Choir. Art and architecture, in the age of Rennie Mackintosh, John Burnet, the Glasgow Boys, and the Scottish Colourists, were both distinctive and internationally respected.

But was there a spectre at the feast? Between 1906 and 1908 the Clyde's output of ships slumped to 50 per cent of its 1905 tonnage. In 1910 and 1911 American competition cut the dividends of the North British Locomotive Company to 5 per cent instead of an anticipated 10 per cent. By 1913 German steel was being unloaded on the Clyde at under the Scottish cost of production. Such developments were ominous for an economy in which eight staple industries — in order of numbers employed: agriculture, coal-mining, shipbuilding and engineering, textiles, building, steel and fishing — produced about 60 per cent of its output.

Yet the Scottish economy was more than a specialized sector of the UK economy. It was disproportionately large for a start. With 10.5 per cent of the UK population, it produced 12.5 per cent of UK output. Its consumer goods industries still made distinctive furniture, pottery, and footwear; English mass-production and food processing still had

1

to contend with the factories of the Co-operative movement. Scottish housing, whether two-roomed stone-built tenement flats, farm steadings, or miners' rows, was quite different from the two-storey brick cottages of England and was (as a Royal Commission was shortly to find out) much, much worse.

Yet Scots workers were, on the whole, better off. Only 1.8 per cent of those insured in 1913 were unemployed, against 8.7 per cent in London. More of them were skilled; possibly 80 per cent in Glasgow, mainly in the metal trades, and large groups in the printing, brewing, and papermaking trades of Edinburgh. Craft pride was reflected in an 'independence of mind', shared also by 150,000 miners and a like number of farmworkers. New tendencies, however, were appearing. In Aberdeen socialism had grown since the 1890s. In Dundee, virtually a single-industry town, whose huge jute-mills were facing increased Indian competition, there had been a Labour MP since 1910. In 1909 the miners' unions had affiliated to the Labour Party, and in 1911 and 1912 severe strikes in the docks, the mines, and on the railways seemed to indicate growing social polarization.

Agriculture and Fisheries

In 1910 agriculture, the fulcrum of modernization of Scottish society in the eighteenth century, contributed 17.2 per cent of UK output. Highly-capitalized mixed farms on the east coast contrasted with subsistence crofting in the Highlands. Rents had fallen by 30 per cent since the 1870s, but by diversifying into cattle and livestock, feedstuffs and pasture — in 1910 they grazed 15 per cent of Britain's cattle and 30 per cent of her sheep — Scottish farmers had fared well. However neither landowners nor substantial tenant farmers felt happy about the Agriculture (Scotland) Act, passed, after five years of struggle, in 1911. Although it set up a Board of Agriculture, it exemplified the Liberal party's commitment to the ideal of a free peasantry, by extending the rights of security of tenure and rent control enjoyed by 27,000 Highland crofters to a further 28,000 Lowland small farmers, permitting the creation of new holdings and the consolidation of existing ones.

Scottish fisheries had likewise been transformed into a major food-producing industry. In 1905 Scottish landings were valued at £2.7m., or 25.5 per cent of the UK total (over 33 per cent if Scottish landings in England are included). In 1911 fishing employed 34,390 men and boys, 25 per cent down on 1893. Productivity, though, had grown as steam trawlers and drifters had replaced sailing boats, and new rail-heads on the west coast enabled more efficient marketing. Besides the men, up to 50,000 women were also seasonally employed onshore, or followed the herring fleet round the coast in its annual migration to the East Anglian fisheries. Of its catch, 85 per cent went for export.

Textiles

Textiles, the motor of early industrialization, had coped with market changes and relative decline. In 1905 cotton was only 1.4 per cent of UK production, and woollens only 8.7. Linen, at 14 per cent, was established in small towns along the east coast, centred on Dundee and Dunfermline, while Dundee had an almost complete monopoly of British jute manufacture — and indeed consumed about a third of the jute imported into Europe. Its greatest days had been in the 1870s, but its magnates often owned and managed its Calcutta rivals. Foreign competition in other textiles was met by a variety of responses. In Paisley J.&P. Coats and J.&J. Clark amalgamated in 1896, to create a monopoly in thread-spinning. Other firms drew on this technology to expand the machine-weaving of lace in North Ayrshire. Woollens — chiefly based in the Borders and the Hillfoots area — tackled Yorkshire competition by concentrating on high-quality products, and carpet manufacturing, in Glasgow, Bonnyrigg, and Kilmarnock, proved an important development. All the textile industries were dominated by exports, chiefly to Europe and North America.

Heavy Industry

Exports also underwrote heavy industry — coal, iron and steel, shipbuilding, mechanical and structural engineering — concentrated in the Clyde basin and the Lanarkshire and Ayrshire coalfields. But the rich mineral endowment of these fields — nearly two-thirds of Scottish coal production in 1913 — was now within sight of exhaustion. Growth was switching to the large new mines of Fife and the Lothians, dominated by Sir Adam Nimmo's equally large Fife and Lothian coal companies, and to the fast growing trade — 10m. out of 14m. tons exported — with east Europe. This caused big port developments at Leith in 1903, Grangemouth in 1906, and Methil in 1907. The Scottish miner was efficient, producing an eighth more than the UK average, partly because of the electric coal cutter, pioneered by Anderson, Boyes of Motherwell. By 1913 this accounted for 21.9 per cent of output.

Coal exports — a reversal to primary production — were a disturbing sign, particularly as iron-smelting, a major market, was declining along with reserves of Lanarkshire 'blackband' ironstone. In 1913 this met only 25 per cent of Scottish demand, and, with obsolete plant, pig-iron output fell. Steel-makers had to use imported pig and scrap and, badly undercapitalized, lacked the modern equipment of Cleveland and South Wales, where 'hot metal' flowed from blast to steel furnace. In 1884 they produced 50 per cent of UK output; by 1913 only 33 per cent.

Shipbuilding, however, was at its zenith. The slump of 1906−8 shaken off, Clyde yards set a record of 757,000 tons and 1,111,000 horse-power of marine engines in 1913 (respectively 33.4 per cent and 49 per cent of the UK total), when all Germany produced only 646,000 tons and 776,000 horse-power.

Although the naval race had increased warship production, this still accounted for only about 10 per cent of total output. More worrying was the Clyde's lag in adopting the new technology of turbines, diesel engines, and welding, and its dependence on orders from Scottish shipowners, who then controlled 4.5m. tons, 27 per cent of the UK fleet.

Engineering, with an output valued in 1913 at £16m. and a workforce of 78,000, involved a wide range of industries — locomotives and rolling stock (where Glasgow had about a third of total British capacity), hydraulic equipment, steam engines, cranes, pumps, prefabricated buildings, and all sorts of structural work. The huge Singer plant at Clydebank, employing over 10,000, the Acme wringer factory, and Barr and Stroud optical instrument factory were evidence that it included more than heavy industry, but the latter firms set the tone: their capital was low, their individual orders small, they relied on a skilled workforce rather than on rationalized production. Innovation wasn't lacking — with Pilcher and Denny's work on aeronautics, Burt's invention of the sleeve-valve engine, and Anderson's electric coal-cutter — but Scottish companies depended heavily on exports. The North British Locomotive Company, sending 48 per cent of its engines to the colonies, and 16 per cent to foreign markets, was probably fairly typical. Increased foreign competition and glutted markets (partly owing to improved engineering efficiency which lessened replacement orders) caused problems. The 'NB Loco's' sagging dividends were one aspect, Beardmore's were another. The greatest engineering conglomerate on Clydeside, it had to be bailed out in 1903 by Vickers, yet its dynamic managing director, William Beardmore, continually broke free of Sheffield tutelage, with attempts at diversification that were imaginative and innovative, but rarely profitable, even after the boost offered by the naval race after 1906. And financial and legal troubles bedevilled and ultimately ended Scotland's pioneer venture into volume car production, the Argyll Motor Company, which went into liquidation in 1912.

Money and Power·

The free market was crucial to pre-war industry. Shipbuilders still haggled with their workers, suppliers, and customers; Glasgow iron dealers still established world prices. Clydeside, and after it the whole Scottish economy, reacted sensitively to fluctuations in world trade and in the shipping freight market. Its great firms were family concerns; their values usually artificially low. Weir's of Cathcart, pump manufacturers, were worth only £60,000 in 1913; Colvilles, the Lanarkshire steel giant, only £280,000 in 1918. Amalgamation and joint-stock companies were still fairly rare — railways accounted for almost three-quarters of the money invested in Scottish industrial joint-stock companies in 1908 — although the North British Locomotive Company, created as a public company by the fusing of the three family firms of Neilson Reid, Sharp Stewart, and Dubs in 1903, with a capital of £2m., a workforce of 10,000, and the second largest locomotive building capacity in the world, was a portent.

In terms of power there seemed to be three Scotlands: the countryside where the gentry held sway; Edinburgh; and Glasgow, culturally further apart from one another than either was from London. Edinburgh was still dominated by an upper caste of the 'old professions' — law, religion, and finance — parasitical on the gentry and to an increasing extent on business, yet keeping the latter at arm's length. (As late as the 1960s the Glasgow Croesus Hugh Fraser was regarded by members of the New Club as 'a mere draper'.) More realistic, though badly flawed, were the plutocrats of the West and Dundee. Energetic, imaginative, and a bit vulgar, they had Corots hanging alongside Faeds in their lobbies, and steam yachts on the Clyde. The fathers had sacrificed everything to technical and economic success; their sons were more ambivalent. They might stick on in the business and marry into other industrial dynasties, like the Bilslands, Colvilles, Weirs, and Lithgows. Or shift from industry into finance, as did many a Dundee jute baron. Or sell out and move into genteel society, like the Tennants or the Clarks. Campbell-Bannerman was one of the few to choose parliamentary politics, for which the mid-nineteenth-century Scottish bourgeoisie had little time — although industralists seem to have absorbed themselves more and more in civic affairs, often to the detriment of their enterprises. Was the 'Westminster carpet-bagger' a response to this abstention? Or was the real inhibiting factor in political life the rigidity of the Edinburgh governing caste? Yet such a union of finance and industry was necessary if the autonomy of Scottish capitalism was to be preserved.

Uncertainty was not confined to the wealthy. Skilled craftsmen, the backbone of the heavy industrial workforce, felt increasingly threatened by new machinery and an expanding labour supply. More women were working, and more boys, who could be sacked on reaching adulthood. For many small-scale industries, facing foreign competition, this was a desperate remedy, but even in the shipyards and engineering shops, pneumatic and self-acting tools were being advocated by employers who had seen their competitors' works in Germany and America, while miners faced competition from immigrant labour, after 1900 from Poland and Lithuania rather than from Ireland.

II Pre-war Politics

Political Scotland existed on two distinct levels: parliamentary and civic. In nineteenth-century England parliamentary elections had supplied the citizenry, in John Vincent's words, with 'the circuses of their lives'. The Scotland of Gladstone's Midlothian Campaign was more serious, but the idea of politics as social drama was even more deeply entrenched. Parliamentary politics were about status, citizenship, religious equality, and, less sublimely, patronage. 'Constructive' legislation played a small part, but the cast was a high-grade one, and Scottish connections abounded. In 1910 nearly a third of the Liberal cabinet were Scots or sat for Scots seats. The prime minister, Asquith, sat for East Fife and had married into the Tennant family of Scots chemical magnates. Balfour and Campbell-Bannerman, his predecessors, had both been Scots; so were the Unionist and Labour leaders Bonar Law and Keir Hardie, and Labour's ambitious secretary Ramsay MacDonald.

Yet there seemed little organic connection between Scottish affairs and Westminster politics. 'Lads o'pairts', moving south to politics and the civil service, passed front-benchers moving north to comfortable and undemanding Scots constituencies – Liberal front-benchers, that is. Although the split over Irish home rule in 1886 had weakened the post-1832 Liberal hegemony in Scotland, it was restored in 1906, and extended at both elections of 1910, even though these saw English Liberal seats fall from 309 to 189.

In 1910 there were 779,000 electors and 72 constituencies, plus three University seats. Voting was by ratepayers, so sons living

Table 1.1: Scotland: Numbers employed in main occupations, 1907—1989 (in thousands)

	1907	1924	1935	1951	1976	1989
Agric. and Fisheries (incl. farmers)	*237* (1901)	*220*	*203*	*167*	*84*	*61*
Mining (Energy in 1989)	132	150	94	120	35	57
Manufacturing total:	622	485	420	767	608	403
Iron and Steel	{ 231 }	61	52	66	39 } { 211 }	
Engineering		130	98	293	258 }	
Textiles	141	122	114	123	57 } { 192 }	
Food & Drink	71	59	66	96	91 }	
Other Manuf.	179	113	90	189	163 }	
Construction	81	64	44	136	171	130
Remaining occupied pop. (mainly in service indust.)		c.402	c.609	1,011	1,208	1,436
Total occupied pop.	(1,982 in 1901)	*1,321* (1923)	*1,370* (1936)	2,201	2,106	1,957 (+ 400 part-time)
Unemployment rate (as % of insured employees)	(3.7 UK)	14.3	21.3	3.1	6.9	10.4
UK unemployment rate		(11.6) '23	(15.3)	(1.5) '50	(5.7)	(6.3)

Note: Estimated figures in italic
Sources: 1907–35 from Census of Production; on agriculture and fisheries from *Scotland's Industrial Future* (1939); 1951 from Cairncross, ed., *The Scottish Economy* (1953) and 1976 from Department of Employment statistics. The total for 1901 is taken from the census returns, and is not comparable with the other totals.

at home and most lodgers were effectively excluded, while businessmen had two votes. Such inequalities may have accounted for the
conservatism of Scottish politics; they probably allowed Scottish
Unionism to survive. It was only really healthy in the south-west and in
a few city suburbs. The ascendancy it had briefly gained in the central
belt, by recruiting the Orange vote, and (in 1900) the Catholics as
well, was curbed by the end of disestablishment as a political issue
(which neutralized the Church of Scotland) and the unpopularity of
Tariff Reform in an exporting area.

The Liberals could draw on a solid tradition of support in east-coast
burghs and counties and in the Highlands, where what the young Tory
candidate John Buchan called their 'tribal incantations' of free trade,
religious equality, and land reform still resounded. Provosts and local
solicitors were still the power-brokers, the 'New Liberalism' seemed
distant, and, unlike England, there had been no concordat between
Liberals and Labour in 1906. What, then, caused Liberalism's continued success? Hostility to the aristocracy seems a plausible explanation in the counties, and the 'causes' of the People's Budget, the
Parliament Act, and the Pentland Land Act are consonant with this.
But in the towns? Old sectarian loyalties remained powerful, but
waters were moving disturbingly under the ice. The Miners'
Federation affiliated to the Labour Party in 1909. Labour gained
three seats — West Fife, Dundee, and Glasgow Blackfriars — in
1910. A lot of the idealism which, in England, went into the New
Liberalism, was passing into heterodox but interlinked radical
groupings, from the home-rulers of the Young Scots to the 10,000-odd
readers (mainly Independent Labour Party) of Tom Johnston's
Forward, while the government attempted to conciliate trade unionism by reforming its legal status, and setting up Royal Commissions
into housing and railways. By 1914, in response to union and woman
suffragist pressure, a further reform bill was in prospect, yet neither
the home rule bills moved in 1913 and 1914, nor the attempts to co-
ordinate socialist activity, made much impact. Socialism and
Liberalism were on the defensive; the Unionists won 4 out of 15 by-
elections, 1910–14. Under pressure of the Ulster crisis, a revival of
Unionism seemed imminent.

Perhaps this upheaval reflected a more fundamental institutional
shift. Until 1906 the politics which actually affected Scots people's
everyday lives had been civic ones: the affairs of the great cities (37 per
cent of the population), of the burghs, and 900-odd parishes. These
traditional units had, during the nineteenth century, continually

acquired new powers. The process of rationalization had yet to begin. The parishes, not Poor Law Unions, controlled poor relief; and, unlike in England after 1902, remained the unit of education. The result was that the dominance of local élite groups was maintained: landowners, farmers, ministers, and schoolmasters in the parishes; businessmen, rentiers, and shopkeepers in the burghs. After the 1860s this élite had extended the interventionist powers of local government to cope with the social pressures of industrialization and to contain the urban working class, until a 'civic consciousness' had been created which endorsed, both in the theory of such as Edward Caird and Patrick Geddes, and in the practice of bodies like the City of Glasgow Improvement Trust, extensive measures of 'municipal socialism'. Much of this ideology was also common to the 'labour aristocracy' and even to the socialist movement, although it stopped short of any inter-vention which seriously affected the distribution of wealth and power. Yet it was under stress − from the lack of civic power to tackle housing, the most obdurate city problem, from the growing insecurity of skilled labour, and from the developing power of the state.

III Scottish Government

The suture between parliamentary and civic politics was the Scottish administration. Scarcely 'Dublin Castle' − with no Viceroy or separate exchequer − this operated from offices at Dover House in Whitehall and in Edinburgh. Through the Scottish Office, the Secretary for Scotland, a somewhat lowly member of most cabinets since 1885, dealt with political organization, patronage, and a range of Home Office affairs; he was also president of the Scotch Education Department, answered for the Boards (supposedly representing Scottish interests) of Agriculture and Fisheries, and Local Govern-ment, and, more tentatively, for the Lord Advocate's Department, which covered Scots Law.

The Secretary had usually been a peer, but Lord Pentland's Agri-culture Act meant that his successors virtually had to sit in the Commons to handle questions and interventions, over a third of which were on agriculture, and about 10−12 per cent each on fisheries, housing, and public health. Otherwise his portfolio was limited; his control was strong in education but weak in local government and in industrial affairs, liaison with the Board of Trade being minimal. Much routine private bill legislation had been devolved to Com-missioners in Edinburgh, and the Lord Advocate maintained a jealous

control over such legal business: the Secretary only gained official pre-
cedence over him in 1912. He was still politically rather than
administratively important: he reassured Scottish MPs — organized
since 1907 in their own Grand Committee for non-controversial
legislation — that the Cabinet was aware of Scottish issues, and after
1906 he kept the Scottish Liberal majority loyal to the premier.
Pentland was Campbell-Bannerman's confidant, MacKinnon Wood a
loyal Asquithian, and H.J. Tennant Asquith's brother-in-law. Most of
the Secretary's year was spent in the south, with a trip around the
Highland coast in the summer on a fishery cruiser. The 1914 trip did
not take place.

IV Business as Usual?

War broke out on 4 August. The state assumed control of the railways,
enemy ships were impounded and aliens interned. The Territorials —
of whose 14 divisions Scotland supplied 2 — were mobilized. John
Reith (later Viscount Reith), one of their officers, recalled that, for
the first time, they were cheered instead of catcalled in the Glasgow
streets. Not all wanted to be mobilized: the north-east was strong
territorial country, but the war coincided with the harvest and the
height of the fishing, and — so Joe Duncan reported in *Forward* —
there was more enthusiasm for home defence than for avenging the
wrongs of Belgium. Even Reith's battalion would only serve abroad as
a unit. Fears of invasion abounded — troops guarded strategic
viaducts; east coast towns put up barricades; the Shetland police force
arrested all the staff of Lerwick Post Office — not without reason:
Rosyth dockyard was still not completed; there was no boom on the
Forth, nor on the entries to Scapa Flow. On 22 September German
submarines sank three old cruisers off East Anglia and Admiral
Jellicoe, First Sea Lord, ordered the Grand Fleet from the Nore to
Scapa — then south-west to Lough Swilly. On 27 October the new
dreadnought *Audacious* hit a mine and sank. Although the attack did
not come, the Admiralty, in order to tighten its blockade of Germany,
commandeered most of the larger ports on the east coast.

Meanwhile, after a disorganized start, the recruiting of the volunteer army — Ian Hay's *First Hundred Thousand* — began.
Industrial districts and the Highlands alike responded enthusiastically, most employers promising to make up wages to peacetime
levels. The percentage per head taking the colours in the new 'pals'
battalions' was the highest in Britain. In Glasgow James Dalrymple,

the autocratic manager of the Corporation Tramways, made his system a giant recruiting office and furnished a Highland Light Infantry battalion from Tramway staff alone. The army waived height restrictions and accepted 'bantam battalions' of tiny, tough Glaswegians. Of the 157 battalions which comprised the Regular Army, from which the British Expeditionary Force was formed, Scottish regiments accounted for 22. They made up a seventh of the Territorial Army, and almost a sixth of the 'first two hundred thousand'. About 9 of the 70 divisions which would be created by the end of the war comprised Scottish regiments, although by then — their usual two battalions swollen to 15 or 16 — their local identity had ceased to count for much.

The 'pals' could not foresee their slaughter by the thousand on the Somme in mid 1916 and at Ypres in 1917, but spent an idyllic autum training in southern England, strange and wonderful to boys from Glasgow machine shops or, like the famous 'Spud Tamson', from the 'barras'. The Scots battalions were the more distinctive for the relative absence of caste differences between officers and men; in England commissions were almost entirely confined to public school boys.

The wartime threat to an exporting economy soon came to the fore. The *Scotsman* reported panic in Border tweed and Highland tourism, and redundancies in the paper mills. Unions protested that ladies knitting socks for soldiers would drive even more out of work. The Berwickshire Hunt philanthropically decided to carry on hunting, 'to account for foxes, to have the young hounds properly entered, and above all, by keeping on the establishment, to avoid adding to the ranks of the unemployed'. By mid August the Local Government Board had met to propose relief schemes of public works, while a fund for the unemployed had raised £20,000 from Edinburgh and £12,000 from Glasgow, whose former provost, Sir Daniel Stevenson, urged employers to fill up vacancies caused by recruits, and the corporation to accelerate public expenditure programmes.

This panic soon abated. The Germans were turned back on the Marne; the stalemate of the trenches began. 'Business as usual' was now to reign until the carnage of the mid-1915 offensives. At Hogmanay its tone was accurately caught by the Unionist MP Sir William Raeburn in the *Glasgow Herald*:

> The war has falsified almost every prophecy. Food was to be an enormous price, unemployment rife . . . revolution was to be feared. What are the facts? The freight market . . . is now active

and prosperous . . . . Prices of food have risen very little, and the difficulty at present is to get sufficient labour, skilled and unskilled. We have not only maintained our own trades, but have been busy capturing our enemies'.

War brought its own equilibrium. On the debit side, some raw materials and markets were cut off; enlistment reduced the labour force; government borrowing and purchasing increased inflation, insurance premiums escalated. Investment was switched to war *materiel*; the government controlled ports, railways, and ships; enemy attacks began to take their toll. But, on the other hand, imports of manufactured goods from enemy countries were cut off, and they were eliminated as competitors in other markets. Substitutes for imports were demanded, along with war contracts; there was less unemployment but also more opportunity for dilution and rationalization, and a substantial rise in profits. The 'impact of total war' was to be long in coming and the traumas it caused when it came were partly attributable to this equilibrium, and the need to change it.

Few protested against the war. Once Belgium was invaded, the Liberal pacifist movement, so nearly led by Lloyd George himself, was dispersed; the old Scottish radical and jurist James Bryce, one of its potential leaders, was to chair the committee that publicized 'German atrocities'. The newspapers, the Unionist and the vast mass of the Liberal party, and the churches, were totally pro-war; opposition was confined to the socialist left (although *Forward*, its main organ, reflected the division of opinion in the Labour Party), to one or two ministers in the United Free Church, and to a few Liberals, notably Sir Daniel Stevenson, who supported efforts in December 1914 to found the Union of Democratic Control, subsequently a meeting point for dissident radicals and anti-war socialists.

V Disruption

'Business as usual' complacency, which Raeburn exemplified, was understandable. The new army battalions did not see action until Loos in October 1915; casualties, though severe, were still only a fraction of what was to come. A sense of unreality pervaded the process of adapting to war production. The first problems — affecting the main institutions of Scottish finance, and some though not all industrial sectors — were mainly caused by disruptions to imports and exports and the financial system. The most obvious result, oddly, was an assimilation to Scottish banking practice. On 6 August 1914 pound notes, which had always circulated in the north, supplemented gold sovereigns in England. Otherwise the City of London rapidly took over control. The eight banks — the Bank of Scotland, the Royal Bank, the British Linen, the National, the Commercial, the Union, the Clydesdale, and the North of Scotland — were still Scottish-owned. Their ruling 'conference of general managers' got them to subscribe generously to the War Loans, and, in response to the Bank of England's fear of the High Seas Fleet staging a 'gold raid', shifted their bullion south. The investment trusts used their huge stakes in American railroads, mining companies, farms, and real estate as security for government loans in the US, or sold them to buy government stocks.

Textiles were hit immediately by the rise of 30–40 per cent in freight and insurance charges, and by the invasion of Belgium. The first town to fall was Verviers, the main source of yarn for the Border tweed industry. Substituted Yorkshire yarn wasn't good enough. Border machinery found it difficult to handle khaki (which was 50 per cent shoddy). Trade slumped and stayed down. The closure of the Baltic was likewise disastrous for linen, pushing the price of flax up by 65–75 per cent. The jute situation was more complex. The demand for sandbags was huge, while German commerce raiding checked the supply of jute and the products of Calcutta. Dundee was hit by a profiteering wave: spinners charged the inflated market price for yarn, but used jute bought at pre-war prices. Their profits soared to 56 per cent, while those of the weavers — subject to government price control — stayed at around 10 per cent. The only way of ensuring equity was for the War Office to organize the whole process, which it did after 1 June 1915. Since by 1918 a thousand million sandbags were to be shipped to the fronts, this early experiment had far-reaching consequences in the development of state control.

War affected the coalfields instantaneously. The German market — 2.9m. tons — was lost, and took the Baltic market with it. Substitute markets, hitherto served from Belgium and northern France, might have been found, but a second disruption supervened. Because of Rosyth's unavailability — until May 1916 — the Admiralty requisitioned the Forth coal ports. By 1918 exports had fallen away to under 2.5m. tons. Although, boosted by the demand for steel for munitions, production in the western coalfield was kept up, the troubles of the eastern field were rapidly reflected by the recruitment of miners into the forces. Scotland had the highest percentages in Britain: 26.5 per cent compared with 22.9 per cent in England and 22.5 per cent in Wales. But over 36.5 per cent of East Lothian miners were in uniform by August 1915, compared with barely 20 per cent in Ayrshire. With the coalowners guaranteeing (at least initially) to make up the difference between army and civilian earnings, there was obviously a strong incentive to enlist — where the alternative was parish relief.

Enlistment resulted in a serious decline in efficiency, as the remaining miners were less skilled, older, or less fit. By November 1915 the Government effectively shut off recruiting and in February 1916 its Coke and Coal Supplies Committee was set up to make the Scottish coalfields self-sufficient. This was not ultimately achieved until September 1917, when zoning of markets was introduced, and railway wagons were pooled and regulated. Government attempts to control prices were less successful. The limitation of home prices in July 1915 simply meant a switch to exports, and although regulation by local committees was ultimately achieved this was not effective until late 1917. Fundamental disruption had been caused to the industry. Manpower was depleted, the more productive eastern coalfield starved of capital and transport, and vital markets lost — as matters turned out, for good.

For fishing the war was from the start disastrous. The herring industry saw two-thirds of its market, in Germany and Russia, vanish. Exports had reached Russia through Germany, and efforts to export via Archangel largely failed. So, few fishermen refused direction into the Royal Naval Reserve, and by 1918 about 25,000 fishermen out of nearly 40,000 were thus employed, with 302 steam trawlers, 838 steam drifters, and 100 motor drifters.

The Highlands, a neglected backwater for so long, suddenly became the scene of frenzied activity. The anchorages of Scapa Flow and Invergordon had been designated in 1912 as out-stations to Rosyth; they became fully protected bases late in 1914. Their importance increased with the Northern Barrage project of 1917 for a continuous mine-field between the Shetlands and Norway. Over the metals of the single-track Highland Railway north of Perth thousands of special trains carried coal, sailors, mines, and ammunition; they returned south with the trees of Highland plantations, chopped down by the Canadian Forestry Corps. In mid 1916 the whole land-mass north and west of the Great Glen became a 'restricted area', which the traveller needed a pass to enter (Richard Hannay fell foul of this in John Buchan's *Mr Standfast*). Behind this new frontier places like Invergordon (population 1,110 in 1911) grew sevenfold. The aluminium works at Kinlochleven and Foyers underwent rapid expansion; in Raasay low-grade iron-ore was mined, railways and blast furnaces built, later to remain for decades as bizarre ruins.

Thus, leaving recruiting and armaments production aside, 'business as usual' was an illusion, bred of military complacency and the supineness of the Asquith government. A rational adjustment to war production was equally impossible. The machinery simply didn't exist, and its ethos was utterly remote from Scottish *laissez-faire* — a situation dramatized by the Jacks case, of June 1915. Partners of a Glasgow iron firm run by Andrew Bonar Law's brother were found guilty of supplying ironstone to (*inter alia*) Krupps in the early weeks of the war. The case was complex but it seems that the Lord Advocate may have been persuaded to drop charges against John Law, whose brother joined the government on 23 May. The relevant papers are still kept as confidential in the Scottish Record Office, but Bonar Law subsequently wrote that the firm's action would have been repeated by 99 out of 100 businessmen.

To the far-sighted, and notably to Lloyd George, Chancellor of the Exchequer in 1914, the drastic use of state power both in the industrial and social field was essential. In 1915 this was to result in accessions of power both to the Scottish Office and to the business classes, via the new Ministry of Munitions, and this challenged many of the institutions of Scottish politics.

VI 'The Red Clyde'

By 1917 some 250,000 men and women were producing munitions in Scotland. The government had invested over £11m., mainly in the vast explosives works at Gretna, but the Clyde Valley had the biggest concentration of production in the United Kingdom. Here 'munitions' — meaning all war *materiel*, from boots and blankets to tanks and battleships — inevitably expanded the heavy industries above all else, rapidly dispelling August 1914's fears of mass-unemployment. As the *Glasgow Herald* reported in December, when over a seventh of the workforce of the shipyards had enlisted: 'Now their greatest difficulties are those of obtaining sufficient labour, even at the high wages now ruling, and sufficient materials even at the equally high prices which are charged'. The Admiralty, which assumed overall control of the shipyards, experienced few problems. Production (an average of 520,000 tons) was never as high as in the pre-war peak of 1913, but warships required powerful engines and horsepower output rose by 58 per cent between then and 1918. Along with gun and shell demands, this multiplied problems for the engineering industry, which was losing skilled labour both to the front and to the shipyards. Management became determined on a drastic programme of modernization and rationalization.

The scene was thus set for the legendary episode of the Red Clyde. Left-wingers came to equate events in wartime Glasgow with Russian Bolshevism and the French army mutinies − both 1917 − and the German revolution of 1918, as part of a Europe-wide communist *démarche*. The problem was: why had it not been successful on the Clyde? Its leading figures, particularly that of the Glasgow schoolmaster Marxist John Maclean (1879−1923), briefly Soviet consul in Glasgow in 1918, have come to be venerated. Fifty years later, nuclear disarmers and nationalists alike would sing Hamish Henderson's 'Freedom Come All Ye' (1949):

> When Maclean meets wi' freens in Springburn
> Aa the roses an geans will turn tae bloom,
> An a black boy frae yont Nyanga
> Dings the fell gallows o' the burghers doon.

The Second Coming apart, there was a serious issue of Marxist politics here. Clydeside, 1914−18, showed an apparent convergence of Marxist political theory with industrial fact. A crisis-ridden capitalism's attack on the identity of the skilled workers − their 'actual humanity' − had coincided with their consciousness of their power and position: the classic situation of 'praxis'. Clydeside, a key arms production district where skilled workers were in a majority, should have provided a powerful lever for revolution. As such, its problems have never lacked committed historians, who see in it either useful morals for contemporary industrial struggles or else a terrible wrong turning − a socialist and nationalist revolution betrayed by orthodox Labourism.

But − was there ever actually or potentially a revolutionary situation? This would have needed (1) capitalists determined to use the war situation to solve peacetime industrial problems by 'dilution' − mechanizing work and reducing the element of skill; (2) militant and class-conscious activists consistently mobilizing support among a widening labour force; (3) government losing control both over public morale and public order. There was certainly evidence − at times − of all three. There was a serious industrial problem. Government, latterly, became badly rattled. Selective quotation can produce a scarlet ferment. During the Forty Hours' strike in February 1919 the Scottish Secretary Robert Munro, for example, informed the Cabinet that 'in his opinion it was more clear than ever that it was a misnomer to call the situation in Glasgow a strike — it was a Bolshevist rising'. Even more blood-curdling reports found their way south from the military intelligence outfit of Sir Basil Thompson. The treatment of John Maclean bears out a sense of panic. What is lacking, however, is a consistent and developing pattern of working-class resistance and leadership. In fact, beneath the rhetoric of both sides, actual conflicts were episodic and widely separated in time, occupying in all only a few months in the space of eight years. They consisted of:

1. The 'tuppence an hour' Engineers' strike of February 1915.
2. The Fairfield Strike of August 1915.
3. The rent strike of October–November 1915.
4. The imposition of dilution in Glasgow engineering shops, January–April 1916, culminating with the deportation of the shop stewards.
5. Then (after a gap of nearly three years, when the Clyde was practically free of industrial trouble) the Forty Hours' strike of January–February 1919.
6. The election of November 1922, at which 10 Labour MPs were returned in the 15 Glasgow constituencies, of whom James Maxton and John Muir had been prominent in the industrial and anti-war campaigns. These subsequently represented a fundamentalist socialist group in the Labour ranks.

However, when such episodes of conflict are examined, even this limited consistency gives way. The situation becomes complex, individual crises and personalities become important. And the key figure was not from labour but management: William Weir (Viscount Weir, 1877–1959), the managing director of G. & J. Weir Pumps of Cathcart, who became munitions controller in Scotland on 13 July 1915. He was young and innovative, but was he the most appropriate appointment? Responding to engineering's problems, Weir was already familiar with new American labour-saving machinery and 'Taylorist' scientific management. He wanted wholesale industrial reconstruction, and saw the war facilitating this:

The shortage of men now, and still more after peace, is giving their chance to working women, and even to boys and girls. In regard to our workers, whatever the unions may do, and notwithstanding any guarantee given, employment can and never will be the same again.

If this, in the *Scots Law Courts Record*, wasn't by Weir, it certainly reflects his attitude. It wasn't shared by the rest of Clydeside management — with the possible exception of Beardmore — which treated its periodic clashes with its workforce as a fact of life. But the war gave the innovators their chance. It also injected into their attitudes an aggressive, and genuine, element of moral fervour — Weir gave all his firm's war profits to charity — of the same sort that took Reith into the trenches. So when, in January 1915, the engineers threatened to strike for tuppence an hour, his response, in a pamphlet *Responsibility and Duty* of 30 January 1915, was scarcely tactful:

> Every hour lost by a workman COULD HAVE been worked, HAS been worked by a German workman, who in that time has produced, say, an additional shell . . . to kill the British workman's brother in arms.

The engineers had been in dispute before the war but action was now provoked by a rise of over 50 per cent in the cost of living. Co-op members to a man, they saw inflation, correctly, as caused by the profiteering of wholesalers, shippers, and insurers. Weir himself, bringing in American workers at well above the Clydeside rates, triggered off the strike on 15 February.

A fortnight later on 4 March it was settled by a compromise. On 17–19 March government and most of the unions signed the 'Treasury Agreements' on wartime industrial relations, and on 30 April the government set up the Clyde Armaments Output Committee, with equal management and labour representation. Weir continued his fulminations. He was given more ammunition by a report of 1 May alleging poor productivity through absenteeism and drink. This was a piece of temperance propaganda, which failed to take account of the impact of enlistment and the resulting less-skilled labour force, as Bonar Law pointed out in the Commons. Yet by 15 May Weir was calling for martial law in the munitions districts. Such scaremongering served a political purpose. By 1 May Lloyd George was Minister of Munitions, determined to dynamize production, and on 7 July the great Jacobin appointed Weir munitions controller in Scotland with an office that was 'in fact a miniature ministry of munitions'. On 30 August Weir abolished the Committee and replaced it with a nominal board dominated by management. As the unpublished *History of the Ministry of Munitions* comments:

> Just at the moment when these novel conditions called for free interchange of opinion between employers and workmen, rapid exploration of grievances, full explanation of the difficulties to be faced on either side, mutual goodwill and readiness to adjust habits and prejudices, the round table was broken up.

Weir had to set up a production plant which would be in operation before the big offensives scheduled for mid 1916; thus he had to spend and build before he had secured the full agreement of capital or labour. By August, however, he had set up a co-operative shell production scheme for 28,500 shells a week. The individual firms drove hard bargains: David Rowan took until mid October to agree 'owing in the main to the firm's determination to protect themselves at all costs against possible loss'.

He was — not surprisingly — less tactful with the labour force. He had to secure dilution before the factories came into production, but the Amalgamated Society of Engineers, sensitive to its members' privileged status and to ham-fisted attempts to enforce the Munitions Act regulations, was slow to negotiate; management, too, wanted a quiet life. Conflicts over the Act bubbled away: in August Fairfields struck work, over leaving certificates, and some shop stewards were jailed. Lord Balfour of Burleigh, the Conservative ex-Secretary whom the government appointed as conciliator, found the strikers to be otherwise exemplary citizens, pillars of the Kirk with sons at the Front, driven to revolt by what they regarded as arbitrary interference with their liberties. The tact of Burleigh and Bonar Law contrasted with the ineptness of MacKinnon Wood, who insisted on the strikers being kept in prison, and the strike — the only major one in the shipyards — was settled equitably. It was swiftly followed by the Rent Strike. This was less an aspect of industrial militancy than the culmination of a pre-war Labour campaign against the rigorous terms of Scottish house-letting and in favour of subsidized public housing. Engineering management, eager to keep wages down, heartily concurred with it, while government, expecting to have to legislate on Scottish housing anyway, ended it by promising a Rent Restrictions Act, which was passed in May 1916.

Dilution, however, remained a battlefield. On one side were Weir, Lloyd George, and — playing an increasingly influential rôle — the Munitions Directorate in London under William Beveridge. On the other was the A.S.E., London-based but traditionally very decentralized, whose leaders had never faced a situation like this before, and manufacturers more concerned with remuneration than with productivity. Somewhere between the two were the workers, torn between alarm at the threat to their status and solidarity with their colleagues at the front, and all the time more dependent on their local union representatives, the shop stewards, a minority of whom were radical socialists of one sort or another. The attitudes of these, too, were ambiguous. Some welcomed dilution on theoretical grounds, as destroying internal barriers to working-class consciousness; others took a revolutionary anti-war stance. Some of the non-socialist shop stewards were the most bitterly obdurate of the lot, resenting deeply the inroads being made by women, and the Irish, into the preserve of the skilled male worker.

The main organization of the shop stewards was the Clyde Workers' Committee, founded during the 'tuppence an hour' strike. While purporting to speak for the mass of munitions workers, it was scarcely representative. Evidence to a Labour Party enquiry submitted that 'it was a heterogeneous crowd which had practically no constitution . . . you could represent a minority in the shop just the same as a majority, even though the minority was one'. This gave the far left its opportunity, and brought on to the scene such as John MacLean, who attended its meetings, though a schoolteacher, and others of Glasgow's rich collection of radical agitators from Christian pacifists to anarcho-syndicalists. This played into the munitions directorate's hands: to the industrial imperative they could add the tempting themes of sedition and revolution, and there was no shortage of volunteer martyrs.

The conflict came to a climax between December 1915 and April 1916. In December Lloyd George came to Glasgow, to win over the workers with his eloquence. He met the leaders of the shop stewards, to no avail; the great rally was a disaster. The Lord Advocate was obliged to seize an issue of *Forward*, which carried a report. But the Clyde had now nominated itself as a test case, and Beveridge and Weir moved rapidly to enforce dilution and thus break the A.S.E.'s resistance. On 28 January 1916 they appointed dilution commissioners, who rapidly drafted agreements covering most of the Clyde's engineering shops. A rearguard action, a strike at Beardmore's at the end of March, was broken by Weir arresting an assortment of shop stewards — including David Kirkwood and William Gallacher — and deporting them to Edinburgh.

Dilution was already going smoothly in most works before the Commissioners were appointed, so the March crackdown was helpful but by no means essential. The shell-forging and turning works opened by May, when the apparent defeat of Jutland (31 May–1 June) gave a new urgency, and reached full production by November, their products bound for the Battle of the Somme. By then Weir was in London, eventually as Air Minister, and the government munitions works were employing equal numbers of men and women; at the end of the war this ran at 30,000 women to 27,000 men. They caused little trouble, even when severe strikes reached the English munitions areas in May 1917. By late 1917 shop-floor co-operation — now led by men like Gallacher and Kirkwood — became such that the *Glasgow Herald*, earlier stridently anti-worker in tone, concluded in December 1917 that:

> The arrangements regarding the recognition of shop stewards are also significant as a sign of the times. They may portend syndicalism or they may not, but they certainly mean that the actual workers will be in closer touch with the machinery of their unions, and also with their employers, and familiarity is more likely to breed friendship than enmity.

By then, of course, the Bolshevik Revolution was a fact. In August the radicals had formed a Glasgow Soviet, greatly worrying Secretary Munro, and other members of the Cabinet, but it folded up when the Corporation would not provide it with a school classroom to meet in. Stories of vast meetings of revolutionary militants must likewise be treated with scepticism: Nan Milton, his daughter, tells us that, to demand John Maclean's release from prison in May 1917 '70,000 or 80,000 marched in the procession, while 250,000 lined the streets', but this was in fact the Glasgow May Day, and most of the demonstrators were protesting against the Munitions Act and discrimination against the Co-ops.

For the remainder of the war the Clyde was quiet, the Clyde Workers' Committee moribund. It was to be three years before there was any more trouble, in the Forty Hours' strike of January–February 1919. This strike was more a portent of the future disunity of the left than a climax to wartime discontent. On 14 March 1918 the Scottish Trades Union Congress (STUC) had called for a post-war 40-hour week, to prevent mass unemployment among demobilized men. After the 1918 election — in which the Unionists won 10 out of 15 Glasgow seats — this demand was echoed by a special conference in Glasgow on 27–8 December. The CWC revived itself to demand a 30-hour week. The strike actually took place in co-ordination with the Orange workers of Belfast, and on 27 January 40,000 came out, rising to 70,000 on the 28th, but, on the 30th, the Carters' Union settled for a 48-hour week. The government called a conference on this basis but, under pressure from Munro despatched 12,000 troops, 100 lorries, and six tanks to Glasgow. The climax came when a huge crowd — not wholly composed of strikers or even the unemployed — assembled in George Square on Friday 31 January to hear the government's decision on the conference. Suddenly the police (whose own relations with the government were edgy) staged what could only be described as a riot and charged the crowd: the response of the leaders, Gallacher and Shinwell, was to get the strikers out of the square and calm the situation down, in which by and large they succeeded, although at the cost of their own freedom. For a couple of days afterwards Glasgow was alive with troops, but the strike fizzled out at the news of a conference and continuance of the statutory regulation of wages and rents. The 'ringleaders' were subsequently tried and, incriminated by rather hypothetical plans for sabotage, given short prison sentences. In this way the 'revolution' ended, with less violence than 1848, when six had been killed in Chartist riots, and less destruction than the pre-war suffragettes had carried out. Although Sinn Feiners chipped in with sabotage and gun-running later that year, this had no connection with the industrial unrest. Pending the 1922 election, the Red Clyde was over.

Initially, the post-war situation seemed a draw between management and labour. Weir's notions of industrial reconstruction were not followed up by action; the practices of the skilled trade unions were restored. Peace, and the promise of widespread social and economic reconstruction, made even labour unrest seem an indication of vitality. Had not Lord Leverhulme, on the verge of his ambitious Scottish projects, declared in the *Glasgow Herald* in 1917 that it was 'the healthiest sign we have got today?' He — and those who confirmed the coalition in power in December 1918 — expected that the enormous investment in war production, and reparations from Germany, could be channelled into diversification of Scottish industry. The expansion of munitions production had depended greatly on electricity; so new schemes to tap hydro power were canvassed. The capacity to make tanks, motor lorries, and aircraft on a large scale seemed to promise a fresh start for the motor industry, and Beardmore's announced an impressive investment programme — 'The firm's enormous resources will enable them to put "mass production" into practice'. Yet left-wing distrust was not fanciful. Allegations of profiteering were well-founded. For all Weir's high-mindedness, the *History of the Ministry of Munitions* admits that profits on completed shells ran at 'a somewhat high rate' throughout the war, and in 1916 profits on completed shell forgings rose as high as 40 per cent. Little of this money was reinvested in industry. The Scottish banks in 1919 were glutted with huge capital balances, while the fashionable artist Sir James Gunn remembered that *annus mirabilis*, 40 years later:

> painters . . . benefited from the desire of war profiteers to translate their gains, pictures and prints providing a ready means. The one-man show at Cassells or Davidson's might sell out in a day . . . There was a boom in etchings: these were easy to store and prints soared to fantastic prices on a sellers' market: if I remember aright one of MacBey's reached the peak at 500 guineas.

But where else could the money have gone? Much war investment could only serve war purposes — like the vast development of engine works for powerful naval vessels. With inflation out of control until 1921, industrial investment carried penal interest charges, as Beardmore's found to its cost. It was simpler, many Scottish capitalists found, to sell out their shareholdings, buy land or invest abroad or in the south. The revolution myth obscures the real change, and the real loss, on the Clyde: co-operative decision-making over innovation had been a genuine possibility. The shop stewards, who represented the 'Labour aristocracy', could be reverent as well as critical of their bosses. But the tactlessness of Weir and the munitions directorate, and the post-war slump, effectively threw this chance away. The workers' distrust both of management and of new technology was confirmed, but it was also plain that their own power was waning. The heroics of the Red Clyde, faithfully retailed by further generations of activists, masked a fundamental defeat.

VII 'A Land Fit for Heroes'?

For the Scots, the supreme sacrifice had also been a disproportionate one. Although the parliamentary return of 1921 simply divided 745,000 British dead by 10 to produce a Scottish toll of 74,000, most Scots probably agreed with the National War Memorial White Paper of 1920, which estimated 100,000 or over 13 per cent of Britain's dead. Scots territorials, at 5 per cent of the male population, nearly double the British average, suffered particularly badly in the mauling of their battalions in 1915.

Although men were retained by war industry and mining, casualties in urban areas still reached the British average — Glasgow's 18,000 dead tallies roughly with the British proportion of 1 in 54 — and the impact in the country areas could be twice as severe. The dead were overwhelmingly infantry privates; one officer died for every 13 men. Few Scottish working-class families escaped; still fewer lacked ex-soldiers who emigrated rather than face the dislocation and depression of the post-war years.

During and after the war both wages and prices escalated but, between 1914 and 1920, wages kept ahead in real terms by something like 25 per cent. The gains, however, were redistributed within the working class in a way that probably penalized Scotland. From a 1914 index of 100, a skilled shipbuilder's wage only rose to 223 in 1920, while an engineer's labourer's wage rose to 309. Women's wages seem to have risen to about 250. Welfare changes made notable additions to real wages: in particular, the extension of national insurance in 1920 to cover practically all manual occupations, and the retention of rent control. Although they were the prelude to an unprecedented depression, such changes meant that poverty would never again be as widespread as in the 1900s.

Even in the euphoria of early 1919 Scottish businessmen felt themselves in a new world. The control of much of their economy had moved southward through English takeovers or government intervention. Banking had shifted south from the start; the Ministry of Munitions ended dealing in iron on the Glasgow exchange on 31 May 1916. In 1918 Barclays and the Midland 'affiliated' the British Linen and Clydesdale banks. After the Midland took over the North of Scotland in 1923, three out of the seven banks were under English control, while the others had switched much of their investment, either into government stocks or the south's more profitable commercial concerns. Even the *Glasgow Herald*, usually no friend to nationalism, feared 'that ere long the commercial community will be sighing for a banking William Wallace to free them from Southern oppression'.

Because the Scottish economy was more complex, government intervention struck deeper than in north-east England or Wales. No major industry escaped. Besides coal and jute, heavy linen (another Dundee speciality), wool purchases, hides, leather, and meat, all important Scottish agriculture-based industries, were controlled through *ad hoc* mixtures of local supervision, compulsory purchase, and price-fixing. In agriculture and fisheries control went even further, using existing Scottish machinery. In response to soaring shipping losses, government in 1917 both introduced a measure of food rationing and demanded the conversion of grassland (which had a low calorie-yield per acre) into arable. An expanded Board of Agriculture carried this out through county agricultural production committees with paid executives and in 1918 expanded Scots arable acreage by over 30 per cent. As elsewhere, recruitment and later conscription forced wages up fast, and while the War Office plucked labourers from the farms, the Board sought to bring them back for ploughing and harvest. The Corn Production Act of 1917 established minimum wages, on a somewhat lower scale than in England, to be fixed by joint negotiating committees. Joe Duncan, the farm workers' leader, saw this as confirming his idea of the worker as a skilled highly-paid expert, rather than the Liberal idea of the peasant small-holder. But the promise of land for crofter soldiers remained, and was to prove troublesome.

Although the Board of Agriculture enthused over its new system, the Geddes Axe cut it down at the end of 1921, along with guaranteed prices and minimum wages. Scottish agriculture reverted to livestock, and initially declined less than the wheat-producing south. The case was worse in fishing.

With boats absorbed in Admiralty service, as minesweepers, patrol boats, and tenders, the loss of markets was not immediately noticeable. Indeed, the fishing fleet modernized its operations in the parts of the North Sea not covered by naval operations. Eight hundred sailing vessels were fitted out with motors during the war and a total of some 4,614 boats (just over 50 per cent of the fleet in 1914) managed to make 1918 'the most lucrative season ever experienced', in the opinion of the Fisheries Board. The Board had co-ordinated wartime purchasing and saw canning and increased fresh fish consumption as post-war options, but its main hopes still rested on the resumption of herring exports. In vain, because of the impact of the Russian civil war, Britain's hostility to Bolshevism, the collapse of the German economy in 1923, and the competition of the neutral and efficient Norwegian fleet. Although the industry's money income was £4.1m. in 1922, against £3.3m. in 1918 and £4.0m. in 1913, its real income had fallen by 53 per cent. Burdened with old equipment and decaying boats, the fishermen were faced with a future which promised no more than bare subsistence, derived largely from dumping herring at fish-meal factories.

To the Highlands the war brought a new desolation. The forests were felled, fishing boats rotted on the crofts where their owners had left them in 1914 — often never to return. Deaths and emigration ended several industries, such as slate quarrying in Lorne and Caithness; prohibition and liquor control closed down distilleries. The government, in a report of 1919, promised 250 miles of new railways (to be built with equipment salvaged from the western front), roads, bridges and piers, and an extensive forestry programme under the new Forestry Commissioners. Lord Leverhulme, who had bought Lewis in 1917, planned the industrialization of the islands on the Scandinavian pattern, around tweed and deep-sea fisheries. But all these schemes depended on continuing British economic prosperity. The returning servicemen were sceptical of this hypothetical new world and demanded their own land. The resulting friction hamstrung Leverhulme's plans; the depression swept both these and the promises of the government away. Population had held up in the 1911–21 decade, because the war inhibited emigration and the peace promised prosperity. In the 1920s it declined by 10 per cent.

Support grew during the war for collectivist 'reconstruction', but with Lloyd George the hostage of the Conservatives, the retreat was rapid. In Scotland, however, positive state policy was essential to remedy state-induced wartime distortions of economy and society. Without this, the Scots tended to surrender economic responsibility.

The instance of railway reorganization is of critical importance. In 1919 Sir Eric Geddes, the newly-created Minister of Transport, suggested nationalization, with an autonomous Scottish region. Under pressure from the Conservatives this became, in the White Paper of February 1921, the 'grouping' of lines into five private companies, substantially regional monopolies. The project for a separate Scottish company was maintained. The reaction of the business community, burghs, MPs, and trade unions in Scotland was alike furious. National control during the war had upgraded hitherto low levels of maintenance and wages on Scottish railways, whose costs had risen 291 per cent on 1913, compared with 227 per cent for the largest English companies. A separate Scottish company would be forced to maintain these standards, while carrying only 45,000 tons of traffic per annum per route mile, compared with 82,000 in England. The compromise between state and private enterprise would thus make the Scottish system uneconomic, jeopardize lines in rural areas, and reduce wage levels.

The result was a campaign, headed by Conservative, Liberal, and Labour MPs, in which the rhetoric of nationalism was used to secure the amalgamation of the five Scottish companies 'longitudinally' with the London Midland and Scottish (Caledonian, Highland, and Glasgow and South Western) and London and North Eastern Railways (North British and Great North of Scotland). This took effect in 1923.

VIII Reconstruction

This situation demonstrated the challenge to, and failure of, traditional Scottish government. There was certainly, in the law, the Church, and the educational system, a will to reform. The collectivist-inclined report of the Church of Scotland's Commission on the social and moral issues of the war (1919), admitted that 'in its teaching [the Church] has not explained either to the few or to the masses the urgency of social justice and Christian brotherhood'. The United Free Church, too, shifted from the Charity Organization Society-style liberal individualism of its 1911 conference on social welfare to a similar approach. School boards and teachers pressed for a comprehensive educational settlement. The whole reform movement was given enormous impetus by the Report of the Royal Commission on Scottish Housing, in October 1917 (after being adjourned from February 1915 to October 1916). Its indictment of landlords, local government, and the Scottish Office was as pungent as its descriptions of the state of Scottish dwellings:

> unspeakably filthy privy-middens in many of the mining areas, badly constructed, incurably damp labourers' cottages on farms, whole townships unfit for human occupation in the crofting counties and islands . . . gross overcrowding and huddling of the sexes together in the congested industrial villages and towns, occupation of one-room houses by large families, groups of

lightless and unventilated houses in the older burghs, clotted masses of slums in the great cities.

Its demand that a reconstructed Local Government Board for Scotland ensure minimal standards presaged a revolution in the powers of the Scottish Office. Yet, although this responsibility, and the new Board of Health, were enacted in 1919, it took until 1939 for the Scottish Office to integrate fully its social, agricultural, and industrial responsibilities. And even the 1919 act had been piloted through, not by the Scottish ministers, but by Dr Christopher Addison, the English Minister of Housing.

Much of the responsibility for the failure must rest with the Scottish Secretaries. MacKinnon Wood and Tennant made little mark on the Commons. When Tennant departed with Asquith in December 1916, Bonar Law, with an eye on the Clyde, stressed policy enforcement and a strong Lord Advocate, and appointed James Clyde (shifting his predecessor, the Liberal Robert Munro, to the Secretaryship). 'Parliament House rule', which the creation of the Scottish Office in 1885 was supposed to replace, was restored and at a critical legislative period. Disastrously. Munro's actions apropos the Forty Hours' strike have already been quoted. He frustrated Leverhulme's aims in the Hebrides; his Education Act lasted only 10 years. As Tom Johnston was to show in World War II, personality was critical in exercising the Secretary's powers. It was Scotland's tragedy that at this important period the Office fell to the dim representative of a failing political party.

IX   The Political Reaction

In Britain the war and its aftermath saw the destruction of the Liberals and the rise of Labour. From 42 seats in 1910, Labour became the governing party, with 191 seats, in 1923. By 1922 Scotland took a leading rôle, returning 29 MPs (plus a Prohibitionist and a Communist) out of Labour's 142; and the Clydesiders helped elect Ramsay MacDonald, whom they respected for his anti-war stance, leader. But was war the motor of change? Arthur Marwick and Jay Winter have argued that it stimulated trade unionism and collectivist ideas, discredited New Liberalism and forced the Labour Party, in its 1918 constitution, to bid for mass support. The war gave this a distinctive dynamic − Arthur Henderson's admission into the war cabinet (1915) legitimated Labour as an interest, while subsequent conflict with the coalition over conscription, Russia, and a negotiated peace gained it support from disillusioned radicals. In the 1920s it became, in MacDonald's words, 'a party of the people', not of a class.

Against this Dr Ross McKibbin has argued that pre-war tendencies would anyway have led to the rise of a trade unionist, collectivist Labour – but not socialist – party. The expanding unions were already imposing their will on Labour. The factor, which 'transformed the conditions under which Labour grew', was the Reform Act of 1918, which expanded the electorate from 7.7m. in 1910 to 21.4m. in 1918, not only adding women over 30 but greatly expanding the male working-class electorate. This would have happened anyway, war or no war. While the war destroyed the Liberals' ability to control the situation, it did not change the tendency towards a working-class party. They would have had to cope with this in any case. The post-1918 Labour Party was not, however, socialist but a premature development of one wing of the Liberals. From that stemmed the tensions of the 1920s, which destroyed much of the ideological and constitutional liveliness of both radicals and socialists.

Scotland's wartime politics resembled the rest of Britain. Opinion at by-elections (only 4 out of 11 were contested) was overwhelmingly pro-government. On two occasions, in fact (Glasgow Central, 28 May 1915 and Aberdeen S., 3 April 1917) the main opposition candidate was more bellicose than the successful government candidate. A 'negotiated peace' candidate gained only 15 per cent on 10 October 1916 at the North Ayrshire by-election, against the local laird, Aylmer Hunter-Weston, despite three months' slaughter on the Somme, where Hunter-Weston was a general. Edward Scrymgeour, Churchill's prohibitionist and pacifist opponent, gained only 21.8 per cent against him on 30 July 1917 at Dundee.

The Unionists continued their pre-war recovery in the election of 14 December 1918. Although the Liberals won 43 seats, half of them were 'Lloyd Georgeites', and this, with 22 Tory gains, mainly in the west, aggravated chronic divisions and organizational weaknesses. Of the seven Labour MPs, two had gained mining seats, South Ayrshire and Hamilton, and the other three gains were in Aberdeen, Govan, and Edinburgh Central. Dundee and West Fife were retained. The Clyde failed to show Red, and the 'collaborator' Coalition–Labour Cabinet Minister George Barnes was returned for Tradeston. Polls were low, as many servicemen had yet to be demobilized, although high in mining areas, where many had already been brought home. But neither the war nor the 1918 Act seemed to have caused a major shift. In 1910 the average Labour constituency vote was 4,926; in 1918 it rose 28 per cent to 6,813, but the electorate had, over this period, risen 183 per cent from 779,000 to 2,205,000.

However, some loyalties had changed — notably in the Co-operative movement. The creation of the labour aristocracy between 1860 and 1914, this was still at its strongest in textile areas, like Angus and the Scottish borders, and in the coalfields. In Clackmannan in 1911 practically every family in the weaving and mining county must have had more than one member. Scots membership was about 10 per cent of the population; the UK figure was 7 per cent. It began the war jingoistically, the 1915 Congress refusing to aid German and Austrian co-operators interned in Britain. It also grew rapidly, because of its low prices and absence of profiteering, and by 1918 its membership was about 30 per cent up on 1911. In Lanarkshire, for example, it grew from 7.61 per cent to 11.46 per cent, in Edinburgh from 12.89 per cent to 17.39 per cent. But its societies were hit by the advantages that Lloyd George's policies of food control gave to its old enemies, the private wholesalers and retailers, and in 1917, led by Sir William Maxwell, the chairman of St Cuthbert's Co-operative Society, the Congress decided to organize as part of the Labour movement. In demonstrations in Glasgow in 1917 the problems of the Co-op came second only to the iniquities of the Munitions Act, and in December 1918 three Co-op candidates polled, collectively, over 19,000 votes and two came very close to being elected; elsewhere the shift of Co-op support to Labour gave the party a major boost. Such collaboration had been envisaged in pre-war negotiations, but it was not in fact to be formalized until 1926.

Left to itself then, the war would certainly have caused an improvement in Labour representation: eventually some 18 – 20 MPs might have been elected, mainly in the coalfields, with a few more in the cities. But economic circumstances were changed. In mid 1919 there were already danger signs; by 1920 definite alarm. Shipbuilding on the Clyde had gone above 650,000 tons in 1919 and 1920; in 1921 it dropped to 510,000 and in 1922 to under 400,000. With few orders in hand, the prospects for 1923 were dismal (less than 170,000 tons was actually completed). The fate of the shipyards was shared by the other heavy industries. North British Locomotive Company production dropped by two-thirds between 1920 and 1921. On top of this, promises were frustrated; the government's 'homes fit for heroes' programme, following a year after the report of the Royal Commission, and after a large pre-war building back-log, failed. Scarcely 2,000 houses were built in 1920, compared with 48,000 in England; in 1921 this was still only, 6,000 against 120,000. Costs were inflated, labour was scarce and expensive, and Scottish local authorities (in which landlords, already battered by the Rent Restrictions Act, were still trying to keep ahead of a Labour Party that was shrewdly exploiting the housing issue), dragged their feet.

This was evident to the Scottish Office. A report to the Board of Health on 'Industrial Unemployment and Distress' compiled in 1921 observed: 'it is difficult to pick out any industrial occupation as being principally affected by unemployment; almost all are in bad condition . . . those engaged in export trade and the means of export are worse than those engaged in the home trade', and urged a radical extension of relief measures, fearing that 'very inflammable elements which, while subjected during ordinary times to damping down by the saner and much larger section of the community, will not improbably be fanned into activity as the endurance of that more sober section is broken by the continued tightening of waistbelts around empty bellies'. Four years earlier the Royal Commission on housing had positively welcomed social discontent; now government feared it, with some reason. Extremist agitation — after the spring of 1920 directed by the Moscow-organized Communist Party — was giving new focus to the discontents of slum-dwellers and the unemployed, while Sinn Fein was active in support of the campaign against the British. The Labour Party — ably organized in the west of Scotland by Patrick Dollan — incorporated as much of this agitation as it could by a positive policy on rents and housing, and the Catholic Church and *ci-devant* Irish Nationalist organization switched its support. Although Labour won Bothwell and Kirkcaldy at by-elections, this came only just in time, as the slump struck severely at its working-class base.

The 1922 election, held on 15 November, set a qualified seal on this shift. The *Scotsman* found its pattern 'vague and confused', as well it might, since Lloyd George's forces acted in unison with the Unionists who had flung him from office three months before. There were 4 four-cornered and 19 three-cornered contests, but in another 43 the 24 'National Liberals' and 18 Unionists acted together. Away from west central Scotland there was, in fact, little change from 1918. Labour maintained an 'armed neutrality' with the Asquithian Liberals, and found itself hard put to maintain itself outside the 11 coalfield constituencies, where 9 of the MPs returned were miners' agents. It — or the left in general — scored a remarkable victory in

Dundee, where the pacifist E.D. Morel and the local prohibitionist Eddie Scrymgeour beat Winston Churchill, but it gained no more seats in Edinburgh and Aberdeen. The mobilization of a rural socialist vote, apparent in 1918, was not repeated — probably a consequence of the setback to Joe Duncan's Farm Servant's Union.

But it was in the Glasgow area that the real turn-round occured. Labour captured 10 of the 15 city seats, and Dumbarton, East and West Renfrew, and Rutherglen, while a Communist (Walton Newbold) got in for Motherwell. Many of those elected had played a prominent part in the labour unrest and anti-war movement on the Clyde, but their success probably owed less to this than to the post-war depression, the housing problem, and the alienation of the Catholic vote from the coalition government because of the Irish troubles. The right-wing press blamed the socialist exploitation — directed at working-class women — of a recent House of Lords decision that, due to a technical formality, all rent increases since 1916 were illegal: 'The technical right of the tenant to recall money which has been illegally taken from him has been worked upon by base appeals and has been used to the utmost to stimulate the virus of Socialism in the community', and observed of the Catholic voters, some 75,000 in Glasgow, who on 10 November had been instructed by the *Glasgow Observer* to vote Labour: 'Their vote, as it always is, has been organised from the top, and they have recorded the dictates of their leaders with the authority of automata'.

Such calculations were, however, far from the minds of the 8,000 who crowded into the St Andrew's Halls to send the new MPs south. With a religious service that had all the fervour of the signing of the Covenant nearly 300 years earlier or of Gladstone in Midlothian some 40 years before, the new MPs pledged themselves to a range of lofty generalities, at few of which would any Victorian radical have baulked, then left by train for the south. When David Kirkwood arrived at Westminster he remarked to John Wheatley 'John, we'll soon change all this', yet the Clydesiders were themselves the proof that parliamentarianism and political organization could tame revolutionary fervour, and emasculate the reactions to the changes which had so brutally altered the expectations of industrial Scotland.

By 1922 Scottish capitalism had changed profoundly. Markets were no longer expanding, nor was the free market any longer the principal mechanism of industrial co-operation. In significant areas near-monopolies had been set up — as in shipbuilding, steel, and coal — or mergers with English concerns, as with the banks and railways. The whisky industry was consolidated by the Distillers' Company. The majority of Scottish shipowners sold their fleets to the 'big four' (Ellerman, Furness Withy, Peninsular and Oriental, and the Royal Mail Line). Imperial Chemical Industries and Anglo-Iranian Oils took over the petroleum and petroleum-based chemical industries. The remaining Scots-based firms faced a difficult future: distilling, its profits low through wartime liquor control, faced prohibition in America; shipbuilding faced a dwindling freight market, and jute even stronger competition from an increasingly autonomous India. Many magnates got out while the going was good, vaulting on the post-war boom to the head of a British consortium. Was there an age-factor behind this? Were the sons of entrepreneurs born and based in Scotland less loyal to their country because of southern education, and possibly less confident of their ability to cope with the Scottish future?

During the war collectivism expanded in two areas: economic co-ordination and social policy. Scottish entrepreneurs, providing expertise unknown to the traditional civil service, helped to co-ordinate business and government – besides Weir, these included the shipping controllers Joseph (Lord) Maclay. Lord Inverforth, and Lord Inchcape, the remarkable Geddes family, Eric, Auckland, and Mona, who between them virtually took over ancillary military services, Sir Andrew Duncan and Sir James Lithgow. None of these were collectivists in any socialist sense, but they recognized the difference that the state could make to the economic health of their class. Their fathers had done without a state. After 1916 such entrepreneurs realized they needed one – to control the terms of trade, regulate supplies, and keep the workers in order – but they realized that this state was directed from the south. What had developed in Scotland was a 'welfarism' that restricted business autonomy. The emigrés to the south used their wartime experience to develop a modified capitalism, based on cartels, understandings with government, and the stimulus of consumer demand, while the autonomy of Scottish capitalism, already weakened by these defections, was further encroached upon at the margin by rent control, public housing, and the effective civic emancipation of the Catholics, traditionally the lowest-status segment.

And who lost? Old Liberalism was mortally wounded, not simply because of its election setbacks, but because the challenge of Labour's municipal success led rapidly to coalitions with the Unionists. The basis of 'civic reform' politics had been destroyed, crushed by economic decline on one side and by increasing working-class organization on the other. Yet the working-class itself had been hit. The hierarchy of the 'skilled men' was never to be the same again. The miners and fishermen had over two decades of economic depression before them. Agricultural affairs improved somewhat, but at the cost of the Liberal dream of a peasantry on Danish lines. More had died than simply the peasants whom Lewis Grassic Gibbon would commemorate, in the last lines of *Sunset Song*, 14 years later:

> They died for a world that is past, these men, but they did not die for this that we seem to inherit.

2

A Troubled Economy 1922 – 1964

I

There was a mighty paradox about the Scottish economy after World War I, and particularly in the years 1960-76. On one hand accelerated growth, and a fairer distribution of its dividends, was the work of the later period; on the other, these two decades have also seen the collapse of traditional industries, the general weakening of manufacture in both relative and absolute terms, mounting unemployment, continuing emigration, and what seems to be endemic social and political instability.

Table 2.1, based on the censuses of production and other official statistics, attempts to sketch some long-term trends. The real output of the Scottish economy, expressed in an index which takes inflation into account, grew by only 60 points, 1907–60, but by 101 points, 1960–76. The average male manual worker's real wage rose by 108 points in the first period, and by 101 points in the second. Yet unemployment rose from 3.6 per cent in 1960 to 6.4 per cent in 1976 and emigration (see table 3.1) – a reasonable commentary on people's economic expectations – was actually 15 per cent higher, 1951–78, compared with 1921–51, against a rate of natural population increase steadily falling in the 1970s. Scotland's recent gains must, moreover, be seen against much higher gains elsewhere. Real wages, for example, rose between 1960 and 1976 in West Germany by 174 points. This returns us to the gloomy spectacle of the industrial structure and its problems. How much was its funda-mentally parlous condition after 1960 the result of previous events and decisions? And why was its dissolution accompanied not by poverty but by apparent affluence?

Whatever else this affluence did, it deferred consideration of problems of industrial structure which had seemed fundamental before 1939. It has required a lot of research – happily now being carried

Table 2.1: Scottish gross output, in million £s (at current prices)

	1907	1924	1935	1951	1960	1976	1989
Agric./Fisheries	26	54	42	97	113	480	1,004
Mining/1990: energy	23	34	21	50	62	177	1,705
Manufacturing	159	275	220	437	708	2,649	7,935
Iron and Steel	62	94	26	52	70	170	⎫ 4,482
Engineering	29	52	41	157	281	952	⎭
Textiles	31	60	39	54	67	171	⎫
Food and Drink	37	75	65	67	125	605	⎬ 3,452
Other		54	49	107	165	751	⎭
Construction	13	21	15	64	125	902	2,758
Service Sector	42	101	133	590	956	5,652	22,080
Scottish GDP	*263*	*485*	*431*	1,238	1,964	9,863	35,482
estimated % of UK output	*11.8%*	*10.5%*	*8.8%*	9.9%	8.7%	9.1%	8.3%
UK GNP (GDP after 1951)	2,230	4,615	4,902	13,287	22,560	108,384	431,197
Index of Scottish Production (1907 = 100)	100	99	107	126	160	261	232
Index of UK Production (1907 = 100)	100	111	147	160	218	340	332
Value of £(1900 = 100p)	93p	50p	61p	25p	20p	6.5p	1.6p

Note: Estimated figures in italic.

Sources: The data for 1907–35 were gathered from the censuses of production; the agriculture and fisheries figures for 1924 and 1935 from the *Reports* of the relevant Boards and Departments. The (very rough) estimates of (1) total Scottish GDP, 1907–35, and of (2) the Service Sector, 1907–35, were arrived at by assuming that the ratio of Scottish GDP to UK GNP was the same as Scottish industrial production to UK industrial production. The resulting figures give a notion of magnitude, nothing more. Data for 1951 and 1960 from G. McCrone, *Scotland's Economic Progress* (1965), and for 1976–89 from the *Scottish Abstract of Statistics*. Index of Scottish Production (1907 = 100) and subsequent adjustments. Value of £ from David Butler, ed., *British Political Facts* (1980 ed.) and subsequent adjustments. (Edinburgh, 1980, 1992).

out — to determine what these were, and it is still difficult to assess the effectiveness of the responses of the 1930s as possible strategies, as they were superseded by a London-imposed approach of 'demand-management' and 'planning'. Here, of course, the temptation to project back strategies which have contemporary attractiveness is alluring and dangerous. It is no use comparing Scotland with Finland or Sweden if no one in the 1930s was actually thinking in those terms. Professor R.H. Campbell has, as a result of wide reading in the archives of the Scottish economic establishment, argued that its fatalism — in face of the constraints of international demand and Scottish resources — was inevitable.

The problem, however, is broader than this. Post-1945 international demand was a different story from 1922–39, and so was the ostensible degree of planning in the economy. Scottish failures arose increasingly from missed opportunities instead of over-commitment, and from the absence of effective Scottish planning mechanisms. How much was this a legacy from the 1930s? There was then a general conviction among the establishment that diversification was necessary, a conviction also shared by nationalists and socialists. The government's own interventions, in the form of the Commissioner for the Scottish Special Area, his disbursements (amounting to more than £4m. between 1935 and 1938), and the plans propounded by the Scottish Economic Committee, favoured economic planning, explicit in the SEC's *The Case for Planned Development* (1938) and its evidence to the Barlow Commission. But its scheme for a Development Agency was never carried out and while the goals of planning and diversification were ostensibly pursued after the war, the means of attaining them was absent. The heavy industries were either disrupted by contradictory policies from central government, or allowed an independence that amounted, in the long run, to self-destruction. Diversification, divorced from a co-ordinated policy on heavy industry, underlay the 'planning' of the Toothill Report in 1961. In the 13 years between Toothill and the Scottish Economic Planning Enquiry of 1974, which recommended the setting-up of the Scottish Development Agency, the heavy industries dwindled to the extent that they were scarcely capable of supplying 10 per cent of the engineering requirements of the North Sea oil industry.

What influence did Scotland have on the UK economy? In the 1960s, H.W. Richardson and D. Aldcroft argued that the UK economy actually grew faster between 1922 and 1938 than before 1914. New industries — motor vehicles, electrical goods, chemicals, artificial fibres — along with building, expanded rapidly in southern England. Investment shifted from capital goods to serve the domestic market, and this shift was accelerated by the National government after 1931, which safeguarded the domestic market by tariffs, and through reducing unemployment benefit directed funds from the unemployed to the employed. The 'regional problem' was the price to be paid — but in UK terms not an unbearable one. Such historical interpretations have been used recently to argue that post-war regional policies were essentially a misconceived attempt to reverse the inevitable, and have simply resulted in an added incubus on the growing areas of the UK economy. But was the drift south inevitable? Were the new industries optimally-sited, highly productive, well-managed? Or had lack of planning meant that the underused resources of the north were paralleled by congestion and duplication of facilities in the south? Were service industries and white-collar occupations — with no great degree of, or criteria for, productivity — simply absorbing money and management skills needed for proper industrial construction?

II The Structure of Industry

As a percentage of total output, the traditional staples suffered a steep decline between 1907 and 1935, which then levelled off. In 1960 they still accounted for about a third, but by 1976 this had fallen to under a fifth.

Table 2.2: Trends in major sectors of output, in percentage

	1907	1924	1935	1951	1960	1976	1989
Staples: agriculture, fisheries, mining, steel, engineering, and textiles:	53	48	39	33	30	20	30
Other manufactures:	26	27	27	14	15	14	
Construction:	5	4	3	5	6	9	8
Service Sector:	16	21	31	48	49	57	62

Note Estimates in italic.

More serious was the rapid decline after the 1930s of other manufacturing industries — clothing, food and drink, paper, chemicals, timber, and leather goods — frequently as a result of competition from the expanding industries of the south. Although the expansion of services acted as a compensating factor, the result was a narrowing of the industrial base by the 1950s.

The economy remained, however, largely Scots-owned and dominated by small- to medium-sized concerns. Large factories (very common in the new industries of the south) were almost wholly confined to the heavy industries:

Table 2.3: Scottish factories, 1938

	Number of employees	
	1,500 +	250 – 1,500
1. Scotland outside Central Lowlands	2	44
2. Central Lowlands outside Glasgow Area	12	187
3. Glasgow Area (Lanark, Renfrew, Dunbarton)	35	143

Large factories (1,500 + employees)		(Scots-owned in brackets)	
Engineering	12 (7)	Shipbuilding	7 (7)
Textiles and derivatives	11 (10)	Co-operative Works	3 (3)
Metallurgy	8 (7)	Miscellaneous	8 (6)

III The Heavy Industries

Shipbuilding

The health of the Scottish economy depended intimately on international trade. Any fall in this meant overcapacity in shipping and a fall in owners' profits. Fewer ships were ordered and depression spread from the shipyards to the heavy industries. In 1921 not only did the naval market vanish, but the post-war boom collapsed. Shipping was glutted by the products of American shipyards, the confiscation of enemy ships, and the selling-off of the government's own merchant fleet, while trade remained sluggish and the British share of it decreased.

The Clyde's strength in passenger cargo-liners and specialized ships, for which high grades of craftmanship and finish were required, provided partial compensation. But the yards were constrained by old equipment and the restoration of pre-war working practices, while modernization was inhibited by the post-war inflation. Beardmore's, whose reconstruction ruined them, were appalled when their old machinery was eagerly bought up by their Clydeside rivals.

But rivalry was not the rule: shipowners reserved berths or bought shares in shipbuilding firms, which had coped with wartime shortages by buying up steelworks. A tight system of vertical cartelization ensued. For a time in the early 1920s Lord Pirrie presided over an effective amalgamation between Royal Mail Lines, Harland and Wolffs, Lithgows, and Colvilles, which dominated the Clyde. Such

cartels were probably inevitable, but checked innovation and diversification, and the trade slump caused the whole edifice to collapse.

Until 1929 a booming American economy sustained transatlantic
passenger travel by *nouveau riche* and immigrant alike and kept up
demand for passenger liners. In 1930 Cunard-White Star laid down a
£4.8m. 81,000-ton super-liner. But the consequences of the Wall
Street crash ended work on 'No.534' (the *Queen Mary*) at Clydebank.
Elsewhere, orders dried up; by 1933 Scottish output, at 74,000 tons,
was lower than in the 1850s. In February 1930 Sir James Lithgow and
the Bank of England set up the National Shipbuilders' Security
Corporation to 'rationalize' the industry by buying up and 'sterilizing'
under-used yards. It had cut capacity 15–20 per cent by 1935 – at
the cost of great unpopularity – but by then work was resumed on the
Queen Mary (completed 1936), Cunard laid down a sister ship, and
the government started to subsidize cargo steamer construction.
Overshadowing everything, rearmament brought, between 1935 and
1939, £80m. worth of arms orders. But the underlying problems of the
industry remained as far from solution as ever.

Heavy Engineering

Heavy engineering, the other main export staple, was hit even harder.
The fall in raw material prices cheapened imports but meant that
underdeveloped countries had less to spend. UK exports to India, for
example, fell by nine-tenths between 1913 and 1935 and exports
through Scottish ports fell 42 per cent between 1913 and 1937. The
market for railway rolling stock, mineral handling gear, sugar-cane
crushers, and so on declined. The North British Locomotive Company
had produced about 400 engines a year, mainly for overseas, between
1904 and 1914; between 1921 and 1931 this fell to an average of 150.
Although the individual size and value of engines had increased,
annual income fell by over 50 per cent. In 1932 the market collapsed
completely, and never recovered. Much the same could be said of
other heavy engineering works: boiler exports also dropped by
50 per cent between 1913 and 1935, and heavy machine tools, dependent on such industries, experienced a similar decline.

Coal

The problems of the coal industry were even more complex. In 1913
it had produced a record 42.5m. tons; between the wars its average

output was 30m., with much-reduced exports: the 1935 figure was 20 per cent down on 1913. Oil-firing at sea and electrification in Ireland and Europe both contributed to this. Moreover, the great Lanarkshire coalfield was now declining. In 1913 it produced 17.5m. tons, by 1937 only 9m. tons. But the labour force fell faster than production, from 139,500 in 1913 to 86,500 in 1937. Large collieries (20 out of 400) now produced 75 per cent of the coal, output per man increased, and coal cut by machine rose from 22 per cent in 1913 to 80 per cent by 1938. Such were the fruits of victory in 1926. Scottish production per man *vis à vis* Britain had already been 112:100 in 1913; by 1938 it was 141:118. This despite the problems of exploiting the growing Fife coalfield — chiefly a shortage of houses. In the 1930s a tight partnership between the state and owners was created. Labour's Mines Act of 1930 had set up regional production quotas; an international agreement followed, cutting exports but boosting profits. Although mining royalties were nationalized in 1938, shares in coal companies had by then risen by 300 per cent. The losers were the miners. Although they got pithead baths and welfare institutions, their real wages fell by 4.5 per cent, 1913—38, and unionization declined until in Fife in 1934 it was less than 30 per cent. Despite the Fife miners' election of a Communist MP in 1935, demoralization rather than radicalism was the result. In 1942 a Ministry of Information report found the sentiment 'we would be as well off under Hitler' disturbingly widespread in the Scottish coalfields.

Steel

Sixty per cent of Scottish steel (itself about 11 per cent of UK production in 1935) was usually destined for shipyards and the heavy industries, so it was a perilous business. Dwindling local ore, undercapitalization and foreign competition had been followed by arbitrary wartime expansion and shipyard control. This no longer worked, but was the industry to be reorganized as a Scottish monopoly, or allied with English concerns? There was no decision during the 1920s, because of the rivalry of management and firms, and the unhelpfulness of the banks. In 1929 the American consultants, Brasserts, recommended concentration on a single large works using imported ore at Erskine on the Clyde, but it was 1934 before amalgamations produced Colvilles, with about 95 per cent of Scottish capacity. During this period Stewarts and Lloyds followed another Brassert suggestion and moved their works and workforce south to Corby, in the

Northants ironstone fields, in 1932, taking with them most of Scottish tube-making. Rearmament brought vastly increased profits, aided by a 100 per cent rise in productivity 1924—37, but it also meant that the fundamental resiting of the industry was not proceeded with.

Textiles

Textiles scarcely fared better than the heavy industries, the number of employees falling from 137,000 in 1924 to 113,600 in 1935. In wool, changing fashion (a flapper consumed about a quarter of the cloth required for an Edwardian lady) and an extra, mid-twenties slump after the UK's return to the gold standard, drove many producers out of business. However, in the 1930s there was some recovery, notably in the semi-mechanized production of Harris Tweed after 1934, through catering for an enhanced leisure market. This probably also aided the expansion of knitwear in the Hillfoots and Border areas, while Shetland hand-knitting left an indelible mark on the fashion of the period. In carpets, too, Scotland, with a third of the UK industry, profited from the English building boom, not to speak of the invention of the vacuum cleaner. This came as a boost to the hard-pressed jute industry, increasingly subject to Indian competition. In 1938 it was on the edge of a precipice as the English economy faltered. 'Happy as a sandbag' had real meaning for Dundee in 1939.

Aircraft and Motor Vehicles

Scotland had developed substantial aircraft and vehicle industries during World War I, but in the 1920s, when complex passenger planes were a relative rarity, and military orders subject to government defence and purchasing policy, aircraft production vanished. Beardmore's experimented with heavy bombers and Weir's with autogiros. To no avail. Only when defence expenditure went up by 25 per cent after 1937 did production start to come north. Rolls Royce established their 'Merlin' engine plant at Hillington, and Blackburn's an airframe works at Dumbarton.

The failure to develop motor manufacture was more complex and more tragic. Before 1914 more than 40 firms had applied Scots engineering, coach- and bicycle-building skills to the problem. With a big landed and sporting clientele, the Scots 'heavy car' — the Argyll or Arrol-Johnston — up to three tons and 30 horsepower, was famous for finish and reliability. Albion did the logical thing, changed it into a lorry, and survived. Argyll's attempt to take the UK lead in volume production with a very advanced design hit technical and legal problems which ruined the firm in 1912. Reconstructed as a specialist producer, with several other firms, it lasted into the 1920s. Why did the industry then founder? Was it distance from southern markets and the west midlands smallware industry? Possibly failure might have been averted by earlier development of motor-cycles, as popular as cars until the early thirties, and anticipating the small car in terms of market, technology, and maintenance. A large and autonomous American plant might also have turned the tide. But the choice of Dagenham and Luton by Ford and General Motors in the late twenties, the impact of their output, and the 1929 slump, wrote finis to the local industry. In 1935 Scotland contributed only 1.5 per cent of UK production.

Chemicals

Scots chemical output was worth £19m. in 1924, £15m. in 1935; it had fallen from 10.2 per cent of UK output to 7.7 per cent. The reason was a combination of obsolescence and wholesale reorganization in new and gigantic corporations like ICI and Unilever. The Scottish dye-stuffs and bleaching industries crumbled rapidly under the new technologies of Cheshire and Teeside, while compensating developments by the great firms were restricted to petroleum products at Grangemouth and explosives at Ardeer. In the absence of state involvement, this specialization frustrated applied science in general. Pharmaceuticals, for example, remained despite Scotland's medical tradition a tiny sector until World War II.

Food and Drink

The decline of the industrial sector inevitably affected consumer goods, although Edinburgh, as a food-processing and brewing centre, remained an oasis of almost southern prosperity. But British drinkers swilled a third less beer and two-thirds less whisky between the wars, and American drinkers didn't legally exist — until 1933. Amalgamations dominated both industries: the Distillers' Company dates from 1923, McEwan Younger from 1931. Prohibition wasn't an unmitigated disaster for Scotland; it hit Bourbon, after all, harder than Scotch, and when the temperance movement in Scotland made itself felt in veto polls after 1913 there was a compensating movement

towards the ambiguous pleasures of cigarettes, soft drinks, and con-
fectionery — all of which showed substantial inter-war increases.
Several large factories for canning and biscuit-making were opened at
this time; as a result of the modern techniques they used, however,
greater production was achieved with a smaller workforce.

Furniture and Fittings

High family expenditure on food was not repeated in consumer dura-
bles. There was no attempt to create a mass-production furniture
industry, and the cartels that dominated the booming electrical goods
industries had no desire to move their factories north. In 1935 only
2 per cent of electrical goods output came from Scotland, largely in
the heavy machinery sector. Weir and Lithgow's attempt to set up
British National Electric's household goods factory at Carfin met with
little success. Small houses made for a small market, and one already
saturated from the south.

Agriculture and Fisheries

Agriculture was still Scotland's major industry, but its labour force
declined, 1921–38, from 126,900 to 105,300, and its output fell from
£48m. to £40m., in UK terms from 17.2 per cent to 14.4 per cent. This
stemmed partly from a growth in English productivity, partly from
structural changes, and partly from government policy. Lorries and
tractors cut demand for horses by a quarter; whisky decline pulled
barley production down. More seriously, government's first subsidies — for beet (1925) and wheat (1932) — designed to safeguard
English arable farming, penalized Scottish mixed farms (although
these were inherently much more profitable). In fact of total subsidies
of £68.25m. paid by 1935–6, only £4.2m. (6.1 per cent) went to Scotland. With the introduction of cattle subsidies in 1934 things started to
change, but by then many Scots 'marginal' farmers had hit the trail for
the richer lands of the south, like those whom Ronald Blythe recorded
in *Akenfield*:

> News about East Anglia got around fast. It was the land of
> Goshen compared with Scotland. A better climate, easier work-
> ing soil, with no damn great lumps of granite pushing out of it. It
> was, 'Come on, Wully! Come doon here!' It was 'Send home for
> brother Angus and for sister Mary and her man!'

The situation was so bad in fishing that even the Cabinet referred to it in 1934 as a tragedy. The East European market never recovered and Norwegian competition increased. Catches held up, with more efficient motor boats, but the rise in fishermen's real income, 1913−37, was barely 3 per cent. Louis MacNeice's comment was apposite:

> His brother caught three hundred cran when the seas were lavish,
> Threw the bleeders back in the sea and went upon the parish.

Only in 1935 was the Herring Industry Board established by the government to maintain minimum prices and assist re-equipment, but shortly afterwards overfishing brought the white-fish industry, centred in Granton and Aberdeen, into peril. By the time legislation had been prepared to aid it, its elderly fleet had largely been drafted for war service.

Transport

Economic decline meant contraction on the railways, intensified by 'rationalization' like the southward transfer of locomotive building. Staff fell by over 18 per cent, 1924−35. Since less than 8 per cent of mileage was closed down, gains in productivity were considerable, but modernization was delayed until the financial structure of the railways had been safeguarded by the transport act of 1933. Both the LMS and the LNER then introduced fast services to the south and powerful passenger and freight engines, but resentment continued because few orders for these came to Scotland, and government-subsidized electrification schemes were restricted to the English conurbations. Grievances over high freight rates were authoritatively endorsed by the Scottish Economic Committee in 1939.

Ramifying bus services slowed the drift from the countryside, and opened it to coach tourists. Started in the early 1920s, often by ex-servicemen converting old army lorries, these services quickly became dominated by Sir William Thompson's Scottish Motor Traction Company (1906). The railways took a 25 per cent interest in 1928 and increased this to 50 per cent by 1939. Although the tram remained the great symbol of urbanism the bus companies took over and closed down the smaller systems. The lorry and delivery van became familiar in the villages, but commercial road haulage was restricted by the sluggish development of light industry, and the rise of the private car by the small size of the middle class. In 1935 there was 1 car to every 25 people in England, but only 1 to 36 in Scotland.

The railways, along with Coast Lines of Liverpool (who took over Burns and Laird's Irish steamers in 1921), also over-saw the reconstruction in 1925 of David MacBrayne's. In return for a government subsidy of £40,000 per annum, freight and passenger rates were controlled, the elderly steamer fleet modernized and linked to new bus services. Coastal shipping was still important, with regular passenger and freight services to many smallish Scottish ports from England, as well as Leith and Glasgow. After 1932 it faced new competition. The S.M.T. started Scotland's first internal air service. In 1933 Highland Airways began flying from Aberdeen and Inverness to Wick and the Orkneys. Small companies proliferated over the next couple of years, but by 1936, as with the buses, two regional monopolies had taken over. Railway Air Services (a consortium of the 'big four') flew Anson monoplanes to Liverpool and Belfast; while Scottish Airways (incorporating two companies) flew Rapide biplanes to the west coast and Highlands. By 1939 the enduring pattern of Scottish internal services had been created.

Electricity

The provision of adequate electricity by Glasgow Corporation had been crucial to munitions production, and William Weir himself took a leading part in the creation of the State–private enterprise partnership of the national grid. An act was passed in 1926; construction started in 1927, and the Central Scottish Grid, stretching from Aberdeenshire to Carlisle, was complete by 1931. It cost, at £3m.–4m., about 20 per cent of the UK total, and was thus effectively a subsidy to Scottish industry, yet only 18.5 per cent of the work went to Scottish manufacturers. Between 1924 and 1929 the British Aluminium Company spent a further £5m. on a huge hydroelectric scheme to produce aluminium at Fort William, and in the 1930s three further schemes, purely for power supply, were built — in the Tummel area, at the Falls of Clyde, and in Galloway. Yet by 1935 Scottish electricity consumption was only 8 per cent of the British figure — much boosted by new industries in the south-east.

Electricity charges were higher than in the south, and few electrical goods factories moved north. Scottish developments essentially pumped electricity into the English grid, or produced semi-finished materials, and anger at this underlay the parliamentary defeat of the Caledonian power bills of 1936−8 — the only Scottish issue in the inter-war period to absorb the full attentions of the Cabinet.

IV The Problem Defined

The multifaceted nature of Scotland's crisis marked it off from the other 'depressed areas'. Although unemployment (25 per cent in 1932) was less than in Wales (40 per cent) or the north-east (33 per cent), it was also accompanied, as we have seen, by structural upheavals in practically every industrial sector, and in the long term aggravated by the policy changes of firms, financial institutions, and governments. Reduced demand for Scots capital goods coincided with foreign tariffs against Scots luxury goods. Declining landed wealth, and (until 1936) inappropriate government subsidies, hit the rural economy. Foreign unrest, autarkic policies, and loosening imperial ties menaced traditional markets. If revaluation in 1925 was bad, welfare cuts and protection after 1931, which aided southern 'home market' industries at the expense of exporting areas, were worse. To all of this the relief offered to coal by government aid, to steel by protection and rearmament after 1935, while magical for harried entrepreneurs (who suddenly saw an escalation in share values), could only be a palliative.

Scottish unemployment averaged 14 per cent, 1923−30. against the UK's 11.4 per cent. But in 1931−8 this percentage ratio rose to 21.9:16.4. Numbers on poor relief, 1929−36, climbed from 192,000 to 341,000, an increase of 76 per cent against a UK increase of 13 per cent. The contrast with London was even starker. There unemployment was at its worst at 13 per cent in 1932, and was running at 6.3 per cent by 1936, when even prosperous Edinburgh still had 12.3 per cent, Greenock had 20 per cent, and Airdrie 30 per cent. Only in 1930 did J.H. Thomas, for the Labour government (see p.96), commission the first regional surveys, when Professor W.R. Scott and his Glasgow University economists identified some 100,000 men in west central Scotland alone as 'permanently surplus'. Traditionally, the 'surplus' had migrated; an average of 147,000 had left Scotland each decade between 1861 and 1911. Between then and 1930 this more than doubled, but between 1931 and 1939 fell to under 100,000. Emigration had swelled the proportions of the old and very young in the 1920s; in the next decade those in employment became victims themselves.

Unemployment was not a function of industrial decadence. In

certain 'traditional' sectors it actually resulted from industrial advance. Between 1931 and 1935, for example, Scots productivity increased by 8 per cent, against 5.6 per cent in the UK. Unemployment hit family incomes and cut demand for consumer goods. Female labour in such industries fell, making matters worse. The middle class did not do so badly; rarely were more than 5.5 per cent of them unemployed. They suffered pay cuts, but their employment actually grew faster than in England between 1921 and 1931, by 20 per cent against 14 per cent — although there, too, emigration continued to operate as a safety valve. Scotland's demography aggravated unemployment, as the table below shows.

Table 2.4: Demographic trends

| | 1911–15 | | 1936–40 | |
	Scotland	England and Wales	Scotland	England and Wales
Birth Rate per 1,000	25.4	23.6	17.6	14.7
Death Rate per 1,000	15.7	14.3	13.6	12.2
Natural increase	9.7	9.3	4.0	2.5

A rate of natural increase about 30 per cent greater than that of England meant that a larger working population was entering a comparatively stagnant job market. In Scotland in 1923 the labour force was 22 per cent and by 1938 24 per cent of the population. In England, however, the equivalent percentages were 26 and 33, a divergence largely made up by the growth of women's jobs and the service industries. As a result of this, there was 20 per cent less earning capacity in a Scottish family compared to the UK average, and this increased the period at which families were at risk from poverty (chiefly when they had children under earning age).

V Planning a Way Out

Government was not inactive, but scarcely helpful. Faced with over-extended heavy industries (which might yet prove to be of strategic importance) and a labour surplus, Lloyd George and later the Unionists handed the former over to the Bank of England, and tackled the latter by assisted migration schemes, enacted in 1920 and 1928. By 1939 these had shifted 250,000 men and women, largely to the south of England. Labour was more positive; continuing Lloyd George's Trade Facilities Act of 1921, which gave low-interest loans to foreign buyers of heavy engineering products (bringing about £5m. before its abolition by Churchill in 1926), and in 1929–31 instituting a public works programme, mainly involving roadbuilding. Neither Labour nor the Unionists questioned the 'balanced budget' – and defended it against Keynes's and Lloyd George's *Yellow Book* plan for reflation through deficit financing. This involved roadbuilding and electrification, paid for in the long term by an increase in the general tax-paying capacity of the country by its 'multiplier' effect on economic growth. However negative such reactions, the problem remained: could such schemes have revitalized a Scottish economy so deficient in the 'new' industries it proposed to stimulate?

In such situations the banking system played in Europe a critical rôle. Not in Scotland, where the strength and sophistication of its financial institutions – a virtue during industrialization – now channelled investment away from the country. The habit of investing in England was also strengthened by the sheer need to sustain the debts of heavy industry. Although innovative financiers like J. Gibson Jarvie – the founder of hire purchase – struggled to set up a Scottish industrial investment trust, the banks were unwilling to take the risk, and only in 1938 did such a scheme get off the ground. The existing Scots-American trusts had taken a hammering in 1929; where they survived, they were much less adventurous. In fact, most interest in Scottish affairs was taken by the Clydesdale, whose owner, the Midland Bank, was a lone proponent of unorthodoxy in the financial world. The banks continued to cater for the middle-class, not only as clients but by providing a wealth of 'white-collar' jobs in their constantly multiplying branches.

Self-help

The Labour government, in a purely cosmetic move, had encouraged regional groups for industrial development. Partly stimulated by this, on 7 May 1930 the Convention of Royal Burghs set up the Scottish National Development Council, the main resolutions being moved by Sir Alexander McEwen of Inverness and the Duke of Montrose, both later of the Scottish Party. Despite its nationalist origins, by late 1931 it had the support of Sir James Lithgow, and of William Elger of the Scottish Trade Union Congress, and in 1932 it even got a grudging measure of government funding. It took on a full time staff and two years later had produced several reports on economic problems, and a glossy quarterly magazine, *Scotland*.

Lithgow was the SNDC's key figure. He shared many of Weir's strengths and weaknesses: talented, hardworking but undiplomatic, he had a logical case for backing it. Only by drastic reductions in capacity and manpower did he see the heavy industries surviving; other industries were needed to absorb the surplus. At the same time he had no expertise in the consumer goods sector. As the SNDC gathered momentum, so did factory closures. Between 1932 and 1934 58 factories opened in Scotland, 88 closed.

Government Action

Only now did government begin to move. In 1932 and 1933 Walter Elliot, as Minister of Agriculture, stimulated enquiries into health and nutrition in areas of high unemployment, on the advice of his friend John Boyd Orr of the Rowett Research Institute, Aberdeen. As a result the Cabinet on 28 March 1934 agreed to 'informal' investigation of central Scotland, south Wales, north-east England, parts of Cumberland and Lancashire, partly in order to smooth the path of the new Unemployment Assistance Act (see p.77).

As a result, on 24 October the Cabinet suggested a 'Special Areas' Commissioner, with four regional agents. But Sir Godfrey Collins, Scottish Secretary, gained a separate appointment – probably because of pressure from Lithgow and the Unionists for administrative devolution. The original investigator, Sir Hugh Rose, an Edinburgh paint manufacturer and head of the Organization for the Maintenance of Supplies during the General Strike, became the first (unpaid) Scottish Commissioner.

His 'Special Area' covered the counties of Lanark, Renfrew, Dumbarton, Fife, and West Lothian, and parts of Ayr and Stirling. Not Glasgow: to declare the 'Second City' a 'distressed area' was too much. Between 1934 and 1939 Rose and his successors Sir David Allan Hay and Lord Nigel Douglas-Hamilton, spent some £4m. Initially they could only aid public works, but after 1937 they assisted small firms through the Special Areas Reconstruction Association. There were failures: some doomed, eccentric smallholding experiments; several ailing firms, bailed out, going to the wall; but the Commissioners did co-operate imaginatively with the SNDC. Rose recommended in his first report, November 1935. 'An authoritative Scots body . . . financed by the government to explore industrial conditions, and in general aim at introducing into our economic structure . . . [an] element of orderly and planned development'. These proposals went far beyond his local remit, but Collins backed them against the inter-departmental Special Areas Committee and in March 1936 authorized the Scottish Economic Committee, only six months before his sudden death.

The Scottish Economic Committee

The Economic Committee under Sir William Goodchild was formally a sub-committee of the SNDC but the Commissioner paid for it and it co-operated with Elliot, now Secretary of State. It was a timely move, as in March 1937 Baldwin announced the Barlow Commission into the Distribution of the Industrial Population. The SEC reported on the Highlands, light industries, and rearmament policy. It gave evidence to Barlow, published as *Scotland's Economic Future*. It helped promote the Empire Exhibition, Scottish Industrial Estates, Films of Scotland, and the Scottish Special Housing Association, but, on the outbreak of war, it was suspended. Whitehall regarded it with suspicion, and its advocacy of autonomy was, during the war, replaced by the policy of centralized allocation of industry advocated by the Labour Party's 1937 committee of enquiry, under Hugh Dalton, which underlay his 1945 Distribution of Industry Act. But it had, for a few years, focussed Scottish 'middle opinion' approaches to economic and social reconstruction.

It drew on Boyd Orr, whose Rowett Research Station extended its influence from agriculture into welfare, science policy, and propaganda, involving Sir Stephen Tallents, John Grierson, and E.M.H. Lloyd, as well as Elliot, its former research fellow. It rejected the somewhat abstract neo-classicist economics of Sir William Scott in Glasgow and Sir Alexander Gray in Edinburgh in favour of the Keynesian ideas of James Bowie, director since 1931 of the new Dundee School of Economics. Finally, it linked up with the planning movement. Inaugurated by Sir Patrick Geddes, this had been strengthened by the creation of the National Trust for Scotland in 1931 and of the Saltire Society in 1936 by William Power, Boyd Orr, Bowie, and Thomas Johnston, and transformed into an influential advocate of economic and physical planning.

Elliot made the Empire Exhibition of 1938 in Bellahouston Park, Glasgow, the climax of these developments. Costing £11m., it drew on all his connections in science, publicity, and the arts. Architecturally ultra-modernist in design – its architect, Thomas S. Tait, brought in the young Basil Spence and Jack Coia – it was to draw, besides 13m.

visitors, light industries to the new industrial estates. The summer of 1938 was the summer of Munich — and it rained — but it demonstrated that there had been a real advance in analysing the Scottish problem. The SEC, the Clydesdale Bank's report, and Bowie's *The Future of Scotland* (1939) gave the problem a new social dimension. When Bowie, for instance, calculated the investment in a moderate-sized town at £10m., he questioned the sort of accounting which could close its local industry as unprofitable. But such analyses were of an economy distorted by rearmament, while factors seen as underlying — stagnant international trade and an English population decline — proved temporary. The maxims, and many of the personalities, of the 1930s were to prove important after the war. But were they still relevant?

VI World War II

Between 1939 and 1945, in contrast to 1914–18, war production was subject to centralized control. An embryo organization had existed since 1924, and in December 1933, after Hitler had come to power, a small, and mainly Scottish, advisory group of industrialists — Weir, Lithgow, and Sir Arthur Balfour — assessed potential wartime demand. Detailed planning began in 1936 but until 1939 most organization and expenditure was still geared not to total war, but to the finance and facilities that were available in peacetime: only the expenditure of the RAF was placed on a potential war footing. After World War I armaments production had been cut back to a minimum — the Royal Dockyards and Ordnance Factories and a few outside firms. It had also changed in nature. Army and air force demand was for the internal combustion engine and its derivatives; when Lithgow tried to interest Scottish industrialists in these he met with little success. Scottish industry was anyway ill-suited to supply them. Yet, as the most suitable factories lay in the south of England, skilled labour moved south to fill them. Only in Admiralty orders — to the shipyards and Beardmore's — did Scotland do well. When war broke out again Beardmore's again acted as the nucleus of gun and armour production, expanding into factories at Dalmuir, Germiston, and Linwood, and Clyde shipyards turned out an average of 400,000 tons of shipping a year — five ships a week by 1943 — not much under their 1914–18 levels.

At the outbreak of the war, which this time involved conscription from the start, unemployment fell to 20,000 (1.6 per cent) and stayed there. But other effects were serious: 'concentration' of non-munitions production meant that many Scottish factories were simply closed down, often permanently ('other manufacturing industry' fell from 26 per cent of output in 1935 to 14 per cent in 1951), and until late 1941 90 per cent of requisitioned factory space was used for storage. Thirteen thousand girls were drafted to the midlands, causing some political unrest. By July 1942, under pressure both from Scottish MPs, Tom Johnston at the Scottish Office, and the Scottish Council on Industry, storage had fallen to 57 per cent, and by 1945 some 7,000 war-connected projects − 13.5 per cent of the UK total − had been set up, including 119 complete plants: a total investment of £12m. Of these the 26 under the Ministry of Aircraft Production were the largest, employing 100,000 workers by 1945. Scotland became the main staging post both for convoys and for aircraft; Prestwick in 1944 was the busiest international airport in the world.

The workforce changed radically; from 80 per cent male in 1939 to only 60 per cent in 1944. Agriculture expanded: arable acreage increasing 15 per cent to its 1918 level through revived agricultural executives, 75 per cent subsidies, guaranteed prices, and a state holding of 227,000 acres. Wheat and barley acreage doubled, potatoes increased by 75 per cent. Yields − doubtless because of well-fertilized soil − exceeded England and Wales in practically every crop, sometimes by over 30 per cent. The number of tractors more than doubled, from 6,250 to more than 16,000. The fishing fleet was reduced from 5,000 to only 936 boats but, as fishing in English waters was effectively banned, it did creditably, although much of it remained obsolescent.

However, the apparent unity of 'the people's war' masked disturbing trends. Although Johnston could claim several economic gains, such as the creation of the North of Scotland Hydro-Electric Board, and could boast of the absence of a 'Red Clyde', citing a strike record of only 0.7 per cent of working days lost, productivity was persistently poor in munitions factories and very bad in the mines, and Ministry of Information reports cited an undercurrent of discontent, which expressed itself in volatile politics (see p.103). Although the fighting itself claimed only 40 per cent of the casualties of World War I, deaths in the RAF were twelve times and in the Merchant Navy almost two-and-a-half times greater. As the proportion of casualties among officers and warrant officers doubled, Scotland, with 15 per cent of UK secondary pupils, sacrificed too many from a generation in whom even more hope had been invested than in the men of Flanders. Their losses were to echo in subsequent inadequacies of management and innovation.

World War II drastically changed economic and social policy. Labour's 1945 victory made this explicit, but the 'managed' economy, achieved through monetary and especially fiscal policy, really dates from May 1940, when Chamberlain left office and Keynes moved to the Treasury. Chamberlain was not hostile to economic planning — witness the Barlow enquiry — but the new power of 'middle opinion' exemplified by the Beveridge Report (December 1942) integrated the new economics with the 'right' to full employment and health care, and was reinforced by the growing power of Labour in the coalition — personified by Ernest Bevin at the Labour Ministry. The Attlee government's policies were essentially a continuation of wartime practice. Hugh Dalton's Distribution of Industry Act, 1945, actually carried by Churchill's brief caretaker ministry, applied this consensus to regional policy. But, though it drew on the Barlow Report, it rejected the autonomous development authority proposed by the SEC in favour of a centralized system of permits and advanced factories built by the Board of Trade. Although the Council on Industry became the Scottish Council: Development and Industry in 1946, with representation from local authorities, unions, and industry (or at least parts of it), and joint bodies were set up between the Scottish Office and other ministries concerned with industry, the valuable semi-autonomy of the SEC was lost — tragically at a time when increasing numbers of decisions ended up in the hands of less-than-expert Whitehall mandarins.

VII Indian Summer

Was 1940–1951 an economic watershed, as Labour claimed — at least until the late 1960s? Had nationalization of 'the commanding heights', centralized allocation of factory space, investment incentives, and physical planning combated the drift south and promoted diversification? Or did the managed economy, by masking fundamental industrial continuities, increase the problem of readjustment?

For a start financial assistance was limited, even by the standards of the 1930s — in real terms government assistance was only about 56 per cent over the resources allocated to the pre-war Commissioner. The main weapon was compulsion. Yet there was little need to compel plants to the north, because of the lack of factory space and housing accommodation in southern England. Moreover, American companies feared losing European markets through possible tariff increases and shipping shortages, and were anxious to open factories wherever the British government allowed them. Even so, expansion was severely curbed by the financial crisis of 1947, and the prevailing export drive actually restricted diversification, while in the heavy industries the export drive, controls on investment and profits, and the absence of state assistance deferred large-scale re-equipment. After 1947 regional assistance dropped by a third; during the 1950s it was actually less, in real terms, than in the 1930s, and all but nominal.

Although industrial building in Scotland had run at 12.2 per cent of the UK figure between 1945 and 1951 it fell to 6.5 per cent in 1958. Regional policy may have been an article of Labour faith, but in 1951 the Scottish Council's Committee on Local Development concluded that 'the disappearance of large-scale unemployment has by no means been due entirely, or even principally, to the new policy'. The wartime decline in the range of Scottish manufacturing was never made good, and by 1953 Cairncross reported that 'dependence on the heavy industries has grown rather than diminished'.

Shipbuilding

The need to restore wartime destruction — allied losses *alone* came to 23,351,000 tons, compared with total losses during World War I of 15,053,786 tons — and the bombing of enemy ships and shipyards, brought an Indian summer to the Clyde. But Cairncross noted the 'comparative indifference' of the heavy industries 'to new equipment, new knowledge, and new opportunities for development'. They had merely been granted a stay of execution. They did not attempt to reverse the sentence.

The slump of 1957–8 in the Scottish heavy industries, which turned out terminal, started with a drop in demand. But the underlying trend was in fact a quite unprecedented demand for ships and engineering. In 1954 world shipping totalled 97m. tons, freighters averaged 6,000 tons, and the world's largest ship was the *Queen Elizabeth* at 83,000 tons. By 1973 world tonnage was 289 million, largest ship, the tanker *Globtik Tokyo*, grossed 239,000 tons, and the combination of containers and 'inter-modal' transport had completely transformed freight handling. The closure of the Suez Canal in 1956 focussed attention both on oil consumption (Britain's grew 200 per cent, 1950–60) and on its transport. The Cape of Good Hope route both demanded and permitted huge ships, and their pattern influenced other cargos and dock design. Scots had experimented with the new technology for years — Brassert's plan for a waterside steelworks in 1929, Dennys' construction of the first modern car ferry in 1939, the Finnart oil-discharging port in 1952. But these innovations were not capitalized on. Why?

It is difficult to find any simple reason. Development failures for instance, beset car ferries. Scotland's early lead was hit by the 1939–55 decline in motoring, and by the sinking of the roll-on, roll-off *Princess Victoria* off Stranraer in 1953. Several years were to pass before another attempt was made, but by 1964 the Germans and Swedes had cornered the market. As the airlines took their toll, vehicle ferries were the only way that the 'hotel-ship' yards would survive, yet Dennys, the major short-sea builders, were one of the first casualties in 1961. They were soon followed by other specialist firms, like Simons-Lobnitz of Renfrew and the Grangemouth Dockyard Company.

The tragedy was that these yards reached Scandinavian standards of craftmanship and tranquil labour relations. By contrast, the great Clydeside concerns were a mess. Their family managerial dynasties were suicidally conservative, in design, marketing, research, and labour relations. Their equipment was depreciating by £9m. per annum, while only half that sum was being re-invested. Research and development ran at a paltry £250,000. Rationalization was badly needed — in Japan 5 engineering works served 18 main shipyards, on the Clyde 9 works served 16 yards — but it was seldom even discussed, management rivalries and union bloody-mindedness ruling even joint consultation out of court.

Engineering

Heavy engineering initially benefited from its semi-monopoly position. Until 1950 railway orders were almost at the 1920 level, and in 1947 Pressed Steel Fisher established a huge waggon plant at Linwood, near Paisley. Yet diesel and electric locomotives were taking over, and the North British Locomotive Company was unable to supply them successfully. Although reprieved by the £1,050m. British Railways re-equipment programme, which also brought orders for 34,000 out of 46,000 new waggons to Scottish works, and Glasgow electric 'Blue Trains' orders to Pressed Steel, it closed in 1961. Shortly afterwards Linwood was turned over to the motor industry.

It was not all loss, however. Many of the techniques of heavy industry were equally applicable to construction, which grew rapidly in the 1960s, and the reservoir of skilled manpower was indispensable for installing and maintaining the first generation of light engineering 'transplants' — Westclox, IBM, Hoover — and after 1962 the motor plants of Linwood and Bathgate. What had been lost, however, was the link between skill and innovation: something which not even the establishment of the National Engineering Laboratory at East Kilbride in 1947 could remedy.

Steel

Scottish steel largely provided plates and castings for heavy industry: in 1950 15 per cent of its output went to mechanical engineering, 15 per cent to constructional engineering, and 20 per cent to ship-building. Only 0.3 per cent went to the vehicle industry (12 per cent in the UK). Although a 'hot-metal' works was built at Clydebridge in 1938, Motherwell, Hallside, Glengarnock, and Parkhead still used Siemens open-hearth furnaces to reduce a mixture of scrap and imported pig-iron. After 1945 scrap and coking coal were scarce, and steel imports grew. But political uncertainty inhibited planning: Labour announced nationalization in 1945, but did not table a bill until 1948. Delayed by the Lords, the takeover only came in January 1951, 10 months before the return of the Unionists, who in 1953 returned the industry to private hands, subject to overall control by a state board. The nationalized board favoured reviving Brassert's scheme, but its successor in 1954 let Colvilles build a new integrated iron-and-steel works at Ravenscraig, near Motherwell, served by an ore-discharging plant at Glasgow's General Terminus Quay. This opened in 1960, and alongside it in 1962 the company started a steel strip mill to serve the motor industry. Economists had favoured a shore site in south Wales, but mounting government unpopularity in Scotland prompted Harold Macmillan to split the scheme and loan Colvilles £50m. In 1967, when Labour renationalized the industry, Scotland's output of strip steel had risen six-fold, but overall production continued to decline. Twenty per cent of UK output in 1920, it had fallen to 12 per cent in 1960. The industry was badly sited, technically conservative, and its large product range was dictated by its predominately local market: all aspects that the corporate planning of the new British Steel Corporation announced itself ready to remedy.

Energy

Labour nationalized the mines in 1948, and shortly announced plans for major expansion intended to double output to 30.6m. tons by 1965. This involved exploitation of the Fife coalfield and centralization of production in 13 large mines, of which the greatest, Rothes, was to cost £15m. But, partly because of the expenses of mine-sinking, and partly because of the numbers still working in old pits, productivity remained low, and the Scottish region of the National Coal Board slid into deficit. The complete failure of the huge Rothes venture in 1960 sanctioned a rapid contraction of the industry. By 1970 production was down to 12.7m. tons and the labour force to 29,700. Its situation had not been helped by the Hydro Board. By 1961 the Board's construction programme was virtually complete and it supplied over a third of Scottish electricity. Before the war socialist and environmentalist critics of Highland water power had stressed this consequence. Johnston had sold it successfully as an agency for regenerating the Highlands, a national investment, and a triumph for Scots autonomy — and it was subsequently rarely criticized. But it was none of these things; without it, coal might not have hit the trough of the early 1960s. By the middle of that decade the Hydro Board's contribution was plainly inadequate, and a programme of large steam generators — coal, oil, and nuclear — was announced. Power generated, about 1,900 Megawatt Hours in 1939, rose to 2,208 MW in 1950, 3,017 MW in 1961, and 10,378 MW in 1978.

Agriculture

War and Labour government completed the reconstruction of agriculture. After 1947 the state guaranteed prices for farm produce, injecting 20 per cent of UK agricultural expenditure into Scottish farming, against 6 per cent in 1939. Scotland had only 11 per cent of UK output but, as livestock received higher subsidies than arable produce, her dependence on it increased. By 1964 she produced 15.2 per cent of UK livestock, compared with only 9.5 per cent of livestock produce (milk, eggs, etc.) and 7.5 per cent of arable crops. Farms were consolidated and sophisticated equipment bought, as rural electrification was extended. Land workers, 120,000 in 1945, tumbled to under 40,000 in 1964. Although they were better off and could now afford a car, freezer, and television, the differential between their income and that of the farmers widened. It now made sense for landowners to farm their own land, so the 'gentleman farmers', whom the sociologist James Littlejohn had noticed filtering into *Westrigg*, proliferated.

Agricultural-based industry also flourished. Meat- and fruit-canning expanded in Fraserburgh, Dundee, and Fochabers, and was supplemented by freezing and vacuum-packing. Brewing and distilling grew spectacularly. Breweries, increasingly English-controlled, pushed up output from 1.2m. barrels in 1939 to over 2m. barrels in 1960, subsequently soaring to over 5m. barrels in 1980, although enthusiasts regretted the abandonment of traditional ales in favour of lager-type beers for the English market. Distilling's post-prohibition upswing was checked by the war, but it subsequently became Scotland's leading export industry. In 1975 its output was valued at £312m. Shipbuilding brought in only £215m.

The Service Sector

After World War II the service sector rose to dominate the economy. In 1936 its components — transport and distribution, business and commerce, and public service — made up about 32 per cent of output, against 36 per cent in the UK. By 1958 Scotland had almost reached the UK level of 49 per cent; in the 1960s she went ahead. Given the extent of the country, transport and distribution were always important; likewise the public services. But business and commerce lagged: in 1958 income from these was still 28 per cent below the UK level, while in 1961 Scotland had only 7 per cent of UK administrators and managers. The activity of retailing was checked by low expenditure per head, which actually fell from 92 to 90 per cent of the UK level 1953—62. It remained fairly distinctive until the mid sixties: few public markets, a strong but rather stagnant Co-op movement, and enough future in department stores to stimulate the activities of tycoons like Isaac Wolfson and Hugh Fraser. Self-service came late, around 1960, and only in the 1960s did growing consumer expenditure attract the English multiples. By 1978 Scottish consumer expenditure was actually slightly over the UK level, but the incomers had changed the face of the Scottish high streets completely.

Transport

Transport changed slowly in the 1950s. Tramcars dwindled, and finally vanished from Glasgow in 1962. Cars were still relatively rare outside country districts, because of dense and cheap bus services, and the sheer difficulty of accommodating them in the narrow tenemented streets of the big towns. The railways had changed little. Only five trains a day ran from Glasgow to London in 1957; the fastest one took 7 hours 40 minutes, 70 minutes longer than 1939. There were still 3,208 miles of track. New roads were few, save in new towns and housing schemes, but by 1960 even the most local routes had been surfaced, although in the Highlands single-tracked roads were still the rule. MacBrayne's steamers still loaded goods, cattle, and cars 'over the side'; puffers still chugged through the Forth and Clyde and Crinan Canals, out to the beaches of the Western Isles.

Change began in 1955, with the start of the Forth Road Bridge. By the time it opened in 1964, a Tay Road Bridge was also under construction (opened 1966) and road expenditure had risen from £2.6m. to £34m., or in real terms by 1,000 per cent. This was at the expense of the railways, which were drastically rationalized, both by Conservative and Labour governments. This process benefited some areas — intercity passenger, container, and bulk traffic, but the division of responsibility between the Ministry of Transport (railways) and the Scottish Development Department (roads, ferries, and buses) frustrated co-ordination. The fruit of the vast expenditure of 1960–75 was a railway system reduced by 42 per cent and a fall of 50 per cent in bus passengers.

Tourism

Tourism was equally impeded by poor planning. Boosted by holidays with pay after 1938, it roughly doubled in size between then and 1958, to earn about £50m. a year. But it remained unsure of its aim: a mass market or a wealthy one? Although the government set up a Scottish Tourist Board in 1946, it gave it only £20,000 in 1958, and by then the mass market was going: the Clyde was losing out to the Costa Brava. When the state did intervene, stimulated by the Irish example, in the 1960s, it perpetrated some horrid developments — the Aviemore centre — and squandered assets like the Clyde steamers. Business had doubled again by 1970, but grew only a third as fast as the rest of Britain. The Highlands and Islands Development Board, however, served its area well, and also boosted the quality of crafts and souvenirs. In the 1950s families toured the Highlands in Morris Oxfords and complained about Japanese knick-knacks. In the 1970s they could buy quality pottery and handweaves to take home in their Datsuns.

VIII Planning Redux

Scotland's economic problems in the late 1950s were difficult to unravel. Structural changes in the heavy industries were fundamental, but government actions aggravated them. Deflation in late 1957 — the consequence of an overambitious defence pro- gramme — coincided with the phasing-out of National Service. Civilian jobs were shed, while the potential labour force was swelled. The government stopped subsidizing shale and jute and cut back the coal industry's plans. As a result, unemployment in Scotland doubled between 1958 and 1959 from 58,000 to 116,000, while the outlook in the heavy industries and mines, and on the railways, seemed even worse. The general election of October 1959 made Scottish appre- hension explicit.

'The spectre of the 1930s' or the result of labour fractiousness? There were grounds for both views. Productivity was poor: in the mines scarcely higher than 30 years earlier. Incoming American firms placed Scotland, with Italy, at the bottom of their productivity scale. The memory of what productivity had meant in the 1930s went deep. 'Hostile suspicion', Cairncross noted in 1952, 'often flares up in reaction to proposals in which there is any hint of labour redun- dancy'. With some reason. Agriculture saw a rise in productivity of 300 per cent, 1939–60, but this benefited the farmer or the consumer, not the weakly-organized farm workers or the local community. Other unions were more grimly defensive.

But management was often no better. As Tom Burns showed in *The Management of Innovation* (1961), the 'mechanical' relationships between departments in Scottish firms lacked the strength of the 'organic' corporate identity of American firms. Scottish managers found relief from difficult organizational problems either by blaming others or by assuming 'irreconcileable differences of attitudes and codes of rational conduct'. Scottish inventiveness could still produce the marine stabilizer and fibreglass, but long-term planning, state or private, was missing. Too much responsibility had drifted south, and too much ability had followed it. The successors of flawed giants like Lithgow or Weir were, as advocates of 'planning', more diplomatic, but also less original and less energetic. Consensus was preferred to abrasiveness, even if the resulting cosiness made it difficult to ascertain success or failure.

The planners, the Scottish Council and the trade unions had been kept out in the cold by the Unionists. The Council had attracted many

American firms, but could foresee stiffer opposition — both from the EEC (1957) and from Eire after the Whitaker Report of 1958. The grandiose regional plans of Mears, Payne, and Abercrombie had lain in pigeonholes for a decade; as the backlog of war-delayed building was completed in the mid 1950s, the architects and planners feared a repetition of the hard times of the 1920s; they were echoed by property men, the construction industry, and, increasingly, the road transport lobby. The STUC, too, had helped attract American firms by conceding union privileges. It was now worried that militancy would grow with unemployment.

But the spectre of economic decline was not the only motive for 'planning'. British attitudes changed sharply in the mid 1950s; a quite unprecedented hedonism propelled the country out of the 'Victorian straitjacket'. As usual this reached Scotland a bit late, but by 1959 Scots were lumping grumbles about smaller houses, fewer cars, worse food, and more restrictions alongside concern about mounting unemployment. When Gavin McCrone's detailed survey *Scotland's Economic Progress* came out in 1965 it showed a growth rate (9 per cent, 1954–60) running at half the UK level, and income per head 13 per cent lower than the UK average — political factors as (if not more) important than industrial reconstruction.

In 1960 Macmillan, through the Local Employment Act, resumed an active regional policy, and the Scottish Office, acting through the Scottish Council, began 'An Inquiry into the Scottish Economy'. The resulting 'Toothill Report' (November 1961) was politically important: it revived the concept of planning and gained it consensus support. As an economic diagnosis it was much more suspect. The central problem remained that of the heavy industries. Before 1939 their productivity grew but their market stagnated; after 1950 the opposite was the case. Yet was their decline inevitable? Cheap labour and raw material might have gone, but skills, adaptiveness, and a valuable range of ancillary industries remained. Could specialized types of production be maintained, or should heavy industry gradually be phased out in such a way that its ancillary industries became self-standing and its skills were preserved? Toothill ignored heavy industry almost completely, in favour of 'new industry' growth-points, infrastructural improvement, and industrial incentives. By dismissing further measures of economic devolution, it also removed the possibility of a planned adaption from old industries to new. In comparison to the Scottish Economic Committee's realism in 1938, Toothill, despite its similar vocabulary, was a sad decline.

The Scottish Development Department (1962) and the Central Scottish plan (1963) stemmed directly from Toothill, and Labour was quick to use it as a stick to belabour 'stop – go' Unionist policies. But Labour after 1964 dropped Toothill's positive insistance on 'growth points' in favour of a broad Scottish Development Area, only to find itself giving first-aid to the rapidly declining heavy industries. The Scottish Council itself subsequently rejected the Toothill formula: in 1970 it proposed *Oceanspan*, which intended to revive heavy industry by using the Clyde as a transhipment port for western Europe. It seemed a sensible option, but 'to lose traditional industries with comparative international advantages', as the economist Peter Jay told the Council in 1974, was to court 'a perpetual dynamic of decay'. By then, heavy industrial decline had gone too far.

3

The Pillars of Society 1922 – 1964

I

'A separate society', according to Tom Bottomore, in *Sociology*, implies 'political independence along with distinct economic, religious, and familiar institutions'. Plainly, Scotland fails to meet such criteria. Its politics and its economy are clearly those of the United Kingdom, albeit with important variations. Yet Bottomore's more detailed list of 'functional prerequisites of society', in the same book, suggests a more complicated picture. These include, besides economy and politics, systems of communication: 'arrangements (including the family and education) for the socialization of new generations and . . . systems of ritual, serving to maintain or increase social cohesion'. Communications and culture — certainly distinctive — will form much of chapter 5. This chapter will deal with socialization, ritual, and social stratification. Such categories are not, of course, mutually exclusive; they overlap. Different interpretations have seen inherent structure and system as crucial or, in the case of Marxism, have seen the central motive of human action inhering in one part of the system — the economy — which fundamentally influences all other parts.

In Scotland education, religion, and law have functions that are political as well as social. They both legitimate Scottish distinctiveness and require the systematic adaptation of British legislation. Moreover, in the absence of a Scottish legislature, they have a political life of their own, concerned to maintain their status — and that of their members — in a society on the whole more pluralistic than that of the south. This causes problems for the historian. The history of Scots institutions, written 'from the inside', has stressed their distinctiveness over their actual function, while, conversely, studies of British society more rooted in a class-analysis have tended either to exclude Scotland, or to subsume its experience by aggregating its data into

British patterns which it then treats as norms. This co-existence of parochial complacency and metropolitan insensitivity has meant that no real attempt has been made to relate Scottish distinctiveness to class structure.

If Scotland substantially originated the study of 'man in society' in the eighteenth century, and produced Sir J.G. Frazer and Sir Patrick Geddes in the nineteenth, twentieth century Scottish sociology has had an unhappy history. In contrast to inter-war European states, where sociology was an essential ingredient of liberal or social-democratic social planning, the Scots produced only a handful of research papers, and the *Third Statistical Account of Scotland* (commenced in 1943) was a sad declension from Sinclair's *Accounts* of the 1790s and 1830s, — a failure reflected palpably by the planning mistakes of the 1960s. Can this be attributed to the plight of the Scottish universities in the inter-war years, and their lack of investment in research (see p.78)? Possibly, but the country produced some good social scientists, and some of them taught in the universities. If there was little inclination, or external pressure, towards the study of Scottish society this was reinforced by the power of the Scottish institutions themselves. The result necessarily complicates the writings of chapters like this. What follows can only be a sketch, with impressionistic data, and a guide to where further research is necessary, with some hunches and generalizations, pending that massive task.

II The People

Between 1921 and 1961 Scotland's population grew by only 6 per cent. Despite consistently lower rates of natural increase — 5.9 against 7.2 per cent in the 1920s, 4.4 against 6.7 per cent in the 1950s — the population of England and Wales grew by 21 per cent.

Out-migration was the main reason, but this was not simply a function of economic deterioration. It was higher in the Edwardian period and in the Indian summer of the 1950s than in the stricken 1930s, when absence of opportunities elsewhere seems to have checked it by at least 50 per cent, thus contributing to Scotland's persistent unemployment. A positive 'emigration ideology' was certainly present — especially in the post-war period when overseas emigration prevailed over 'drifting south'. As *Scotland* reported in 1956, 90 per cent of emigrants were under 45, and most were 'drawn from the most important industrial groups'. Family ambitions, rather than personal economic circumstances, prevailed as a motive. In the 1960s losses came to

94 per cent of natural increase; in the 1970s they were 163 per cent.

Regional population distribution changed relatively little after the late 1800s. The Scots who lived in the central Lowlands certainly increased from 61 per cent of the total population in 1871 to 76 per cent in 1961, but the proportion dwelling in the 4 cities and 20 large burghs — 51 per cent in 1901 — scarcely changed. The drift from the countries north of the central belt — 8 per cent between 1911 and 1931 — had dropped to 2 per cent by 1951. Some industrial growth and better communications (especially cars, buses, and delivery vans) certainly helped combat farm mechanization and fishing decline, until electrification, oil, and the activities of the Highlands and Islands Development Board came to the rescue. Between 1951 and 1974 population rose by 15 per cent. Lacking such inputs, the southern uplands, where population held stable until 1951, dropped by 6 per cent in the same years.

Buses, council housing, and lack of long-term planning also pre-served, in the central belt, many old industrial settlements that ought to have been evacuated and demolished. As a result an unlovely 'third Scotland' sprawled from South Ayrshire to Fife, merging with outlying city housing schemes, speculative developments, and new towns. The 'third Scotland' was neither much liked nor at all well known. Somewhat isolated, ignored, lacking city facilities or country traditions — even lacking the attentions of sociologists — yet, as the

Table 3.1: Population, 1911 − 1984 (in thousands)

	Scotland (% of UK)	Natural Increase	Net Migration to rest of UK	Overseas
1911	4,760 (10.5) [+]			
1911 − 21		360.2	− 238.6	
1921	4,882 (10.4) [+]			
1921 − 31		352.4	− 330	− 60
1931	4,842 (10.5)			
1931 − 51		502.3	− 210	− 10
1951	5,096 (10.1)			
1951 − 61		339.3	− 140	− 142
1961	5,179 (9.8)			
1961 − 71		346.3	− 169	− 157.5
1971	5,228 (9.4)			
1971 − 81		55.9	− 54.1	− 92.1
1981	5,180 (9.2)			
1981 − 90		21.0	− 99.0	
1990	5,102 (8.9)			

[+] UK included all Ireland

Table 3.2: The New Towns

	Population 1975	
	Actual	*Planned*
East Kilbride (1947)	70,000	95,000
Glenrothes (1948)	32,000	70,000
Cumbernauld (1956)	31,000	70,000
Livingston (1962)	21,000	100,000
Irvine (1969)	46,000	120,000

population of Glasgow plunged 25 per cent, 1951—80, it steadily grew, and showed a fair amount of political volatility in the 1960s, as though nationalism provided some sort of substitute for the community identity it lacked.

One ingredient of 1960s politics absent in Scotland was racial tension. The post-war labour surplus meant little inward migration. As the Irish inflow slackened after the 1920s, most incomers were English (5 per cent of the population by the 1960s) usually in somewhat temporary armed service or management rôles. They found Scottish education and housing sufficiently strange to make major office transfers a tricky business. Hence Toothill's attempts to reassure them. The tension that the Irish had earlier aroused in Scotland, and that coloured immigration provoked in England in the 1950s and the 1960s, was absent. New Commonwealth immigrants were only 0.2 per cent of the 1966 population, compared with 1.1 per cent in the UK, no more noticeable than the communities of Jews, Italians, Poles, and foreign students in the larger towns. As the immigrants either integrated well, or were unobtrusive, working class racialism was absent. Were the Scots more tolerant? Possibly. Despite much anti-Irish propaganda in the 1920s, the Catholic community had become well integrated, and there were few reverberations from events in Ulster. But immigrant numbers were never sufficient to put this to the test.

III Family and Household

Scottish families, in common with the rest of the UK, fell in size in the twentieth century; but they still remained larger than the British norm, even in 1961: something that increased the non-earning section of the population — and thus the poverty figures — in the 1930s. More children survived than previously. Due largely to antisepsis, infant mortality fell from 1 in 6 in the 1890s to 1 in 8 by 1911 (under the UK figure of 1 in 7); this rate of improvement was not sustained. In 1938 it was 1 in 11, but England had improved to 1 in 16, and Holland stood at 1 in 30. This was largely due to Scotland's industrial depression and poor housing, although possibly aggravated by later marriage and inferior antenatal facilities. In the 1930s government and local authorities started to shift confinements to maternity homes, a process continued under the National Health Service. Angus, for example, got its first maternity hospital in 1939; by 1948 60 per cent of births were in such hospitals, and by 1966 97.8 per cent. By then infant mortality had fallen to 1 in 66.

Large families were also due in part to a large Catholic population: 15 per cent in 1961, against 10 per cent in the UK. But among the Protestant middle classes attitudes were changing. In 1918 Dr Marie Stopes, the product of an Edinburgh liberal background, published *Married Love*, her famous plea for the acceptance of sexual pleasure in marriage and, logically, of contraception. This was attacked by all the churches — the Kirk only grudgingly changed its mind in the 1940s — but family planning clinics were opened in the cities, and in the 1930s Aberdeen formulated one of the most advanced family planning and maternity services in Europe, under its Medical Officer of Health, Sir Dugald Baird. 'Artificial' contraception was less important than *coitus interruptus* until the 1950s, but family size dropped from around five to two children. Reduced drinking must have helped this, and doubtless, too, a growing if grudging valuation of the wife's rôle as wage-earner and housekeeper.

In its turn, this exposed marriage to greater stress. Divorces, while more available than in pre-1914 England, were prohibitively expensive, and reform was delayed until 1938. Thereafter the number increased considerably, to 2,000 in 1951 and nearby 3,700 in 1966. Divorce reflected both growing instability and male irresponsibility; the number of single-parent families, 4,000 in 1947, grew to over 25,000 in 1972 — although this also testified to a welcome disinclination among Scotswomen to tolerate the semi-servitude that marriage had often entailed.

Before World War I, and for a long time afterwards in heavy industry areas, women acted as housekeeper: usually to more than one worker per household. But they had become 25 per cent of the labour force in 1921, 35 per cent in 1961. Wages were still poor, and rose from under 40 per cent of male wages in 1921 only to 50 per cent in 1961. But women were arguably more socially mobile than men; they voted with their feet. Littlejohn, in *Westrigg*, noticed that a farmworker's daughter could marry a farmer without the latter losing caste, and otherwise would often move into towns in search of eligible partners.

The same applied to miners' daughters, reluctant to housekeep in male-dominated pit villages. Even before post-1945 light industries set out to attract women, they were in the majority in Scottish towns. This was true of textile communities, but as women usually outlived their menfolk and then moved near to relatives this meant that in the 1950s (when the overall ratio was 101 men to 109 women) a large Scottish town would show only 88 single men to 124 widows, while a country district would show 110 single men to only 81 widows.

Surveys, like Willmott and Young's of East London, stressed the shift from 'extended' to 'nuclear' families. The Scottish case was less straightforward. Scottish farm-workers had moved around almost like nomads although minimum wage and national insurance (1935) was bringing this to an end. The extended family — with its 'hive' of relatives living close to one another — was really an urban phenomenon, and a relatively recent one.

A 1960s survey of Edinburgh housing estates found that in Wardieburn, a 1930s slum clearance scheme, 83 per cent of families had relatives in the city, in 27 per cent of the cases no more than a mile away. By contrast, only 35 per cent of families in owner-occupied Silverknowes had Edinburgh relatives. As grannies and aunts helped bring up children and run the household — an unthinkable activity for men — the working-class 'hive' of interlocking activities (contrasted with the middle class 'network' of optional acquaintances) was relatively female dominated. It was also menaced, both by the growing numbers of working women, and by the impact of rehousing. The Edinburgh survey found three responses to this: 'escalators' aimed at an affluent nuclear family, buying more consumer goods — though not housing or private education. Fathers played a greater part in looking after the family and decorating the house: 'Ubiquitous is the cherry moquette suite, the contrasting wallpaper, the television set in one corner, and the budgie in another'. If the 'escalators' resembled the 'affluent workers' of Goldthorpe's Luton survey, the second group were more characteristically Scots: often composed of people, originally from the same area, who tried to recreate the same interdependent working-class community. Success tended to depend on the 'stair-heid' politics of a dominant working-class woman, such as the one who organized a fry-up on Granton foreshore. Where such were lacking, in the slum clearance estates like Wardieburn, the older residents regretted the 'paradise lost' of their old communities, and were seemingly incapable of integrating either unruly youngsters or the 'problem families' that increasingly were dumped there.

The initial poverty of Wardieburn families diminished their resilience. Working-class community required some degree of affluence: it was no substitute for it. Ultimately, affluence even gave the extended family a new lease of life. Car ownership rose from 1:7 people in 1961 to 1:5 in 1978 and 1:3 in 1990. Telephone ownership rose even faster, from 1:7 in 1961 to 1:2 in 1978. With 81 per cent of homes connected in 1990, families could remain 'extended' even after rehousing.

Family life preserved accents, although broadcasting, 'talkies', and the hostility of the schools to the 'speech of the street' emasculated the old dialects. 'Speaking broad' was a badge of working-class identity, and the English of working-class leaders, who could either be inarticulate (like William Adamson) or else of an almost artificial 'cut glass' or 'plum in the mooth' precision, bore out some of Edwin Muir's suppositions about the consequences of having to be literate in a foreign language. In London, however, Scots was less socially crippling than provincial English. Sean Connery's Edinburgh accent — referred to by one critic as 'Martian' — established him as a very potent 'James Bond': a part that could never have been played by a Brummie.

IV Housing

Family life was limited, above all, by poor housing. In 1911 less than 8 per cent of the population of England and Wales lived in one- and two-roomed houses: in Scotland 50 per cent. High land values, legal peculiarities, rapid urbanization, a tradition of multi-storey living and relatively low rents had led to an acceptance of lower standards.

Despite the Royal Commission's report, after 1918 the situation became, if anything, worse. Those living in one or two rooms had dropped by about 3 per cent per decade, 1871–1911, to 50 per cent of families. But the fall between then and 1931 was only to 44 per cent. The Commission had talked of a target of 250,000 new homes (rather over a quarter of the existing housing stock). Between 1919 and 1939 300,000 were in fact built, but in 1935–6 the first survey to supply equal criteria north and south of the border found that 22.5 per cent of Scottish homes were overcrowded, compared with 3.8 per cent in England. The best Scottish case — Edinburgh with 17 per cent — was almost equal to the worst English one — Sunderland with 20.6 per cent. Clyde valley towns commonly reached over 40 per cent and even council houses (by then, about 12 per cent) were as overcrowded as the national average. In all, almost 50 per cent of Scottish housing stock was now deemed inadequate.

A further inhibiting factor was the tenants' success in winning rent control. As private renting was now inherently uneconomical, landlords had no motive to alter, enlarge, or repair properties.

Even after 1918, the rate of new building per head of population was only 60 per cent that of England, there being no equivalent to the building boom of the 1930s. The conditions which led to it — growing industries, cheap mortgages (building societies were almost non-existent in Scotland) and raw materials, the inward migration of labour, and potential customers — were all lacking.

Finally, local authorities and the state were both inexperienced. Local authorities had, before 1914, rehoused fewer than 1 per cent of Scottish families, but the Housing (Scotland) Act (1919) made them the main instruments of housing construction. This inexperience, coupled with the absence of a proper advisory staff or effective cost controls, meant that the first generation of council houses were overpriced, and the 'Addison Act' was a virtual dead letter by the time of the Geddes cuts. Between 1919 and 1923 only 25,000 houses had been built. The Chamberlain Act of 1923 subsidized privately-built houses for rent by £4 per annum, and built over 50,000. The Act of 1924, however, was largely Scottish in conception and execution, the work of John Wheatley, the ablest of the Clydesiders. By this an annual subsidy of £9 per house per year was paid to the local authority by the state. When passed to the tenant, this meant a cut of between a third and quarter of his weekly rent, or an extra room. The number of houses built 1925–9 went up by 140 per cent on 1920–4.

The theory behind these Housing Acts was that council houses would cater for the better-off tenant, whose relatively tolerable accommodation would then be available to the less well-off. At the bottom of the ladder, slums would thus steadily be cleared. However, this 'stepladder' needed some affluence to work, otherwise it simply subsidized the better-off while the slum-dwellers stayed put. In 1930 Labour shifted the stress to wholesale slum clearance and rehousing on new estates, built to higher densities, while the later Act of 1935 concentrated on more selective remedying of the overcrowding revealed by the report of that year. Walter Elliot placed particular stress on housing, attained an inter-war maximum of nearly 20,000 completions in 1918, and formed the Scottish Special Areas Housing Association, a government building organization using new construction systems. This was to play a remarkable rôle in the post-war period.

The slum clearance schemes of the 1930s were cheap housing and looked it. Wardieburn and Craigmillar in Edinburgh and Blackhill in Glasgow, with their monotonous rows of three- and four-storey tenements, gave their tenants more rooms and a bathroom, but deprived them of easy access to pubs and shops. They separated 'extended families' whose small but closely-grouped rooms and kitchens were often a sort of extended house. They were already acknowledged as centres of social dislocation by the 1940s.

Housing remained an acute problem after 1945. Although 'prefabs', mass-produced in former aircraft factories, were an imaginative innovation, exports took priority over housing, while town planning schemes provoked tension between the planners and the municipalities, particularly Glasgow. Anxious about green belt constraints and the drift to new towns and overspill schemes, the towns turned to technology. Glasgow's first multi-storey scheme, in Partick, was completed in 1952. The Unionists, inspired by Harold Macmillan, boosted the rate of housing completions by over a third. In 1954 they built over 38,000 houses, 12.5 per cent of the UK total. The best pre-war year, 1938, saw only 26,000 completions, 8 per cent of the UK figure. The cost, however, was measured in size and quality: the tradition of the slum-clearance schemes persisted.

The Unionists remained faithful to Elliot's pre-war concentration on public housing. Although private householding trebled, to 20 per cent of completions, between 1954 and 1964, this compared with an English rate of 62 per cent of completions. A comparison between 1921 and 1961 shows a fall in private renting common to both countries, from over 80 per cent of households to under 25 per cent. But in Scotland the main change was to council tenancy (42 per cent compared with under 24 per cent in England), while owner-occupancy lagged badly, because of rent control, low council rents, and the absence of the building-boom. Under 25 per cent of Scots households were owner-occupiers, compared with over 42 per cent in England. Thus, in contrast to other areas of social policy, state intervention actually increased the differentiation between Scottish and English society, and in an area which impinged closely on political behaviour.

V Food

Reports on Scots eating habits and nutrition are plentiful for the pre-1914 period but less so for the period between the wars, despite the fact that it was the research of the Scottish agriculturalist John (Lord)

Boyd Orr that, in his *Food, Health and Income* of 1936, concentrated attention on the effect of malnutrition on between a third and half of the population. On the whole, pre-1914 reports alleged an apparent paradox: diet deteriorated as the population got wealthier and more urbanized. The oatmeal and milk diet of the agricultural labourers, though unvaried, was high in protein and roughage, and thus superior to the growing tendency to consume tea, white bread, and strong liquor. In 1938 a Ministry of Labour enquiry disclosed that, with long-term reductions in the cost of imported foodstuffs, the variety of food increased, with a greater amount of meat, poultry products, and fruit, but its unbalanced and unhealthy aspects continued. Sugar, which produced short-term increases in energy, but at the cost of tooth decay, constituted a disproportionate part of the Scots diet (5.4 per cent against 4.9 per cent in an English family's food budget); the Scots were also deficient in fresh vegetables (11.8 per cent against 12.8 per cent). For those in industries and areas afflicted with unemployment and low wages, standards may even have deteriorated since the nineteenth century. To this end, in the 1930s, the programme of free milk in schools and of domestic science classes was an attempt to cope with the 'secondary' malnutrition of about 20 per cent of the population; but for the lowest 30 per cent nothing short of a guaranteed increase in income could ensure an adequate standard. World War II seems to have brought this about: D.J. Robertson, in 1953, calculated that the index of Scots expenditure on food had risen from 110 in 1939 to 244 in 1951, while the UK figures had only gone up to 228 from 109. Yet peculiarities persisted: more was still spent on cereals and sugar and less on fruit. In general terms, Robertson concluded, Scottish household expenditure was 'more definitely urban and determinedly in the tradition of the working class' than elsewhere.

Scotland remained an austere place in the 1950s. The high alcohol consumption of the pre-1914 period had fallen away. In 1953 the Scots spent 18.4 per cent less than the UK average on drink, and relatively little on eating out. Strict licensing laws and a dearth of good restaurants (one of the main problems faced in its early years by the Edinburgh Festival) were at least a partial explanation. They made up for this by smoking like no one else in Britain, spending 11 per cent more than the UK average on tobacco. 'Can there be life after dark?' was a question asked by others besides Arthur Marwick in the early 1960s, but matters were soon to change.

VI Health

Twentieth-century Scots were eating well, if not too wisely. They were also growing taller and living longer. A Glasgow boy born in 1910 would on average be 4 ft 7 in. tall at 13 and weigh 75 lb.; a 13-year-old in 1954 would be nearly 4 in. taller and 15 lb. heavier. To what extent were these improvements the result of the institution of a national health service in 1948, of incremental increases in general health care, of growing affluence? Again, the detailed research has yet to be done, but a preliminary view suggests that the National Health Service improved rather than revolutionized health care – as with maternal provision. The conquest of tuberculosis and infectious disease in general was another major success. Before World War I the mortality rate from TB was 20.8 per 10,000. Isolation of cases, better public health, inspection of milk products, X-rays, cut this to 10.8 per 10,000, even before the invention of antibiotics – itself a much advertised triumph of Scots medicine, in the person of Sir Alexander Fleming – ended the menace of 'Bluidy Jack' forever. Fever cases also subsided between the wars, for similar reasons. The county of Angus had 231 per annum in 1908, 81 by 1965. The concomitant of a decrease in such 'young people's diseases' was an increase in the death-rate from heart disease and cancer, which struck after the age of 60.

There was a steady increase in hospital provision and treatment, aided by the National Insurance Acts of 1911 and 1920. Hospitals were divided both by type and organization: the disproportionately large number of voluntary hospitals, staffed by consultants and residents in the larger towns, and those provided by the local authorities, sometimes consultant-staffed, more often cottage or isolation hospitals attended by the local GP. The two types were gradually coming to resemble one another: many voluntary hospitals were heavily subsidized by trade unions, while local voluntary organizations, like the county nursing associations set up after World War I, removed the 'poor law' stigma from the local authority hospitals and made them part of an increasingly effective local health service. On the eve of World War II this was further enhanced by the construction of four large 'Emergency Medical Service' hospitals in the rural areas – Law and Strathyre, Peel and Stracathro – designed to cope with bombing raids on the main cities. When these did not materialize, Tom Johnston used them as the basis of improved civilian medical services, a factor that made the transition in 1947 to the five regional hospital boards of the NHS particularly easy. Again, the administrative momentum of the Scottish Office ensured that it would control the new system.

Under the boards were 65 management committees, while a parallel system of Health Executive Councils governed the GP services. The county councils and larger burghs constituted the third segment — the local health authorities covering infectious diseases, school medical and dental services, midwifery, and public health. The new service was not long in making an impact on some of the worst problems. An integrated maternity service helped reduce infant mortality. In Glasgow it fell from 1 in 13 in 1947 to 1 in 28 in 1953. There were much needed improvements in eye treatment and dentistry, and in preventive medicine insofar as it affected the school system. But, despite the fact that the reform was carried through by Aneurin Bevan, the doyen of the left, socialist hopes of a salaried medical service, concentrating on occupational health services and preventive medicine, and otherwise organized in health centres, foundered on the rock of the British Medical Association. With the experience of the Highlands and Islands Medical Service (1913) and the memory of the depression, Scots doctors were more committed to the service than their English counterparts, but by the 1960s inadequate capital expenditure, and the emergence of new problems associated with an ageing population were making their mark, while the gap between the health conditions of the well-off and the poor remained as wide as ever.

VII Unemployment and Poverty

Many of the traditional institutions of Scottish life managed to preempt their own reform, or impress their character upon it to render the result distinctive. In the case of the poor law, however, the process of elimination of such regional differentials was wholesale. Few, certainly, could be found to shed tears for the old system, which before 1914 denied a guarantee of outdoor relief to the able-bodied workman. In practice, this qualification was rarely observed: nine-tenths of relief granted was outdoor, and even Beatrice Webb commended the Scottish poor law on the professional approach of the parochial relieving officers, usually the local schoolmaster. But after the war it was all too evident that the principles of the old poor law were incapable of coping with a situation of endemic industrial depression. In 1921 the unemployed were granted statutory entitlement to outdoor relief. But, while the poor remained a parochial responsibility, rates of relief varied, and depression-struck parishes found themselves imposing crippling burdens on local industries simply to meet relief payments, a factor which tended to accelerate industrial closures. In 1929, therefore, the Local Government Act transferred relief to the counties, and funded it substantially out of block grants from central government.

Compulsory national unemployment insurance, funded by stamps paid by workers and employers alike, had been introduced in 1911 and after 1919 was extended to cover most workers (except those in agriculture or with salaries of more than £250 per annum). As unemployment spiralled after 1929 the fund, administered by the Scottish insurance commissioners, went into deficit, and cuts in benefit were a condition of the loan from foreign bankers in 1931 which split the Labour cabinet and brought about the National Government. These cuts were promptly introduced. They discriminated heavily against women, the long-term unemployed (who could now only claim benefit for 26 weeks), and those who had only paid in a few months' contributions. Those from whom benefit was withdrawn were now paid a transitional benefit from the state, on a scale of hardship assessed by a means test. This was conducted by local Public Assistance Committees, and took into account all family circumstances, like working sons and daughters, savings etc. National insurance had always been regarded as a right honourably worked and paid for. Transitional benefit, and the poor law to which it was an overture, were regarded as stigmas, accepted only in extreme circumstances and rendered all the more unwelcome by the inquisition into family circumstances involved. The bitterness about the 'means test' has lasted to the present day. Government policy, however, had its effect. By 1932 about 50 per cent of benefits were means-tested, and as a last resort, the poor law was by 1935 relieving 59,000 workpeople and 101,000 dependents, where in 1930 it had relieved 15,900 and 34,000. Scales of relief still varied widely from place to place and Scotland was particularly badly penalized by the fact that the block grant was not commensurately increased. Between 1930–1 and 1934–5 Scotland's expenditure increased by £1,800,000 (19 per cent), while the block grant only increased by £100,000 (4.7 per cent); as a result, Scotland's rates were over 6 per cent higher than England's, an additional discouragement to industrial development. Even after the Unemployment Act of 1934 made relief a national responsibility, under the Unemployment Assistance Board, Scottish local authorities still had to raise £800,000 (28.5 per cent) of the £2,800,000 (or 5 per cent of total unemployment relief) not covered by the Board, an anomaly not removed until 1937. The intention of the new Board had been to fix national standards of relief and combat the anomalies of the awards made by the local Public Assistance Committees: in practice it found itself sanctioning such variations, and also expressing more generalized disquiet about working and living conditions in Scotland. Left-wing agitation alleged that the UAB was an instrument for policing the working class, and cited the grim work camps that it operated in Argyllshire, but its rates were not ungenerous and in many ways its reports helped awake government to the need for further expenditure on relief works and housing.

Before the Unemployment Assistance Board came into action, those dependent on the dole in Scotland, in 1935, totalled a staggering 1.16 million, or nearly 250 in every 1,000. After World War II, and the adoption of a full employment policy, the UAB's successor, the National Assistance Board (1948), had to deal with about a tenth of that number, who had fallen through the pensions and insurance 'net'. The NAB's first chairman was George Buchanan, 20 years earlier one of Clydeside's unruliest MPs. He exemplified a shift in the left's attitude to Westminster. Twenty years earlier he and his colleagues had argued that Scotland's comparative poverty constituted part of the case for home rule. James Maxton had said in 1923: 'We mean to tell them they can do what they like about English children but that they are not going to suffer Scottish children to die'. Now, with Scotland still relatively poorer than England, the fact of equal entitlement to benefit was quoted as a clinching argument for the Union.

The welfare state diminished poverty, it did not eradicate it. Gradually, the numbers requiring assistance increased, from 20 per 1,000 in 1947 to 38 per 1,000 in 1961 and 62 per 1,000 in 1972. This was partly the result of unemployment, but also attributable to the growing number of old people, and the casualties of an increasingly unstable society, such as unmarried mothers and deserted wives. Moreover, those entitled to benefit frequently either did not claim it, or mis-spent it, and the results were readily apparent in family breakdown and juvenile crime. This provided the background to the enquiry, chaired by Lord Kilbrandon, into children's courts (1964) which led in due course to the children's panel system and, in 1968, to the Social Work (Scotland) Act, which integrated child care, home helps, mental health, probation, and, later on, prison welfare and hospital social services. The Act was not only an advance on previous practice, but radically different from English arrangements. Thus, even in an otherwise integrated area, a measure of Scottish distinctiveness had been restored.

VIII   Education

If Scotland showed the gulf between groups that characterized an upwardly-mobile society, then education was largely responsible. The Scots had always prided themselves on the accessibility of their educational system to the bright but badly-off. So far this has not been subject to much statistical verification, but it seems that, while valid for the mid nineteenth century, recruitment patterns narrowed before World War I, and the universities had become steadily more middle-class oriented. But all such relationships were altered by the war, and the Act of 1918 was intended to remedy the effects of four years of disruption. Subsequent retrenchment frustrated its main intentions. Its envisaged leaving age of 15, for instance, was not enacted until 1939, just in time to be postponed 'for the duration'. Although Scotland continued to receive about 14 per cent of British educational expenditure, her relative performance declined. She had 18 per cent of secondary pupils in 1913, 15.3 per cent in 1938. Moreover, the day of the all-ability local school was ending. Anticipating the recommendations of the English Hadow Report, the new secondary schools were after 1923 divided into 'junior' and 'senior secondaries', only the latter being academic. Although this made little difference in many county districts, it created a serious social gulf in the larger towns, and also increased the propensity of the gifted to move out once they had their qualifications. Jenny Lee, who left a Fife mining community for university and politics, regretted the fact that most of those who used this stepladder then broke off all connection with the community that had originally given them their chance.

Higher education fared badly between the wars. The number of full-time students at the four universities fell from 10,400 in 1924 to 9,900 in 1937, while the English universities registered a rise of nearly 19 per cent. The decline was worse among women (26 per cent) than among men students, although even here the lack of job opportunities in areas in which the Scottish universities had traditionally excelled — such as engineering, metallurgy, and naval architecture — meant that the development of research and the modernization of facilities was severely curtailed. Although English university expenditure rose by over 90 per cent during this period, the equivalent

Scottish figure was scarcely a third of this. As a result, the best Scottish students tended to move south for postgraduate work, and there was little development of new subject areas. Worst of all was the stagnation of vocational and further education, the development of which had been stressed by the 1918 Act. As late as 1955 only eight local authorities had technical colleges, and barely a tenth of school leavers attended them full-time. Day-release certainly grew rapidly after the war. There had been only 900 students in 1939; there were 24,000 in 1955. But this was only a fraction of the potential. If *Scotland* condemned the 'sheer ignorance' of 18-year-olds in 1961 as 'a bleak omen for the future', it was scarcely the fault of the youngsters themselves.

Discussion of future policy was not made easy by three major reorganizations in as many decades. The elected Local Education Authorities of the 1918 Act lasted barely a decade before being swept away by the Local Government (Scotland) Act. Neither they nor the school management committees which replaced the old School Boards had been particularly successful; perhaps they had simply not been given enough time. The professional organizations tended to fight a series of defensive battles over redundancies, wage cuts, and threatened status. The result of both was an intensely 'political' spirit which militated against real discussion of the nature and goals of education. Radicals, like A.S. Neill, were forced out; where there was innovation it tended more and more to come from the Scottish Education Department, since 1921 situated in Edinburgh, and its inspectorate.

The 1944 Act was anticipated by the re-establishment of the Advisory Council on Education, an achievement of the wartime Council of State, and after 1945 there were some notable innovations in curricula and methods, aided by more determined central direction from the inspectorate and increased expenditure on school building. The main beneficiaries, however, were the academically inclined; as Scotland lacked the English 'O' level system, until 1961 the vast majority — 93.4 per cent — of pupils left school at 15 without any qualification. By 1978 58.3 per cent of pupils gained at least one 'O' level, and 17.2 per cent gained three or more Higher-level passes. As only 3.7 per cent reached this stage in 1951, the wastage of talent was palpable.

IX Law and Order

So far as criminal statistics can be compared — and the means of keeping them varied radically between police forces, let alone between Scotland and England — the Scots were ceasing to be appreciably more criminally inclined than the English. In 1938 crimes known to the police ran at 11 per 1,000 of the total population; the English proportion was 7 per 1,000. By 1951 both countries had increased to 14 per 1,000. Even the 1938 figure was an improvement on the situation before World War I, with a reduction of almost two-thirds in drink-connected offences, which fell further to only one-fifth of the 1913 level. Did types of crime vary with levels of affluence? Some criminologists have argued that periods of economic recession see a rise in crimes against property while periods of affluence see a rise in crimes against persons. Yet violent crime in late 1930s Scotland was running at a level six times that of the south, and subsequently declined. Nor was the impact of the two world wars uniform: crime slumped in World War I, stayed down during the inter-war period, but rose during World War II.

Crime is an area of Scottish society that has been badly neglected, yet that surely offers huge rewards to the Scottish Richard Cobb who can use the plentiful evidence of the courts to explore the pathology of Scottish society. For this period we can at least say that crime was urban, masculine, and relatively unorganized — at least in a commercial sense. For Glasgow gangs devoted to fighting and drinking, petty theft and protection rackets were simply a means to this end. Drinking had certainly much to do with violence in the cities, with two major waves of gang warfare sweeping over Glasgow in the 1930s and 1960s. Yet the Western Isles, statistically awash with booze, were virtually crime-free. The connections between crime and religious communities need exploring, too. In nineteenth century Scotland two-thirds of the Scottish jail population was Catholic, disproportionate for the whole of society, if not for its poorest part. How much was this the result of poverty, how much of discrimination by a Protestant magistracy? It had fallen to 25 per cent by the 1920s, when the Catholic minority had legitimized its position. Irish political violence was not imported, save on Clydeside just after World War I, as Irish nationalists in Glasgow attempted to aid the struggle against the British Army in Ireland. But this was far less conspicuous than the suffragette campaign before the war, when middle-class ladies carried out acts of violence and destruction at which the leaders of the Red

Clyde would have blenched. As a rule, though, the women of Scotland — truly the country's most oppressed group — were consistently law-abiding, and became even more so. The ratio of male to female crime was 4:1 in 1913, 12:1 in 1951.

Violent crime was working class; murder a family affair. Fraud, tax evasion, and embezzlement were traditional middle-class wickednesses, but corruption was relatively new, occurring where business met the local government system, from the 1930s increasingly run by inexperienced men, handling huge budgets on small personal incomes. It came to play an important if tragic rôle in city corporations, quasi-governmental bodies, the trade unions and the co-operative movement, swelling with the complexity of business organization and the drive to attract investment. To the old grandees of local government it resulted from the extinction of civic politics and the rise of Labour, but it was surely also the result of a governmental system peculiarly remote and secretive.

Scottish police forces, like those of England but unlike the Metropolitan Police or the Royal Ulster Constabulary, were local concerns. There were in 1920 32 'joint-county' or 'county-burgh' authorities — of which Glasgow was the largest in Britain. Archaic in equipment and organization, they found it difficult to cope with political disturbances — as 1919 in Glasgow showed — urban violence, and growing traffic problems. Sir Percy Sillitoe, coming to Glasgow in 1933, found elderly officers, a decrepit CID, and (it later turned out) corrupt political leadership. His reforms, soon copied in other cities, ranged from policemen's checked cap-bands to police boxes and radio-controlled cars.

It is more difficult to talk of innovation in the prison service. For the first half-century Scottish prison admissions consistently declined, from 50,000 to under 9,000. There was thus little pressure to modernize the prisons, which dated mainly from the mid nineteenth century. On the other hand, as crime rose during the 1950s, these became increasingly overcrowded. Admissions were over 12,000 in 1961, and peaked at 18,773 in 1975. While readers of the *Sunday Post* were alternately reassured to see enemies of society behind bars and scandalized at the privileges they were alleged to enjoy, it is doubtful whether incarceration in ancient and crowded buildings diminished the anti-social tendencies of the inmates.

Law had, of course, civic and economic as well as criminal functions. It was a central part of the Edinburgh caste-system and the world of the investment trusts, and before 1914 was judiciously assimilating to the south. When assimilation accelerated, after 1918, there were two responses. Lord Macmillan (Unionist Lord Advocate in the 1924 Labour government) personified one, moving south to the English bar and becoming legal handyman to successive governments. Andrew Dewar Gibb, also a Unionist and Professor of Scots Law at Glasgow, personified another, shifting, through a defence of his subject, to the chairmanship of the SNP. In the 1940s another Unionist, Lord Cooper, played a major part in the revival of Scots legal studies, and under his disciple, Professor T.B. Smith, Scots lawyers claimed an almost Savigny-like identification between Scots law and the national *geist*. Lawyers were still over-influenced by the chances of party patronage, but after 1945 they took a prouder line, stressing their law's closeness to the codes of the European nations. Solicitors, with academic qualifications absent in England, took on a more active business rôle, acting as estate agents as well as conveyancers in house sales. The new legislation of the 1960s thus strengthened the internal pressure for reform. The creation of the Scots Law Commission under a leading innovator, Lord Kilbrandon, in 1965, appeared to confirm this, and the difficulty of transferring its recommendations to the statute book subsequently became a major argument for devolution.

X Religion

The disestablishment of the Church of Wales was carried by parliament in 1913. Because of the war, it did not become law until 1920. In the following year, however, the Church of Scotland Act permitted an established presbyterian Church to remain north of the border. This effectively brought to an end the savage sectarian rivalries of the nineteenth century. Eight years later the main dissenting group, the United Free Church, fused with the Church of Scotland. The way had been clear for unity since the early 1900s. When the United Presbyterians and Free Church had merged in 1900, the wrangling and litigation had been such that the dissenting leaders seem simply to have become fed up with their traditional aim of disestablishing the Church of Scotland. There were some differences of view, but not many, over World War I, and complicated negotiations over teinds or tithes, but the upshot was a presbyterian Church more united than it had been for over a century, although no longer reaching the 36 per cent of the population the three churches had reached in 1886.

Formally, Scotland was still a religious country, although its actual religious balance was changing. In 1930 the Church of Scotland claimed 1,271,095 members, 26.2 per cent of the population; the Catholic Church claimed 560,000, or 11.2 per cent (9 per cent in 1886). The Church of England, by contrast, had only 11.0 per cent. By 1960 the rate of decline seemed to have been halted. The Kirk claimed 25 per cent of the population, but the Catholic percentage had risen to 14.9. In the next 14 years the Kirk's percentage was, however, to drop to 20.4. While some of this can be attributed to a more scrupulous weeding out of nominal members, who had hitherto inflated the figures artificially, the evidence of ministers' reports in the *Third Statistical Account* is of a steady drift from regular religious participation from World War I on.

The Kirk was affected by the withering away of its secular rôle — for instance by the end of the parish councils in 1929, on which ministers tended to sit as if of right — by the challenge of slum clearance and rehousing, and by secular alternatives in education and entertainment. The Catholic Church, on the other hand, reinforced its position largely through the 1918 Education Act's provisions for its schools to become part of the state system while retaining their religious distinctiveness, and through a further influx from the Free State and Ulster in the 1920s. This caused a strong racialist reaction both among conservative presbyterians and some nationalists and had some influence in the rise of the Protestant Action in the 1930s (see p.100).

In the united Kirk two tendencies, Catholic and Evangelical, competed. The Iona Community, founded in 1930 by the socialist and pacifist George MacLeod, sought a more mystical and ritualistic religion, as well as a stronger social commitment. Funded substantially by James Lithgow, it devoted itself to work in the slums of Clydeside as well as to the reconstruction of the medieval abbey of Iona. A decade later, after 1947, the Rev. Tom Allan's 'Tell Scotland' movement, which culminated with the Rev. Billy Graham's 1954—5 Glasgow Crusade, reinstated the Evangelical tradition. The two clashed violently in 1961, when a committee of the General Assembly, including MacLeod, recommended the reintroduction of bishops in the Kirk, only to have its report rejected by the Assembly in session, after an energetic campaign by Beaverbrook's *Scottish Daily Express*. The Church remained a paradox. Middle-class in recruitment and leadership, and on the whole evangelical in theology, it nevertheless adopted, largely at the behest of the clergy, a range of liberal policies on race, the arts, sexual morality, and home rule. Until the 1960s it was, effectively, the last redoubt of old-fashioned Scottish liberalism. But its appeal to the progressive young was dangerously limited, and in due course a generation of intellectuals, who could sympathize with the Church's radicals, like MacLeod or Kenneth MacKenzie, personally and on political issues, simply slipped away from formal belief. With an ultramontane dogmatism not far behind that of Eire, on the other hand, the Scottish Catholic hierarchy could observe growing numbers of communicants until the mid 1960s, with a number of distinguished converts, and a high reputation in literature and the arts.

When religious identification expressed itself in politics, however, there was a paradox. While the political choice of Protestants broadly followed class lines, Catholics, including middle-class Catholics, voted overwhelmingly for Labour. This was partly to do with traditional Irish resentment of Unionism, and partly because Scottish Labour was careful to protect the Catholic Church's educational privileges. This had its bizarre side. In 1931 the Catholic *Glasgow Observer* simultaneously anathematized socialism and advised the faithful to vote for Jimmie Maxton! But, given the general weakness of Labour organization in the west of Scotland, the well-organized Catholic lobby consistently exercised a conservative influence on the party. On the Protestant side the links between the Established Church, the Orange Order, and the Unionists seem to have lapsed during the 1920s, prior to the amalgamation with the predominantly Liberal U.F. Church, but as its membership fell in the 1960s, the politics of the Church — as far as one can judge from its monthly, *Life and Work* — seemed to settle to the right.

XI Class

Taken as functional systems, the main institutions of Scottish social life showed variable and sometimes contradictory degrees of assimilation to UK norms. An absence of coloured immigrants, larger families, the prevalence of rented public-sector housing, different eating and drinking patterns, more pervasive religion — all of these provided considerable areas of distinctiveness in everyday life. The economy had, of course, steadily been assimilated to the south, carrying with it the system of social welfare, but in other important areas of public intervention such as law, education, and housing, Scotland radically diverged from England. This complexity is scarcely illuminated by generalizations such as that by Professor Peter Hall, alleging assimilation on the grounds that 'We get the same morning papers, we see the same television programmes, we buy the same goods in identical supermarkets, lured by the same advertising'. Yet a treatment of institutions remains a distorting one if it does not attempt to relate them to the economic structure by dealing with class relationships and their connections with the distribution of economic power. Socialists who attacked Scottish nationalism during the 1960s argued that the real division lay along class lines, and that working-class consciousness was the common property of British working people. Bearing in mind the subsequent fate of Scottish nationalism, that argument still has to be met.

This approach is not, however, proved by saying that Scotland is a more working-class country than England. This can be a mark of divergence, not congruence. Mark Abrams' calculations of income distribution for *The Home Market* show a Scottish upper class, largely based in Edinburgh, actually strengthening its position over the period 1934—49 period, while there is also a growth in the percentage with 'working class' incomes. Both extremes of the social scale grow in numbers, while the middle class actually declines from 21.8 per cent to 18.9 per cent, its English counterpart growing at the same time from 21.3 per cent to 26 per cent.

Table 3.3: Percentages in income categories, 1934 and 1949

	1934					1949	
	Eng.	Scot.	Edin.	Glas.		Eng.	Scot.
Grade A					Grade A		
(£520 +)	5.3	3.4	7.0	2.0	(£1,000 +)	4.0	4.1
Grade B	21.3	21.8	29.0	27.0	B (£650–1,000)	8.0	6.4
(£208–520)					C (£400–650)	18.0	12.5
Grade C	73.4	74.8	64.0	71.0	D (£225–400)	61.9	64.9
(£0–208)					E (£0–225)	8.1	12.1

(Over this period the value of the pound was roughly halved, so the income divisions are broadly comparable.)

Even allowing for distortions, this shows a more proletarian country, and one likely to show strong evidence of class-consciousness. Even if we accept — especially if we accept — that the educational system promoted social mobility, the corollary of this is usually an increase in tension between classes. From what little sociological research was carried out in Scotland in this period — and I am heavily in the debt of James Littlejohn's lucid and perceptive *Westrigg*, a book that goes far beyond the bounds of the 'Cheviot Parish' it surveys — we seem to see class-consciousness developed to an almost pathological degree. In

Westrigg Littlejohn found working people deeply conscious of being, in Marx's phrase, 'of a class, but not for a class'. This penetrated social and recreational life as well as work relationships, and was closely related to the masculine dominance of rural working-class life. Women were more mobile, and in the upper social classes exercised a greater degree of responsibility, but this went along with a greater use of 'managerial' or 'problem-solving' skills by the upper classes as a whole. As a result, 'on any issue the working class is sharply divided while the middle classes are more unanimous, though with a difference of emphasis between property owners and professionals'. This was evident within working-class organizations — where the move of a working-class person to a leadership rôle was itself resented as a breach of class solidarity.

The application of this perception to Scottish politics shows, I think, an analogous development, with the leadership of Scottish working-class organizations increasingly recruited from the middle class, or deferring to middle-class ideologies. How had this come about? Again, in the absence of detailed research, we can only speculate. By destroying the Lowland peasantry, eighteenth-century 'improvement' had, arguably, also removed the local relationships of kin and community, out of which a localized 'organic' society, with its demotic political and leadership structures, had emerged on the continent and in Ireland. The Scottish alternative was the consciousness of the skilled industrial worker, but this was something that lacked both realistic political expression, and was greatly dependent on industrial changes that the working class could not control. Although the aftermath of World War I saw the rise of the Labour Party, it also saw the frustration of this class's bid for political leadership, and the beginning of its decline.

Socialists welcomed the broader working-class solidarity that they expected to emerge from this. As its president, William Leonard MP told the STUC in 1925:

> There can be no denial that the gulf which at one time divided the skilled from the unskilled is fast disappearing, and, as a craftsman, I welcome the change. It is not that we are less capable than our forefathers, but that their dexterity and fine points of craftsmanship are no longer needed by our present methods, and the same tendency is bringing up to our level those who at one time were dubbed 'only labourers'. Unemployment is with us until we dismiss Capitalism. I care not what type of government

we have, if it tries to work this lack of system — the problem will remain.

This was a view sanguine to the point of self-deception. A decade later the Unemployment Assistance Board was more grimly realistic:

> One unfortunate feature is the number of skilled workmen of various kinds who cannot be absorbed into their own industries and who are gradually drifting into the general labouring class. a section which is already over-crowded and which is likely to occupy the Board's attention for many years to come.

The skilled working class had supplied the labour and co-operative movement with most of its leadership, yet its own identity was ambiguous. Its culture, for instance, was almost wholly derived from the middle class. Thus, as it broke up, the more intelligent of its younger generation tended to shift into the middle class, through the educational system, or emigrate, rather than attempt to politicize the unskilled. The two sons of Willie Gallacher both went to university, and were both killed flying for the RAF in World War II. Mrs Gallacher mourned her 'poor, clever bairns'. It would never have occurred to her or her husband to deny them the chance to leave their class.

Thus, although economic change seems to have increased class ploarization, the institutions of Scottish society actually inhibited the development of a positive political class-consciousness. They provided means of 'spiralling' out of the working class, and they also created, through the expansion of public intervention, a range of middle-class organizational and leadership rôles — schoolteachers, local officials, councillors and MPs, social workers — what Stephen Maxwell has called 'a state-sector middle class'. With the dwindling-away of indigenous capitalism, and the relative isolation of Unionism as an agricultural interest group, this class exercised effective dominance over much of Scottish society in the 1960s.

D

4

Politics and Government
1922 – 1964

I

There was an Irish Question in British politics throughout the nineteenth century. It became obsessive after 1880, and refused to disappear even after the setting-up of the Free State in 1921. There was no Scottish Question. Between 1922 and 1964 few specifically Scottish issues preoccupied the Commons for more than a few hours, or Cabinet for as many minutes, even at the pit of the depression. The only one that did, the Caledonian Power Bill of 1936–8, had implications for national defence. This may give a clue to Scotland's unobtrusiveness. Before 1945 high politics in Britain meant the Empire and foreign policy. The Irish took constitutional issues away with them; the subtraction of their 70-odd anti-Tory votes helped account for Conservative hegemony until 1945 and, by implication, for Parliament's restricted preoccupations. The Government of India Bill, not the slump, took up 84 per cent of legislative time in 1934–5. Things had changed by 1964: in real terms government expenditure was 300 per cent more than in 1914: from 28 per cent of a pre-war budget of £207m. it had risen to 77 per cent out of £6,727m. Plainly, only when government became preoccupied with social policy, after 1945, could Scottish issues intrude themselves — unless they were constitutional issues. But the nationalist movement was never strong enough to create these.

Scottish politics had, however, patently changed after World War I and the 1918 Reform Act. What, then, were they about? Old Liberalism viewed the new electorate and new politicians with vast distrust. To Asquith the Paisley voters in 1920 were 'for the most part hopelessly ignorant of politics, credulous to the last degree, and flickering with gusts of sentiment like a candle in the wind'. Did they want, or even know very much about, socialism? Margot Asquith fairly accurately nailed Rosslyn Mitchell, who beat Asquith in 1924, and who had drafted the Clydeside Labour members' dramatic pledge in 1922, as 'highly educated and no more Labour than you'. Nineteen thirty-one was to show that Scottish loyalties to Labour were thin, and its inter-war career was scarcely consistent or imaginative. Labour may have replaced Liberalism on the left of a continuing two-party system, but the latter's collapse, sudden and still not fully explained, left a vacuum not filled until 1945.

What filled it? A class-based loyalty to Labour's welfare pro-gramme? This may have fitted the 1950s, but the 1960s and 1970s have suggested greater complexity: class-politics were skewed by the dis-tinctive nature of Scottish local government and its close relationships with a largely Scots-based administration. If Scots made 'secular' political choices, they did so in an increasingly Scottish context, but there was nothing determinate about this evolution. It was as much the work of Unionists as of Labour, and of the momentum within Scottish administration itself.

II Labour contained 1922–1935

Unionists and Liberals

November 1922 inaugurated a brief period of three-party politics, but by December 1924 the Unionists were dominant. Their breach with Lloyd George had preserved their independence. They had 335 seats in 1918, 345 after November 1922. In Scotland, however, they lost 17 seats in 1922 and gained only one in 1923. Only in 1924 did the party sweep forward to 38 seats — although in 1935 it still held 37; not until 1964 did its representation drop below 30.

The reasons for this success were the result of organizational rather than social change; its total vote changed little from 1924 to 1955. The formation of the Scottish Unionist Party in 1911 united rural conser-vatism with right-wing urban liberalism. The SUP had five regional councils, but remained firmly under the control of the parliamentary leadership and of Conservative Central Office, a relationship strengthened by the virtually unbroken line of the Scots who chaired the party: Sir Arthur Steel-Maitland from 1911 to 1917, George Younger from 1917 to 1923, J.C.C. Davidson from 1926 to 1930, and John Baird from 1931 to 1940. Steel-Maitland and Davidson, in particular, modernized local party organization, with regular sub-scriptions and (at least nominally) elective committees, provided an

Table 4.1: MPs elected for Scottish constituencies 1900 – 1983 (showing number of MPs and % of vote)

	Unionist		LU/NL[1]		Lib.		Lab.		Others	
	MPs	%	MPs	%	MPs	%	MPs	%	MPs	%
1900	21	+	17	(49.0)	34	(50.2)				
1906	8	+	4	(38.2)	58	(56.4)	2	(2.3)		(3.1)
1910 (Jan.)	8	+	3	(39.6)	59	(54.2)	2	(5.1)		(1.1)
1910 (Dec.)	7	+	4	(42.6)	58	(53.6)	3	(3.6)		(0.2)
1918	32	(30.8)	19	(19.1)	15	(15.0)	7	(22.9)	1	(12.2)
1922	15	(25.1)	12	(17.7)	16	(21.5)	29	(32.2)	2	(3.5)
1923	16	(31.6)			23	(28.4)	34	(35.9)	1	(4.1)
1924	38	(40.8)			9	(16.5)	26	(41.1)	1	(1.6)
1929	22	(35.9)			14	(18.1)	36	(42.4)	1	(3.6)
1931	50	(49.5)	8	(4.8)	8	(8.6)	7	(32.6)		(4.5)
1935	37	(42.2)	7 + 1	(7.6)	3	(6.7)	20 + 4	(41.8)	2	(1.7)
1945	25	(37.4)	5	(3.7)		(5.0)	37 + 3	(49.4)	4	(4.5)
1950	26	(37.2)	5	(7.6)	2	(6.6)	37	(46.2)	1	(2.4)
1951	29	(39.9)	6	(8.7)	1	(2.7)	35	(47.9)	1	(0.8)
1955	30	(41.5)	6	(8.6)	1	(1.9)	34	(46.7)		(1.3)
1959	25	(39.7)	6	(7.5)	1	(4.1)	38	(46.7)		(2.0)
1964	24	(37.3)		(3.3)	4	(7.6)	43	(48.7)		(3.1)
1966	20	(37.7)		–	5	(6.8)	46	(49.9)		(5.6)
1970	23	(38.0)			3	(5.5)	44	(44.5)	1	(12.0)
1974 (Feb.)	21	(32.9)			3	(8.0)	40	(36.6)	7	(22.5)
1974 (Oct.)	16	(24.7)			3	(8.3)	41	(36.3)	11	(30.7)
1979	22	(30)			3	(10)	44	(42)	2	(18)
1983	21	(28.4)			8	(24.5)	41	(35.1)	2	(12.1)
1987	10	(24)			9	(19.2)	50	(42.4)	3	(14.3)
1992	11	(25.7)			9	(13.1)	49	(39)	3	(22.2)

[1] Liberal-Unionist to 1912; 'Coalition Liberal' 1918–22; 'National Liberal' 1931–64.

Note: The totals of MPs include two university MPs 1900–18 and three 1918–45. These seats were abolished in 1948. As they polled by proportional representation, party percentages cannot be established.

efficient agency service, and greatly increased income from business sources — aided greatly by the rightward shift of former Liberals. This was reflected in a rise in membership: in Glasgow it increased from 7,000 in 1913 to 20,000 in 1922 and 32,000 in 1929, a figure almost double the individual membership of the Labour Party *and* the ILP for the whole of Scotland.

Unionist cohesiveness triumphed over Liberal disorder. Traditionally the nominal independence of the Scottish Liberal Federation had been countered by the combination of front-bench MPs and reliable local managers — usually solicitors. The wartime split was fatal to this. Even the rallying-call of 'free trade in danger', which unified Asquithians and Lloyd-Georgites in 1923 — not to speak of the mysterious Lloyd George fund — brought no recovery, and in 1924 organization collapsed. Only one candidate had been nominated for a Glasgow seat on the eve of the October election, and only eight MPs survived it, mainly in rural areas. When Lloyd George at last succeeded Asquith as leader in 1926, he found all but one of them —

Table 4.2: The backgrounds of Scottish Members of Parliament at selected elections, 1910 (December) – 1979

	1910			1922			1945			1964			1979				Totals
	U	Lab.	L	U	Lab.	L	U	Lab.	Other	U	Lab.	L	C	Lab.	L	SNP	
Business	1	—	24	3	3	5	14	1	—	3	4	—	7	2	—	1	68
Landowning/farming	4	—	5	1	—	2	6	—	—	9	—	2	3	1	1	—	33
Law	3	—	17	6	—	7	1	2	—	4	1	1	7	2	1	1	53
Education	1	—	—	—	4	1	1	5	—	—	7	1	2	8	1	—	31
Other professions	2	—	11	5	5	12	9	7	1	6	7	—	3	9	1	—	78
White collar	—	—	—	—	1	—	—	4	—	—	9	—	—	9	—	—	23
Trade union and labour organisers	—	3	—	—	16	—	—	6	—	—	4	—	—	7	—	—	36
Skilled workers	—	—	—	—	2	—	—	14	1	—	10	—	—	6	—	—	33
Others/unidentified	—	—	1	—	—	1	1	1	—	2	1	—	—	—	—	—	7
Totals	11	3	58	15	31	28	32	40	2	24	43	4	22	44	3	2	362

Archie Sinclair in remote Caithness — intractably Asquithian. In 1929 it was farmers' discontent about falling prices, not Lloyd George's imaginative 'Yellow Book' programme (see p.49) that brought five gains. But Liberal performance in Scotland was almost 30 per cent worse than in the UK as a whole, largely because the rise of urban Labour had led, even more swiftly than in England, to 'anti-socialist' mergers with the Unionists. Nineteen twenty-nine proved to be the last rally. Party discipline collapsed, Lloyd George fell sick; in 1931 Scottish Liberals were to support the National Government over-whelmingly.

Labour

But the greatest blow to the Liberals was the first Labour government. In December 1923 Ramsay MacDonald formed a minority adminis-tration. Scots made up a quarter of the cabinet, and provided its major successes, with MacDonald's conciliatory foreign policy and John Wheatley's Housing Act (see p.71). Otherwise little could be achieved — save proof that Labour could govern and that the Liberals were devoid of strategic alternatives. The electorate con-demned them in October 1924. But in Scotland Labour lost eight seats, and by the time of its next victory in 1929 inadequacies of organization and the setback of the General Strike had taken their toll.

As an organization, Labour occupied a median position between Unionist integration and Liberal autonomy. But its structure after 1918 was an awkward compromise between federation and mass organization. The executive of its Scottish Council had six union representatives, four from constituency parties and trades councils (often more or less the same thing), four from women's sections, two from the ILP, and one apiece from the moribund SDF and the Fabians. Less than half of the 80-odd unions affiliated to the STUC sent delegates to Scottish Conference — only 31, for example, in 1930. These represented just 42 per cent of engineers, 39.5 per cent of textile workers, 45.5 per cent in the distributive trades. Strongly affiliated unions, like the miners (89 per cent) and railwaymen (83 per cent) had been hard hit by the depression, and only five of the 36 Scots-based unions sent delegates. Were they represented through the trades councils, or simply uninterested in politics? Labour was less nationalist than the STUC, and also weaker at the grass-roots; individual membership per head of population was only a third of that in London in 1929. This was partly due to the strength of the ILP, and partly to trades council representation — although this opened them to Communist influence.

If in 1922 the Clydesiders had acted as kingmakers for MacDonald, they faced competition. In the same year the Cambridge-educated former conscientious-objector Clifford Allen became ILP chairman and moved the party to a left-liberal position, appealing to middle-class reformers as the intellectual power-house of the left. With success: membership increased from 25,000 in 1922 to 60,000 in 1926. But Allen's aims conflicted with the Glasgow MPs' desperate concern with unemployment and, to a lesser extent, with their nationalist inclinations.

At the industrial grass-roots, moreover, the ILP had to face the British section of the Communist International or Comintern. The Communist Party of Great Britain (CPGB), founded in July 1920, included some Clydeside revolutionaries, but its structure implied obedience to Russian directives. Leaders who survived tended to be former Scots Catholics, accustomed to ultramontane control; less docile radicals followed the example of John Maclean and retreated into obscure and uncompromising sects. The CPGB had some electoral success before 1924, while its relationship with Labour remained undefined. Walton Newbold held Motherwell from 1922 to 1923; James Geddes came second in both years at Greenock. But, although its housing agitation helped increase Labour support, its attempts to affiliate were rebuffed in 1924. Thereafter it attempted to penetrate the unions through the Moscow-funded National Minority Movement which helped to raise the political temperature in the months before the General Strike of 4–12 May 1926.

The General Strike

The strike — MacDiarmid's 'Camsteerie Rose' — arose from the declining economic position of the coal industry, and the attempts of the mineowners to force wage reductions. The vacillations of the General Council of the TUC, pledged to support the miners, were reflected by the leaders of the STUC and the 'first-line' unions — in transport, mining, docks, and printing. Preparations were sketchy, save in some coalfield areas where the Minority Movement organized 'Councils of Action' to enforce picketing and control food supplies. The government, by contrast, had been preparing since 1919. The Lord Advocate had organized an emergency administration, with Scotland divided into five regions; their officials could call on the forces and the Organization for the Maintenance of Supplies, a private body of volunteers — some from the extreme right.

The initial impact was most dramatic in transport. Trains stopped, even on the remotest branch lines. But the government machine got supplies moved by car and lorry, while student-manned trams (which were fairly easy to drive) provided a skeletal public transport service in the cities. There were many acute confrontations: the working-class solidarity demonstrated by the strike extended far beyond the limits of union membership. Even Orange flute bands joined the picket lines, although the Grand Masters were as hostile as the Catholic hierarchy. On 11 May the 'second line' unions downed tools, but that evening the General Council in London backed down:

> The thistle like a rocket soared,
> An' cam' doon like the stick.

'Demoralized by the utter and absolute capitulation' — in the words of a young participant, Jennie Lee — the strikers went back to work. Many were sacked, demoted, or otherwise victimized. The miners stayed out until November when, driven by hunger and the approach of winter, they surrendered. For a former élite, it was a terrible defeat, with wages and status reduced to a level little above that of the unemployed. In other respects, however, political Labour benefited. The strike destroyed such working-class loyalty to Liberalism as remained: Simon and Asquith had condemned it as fiercely as the ex-Liberal Churchill. Municipal Liberals had acted with Unionists to assist the government and penalize strikers. Although the Communists gained support during the miners' lockout, they lost most of it when it ended, but the Labour Party moved forward strongly in municipal politics — in Edinburgh after the November elections its seats rose from 6 to 14. The strike cut at the roots of revolutionary millenarianism; it also enhanced the notion of 'British' class politics, and so diminished the nationalist element in Scottish Labour, while the subsequent victories on the councils made local power a real possibility — especially in the eyes of astute managers like Patrick Dollan.

Unionist Reform

Baldwin remained in power until 1929. Because of Winston Churchill's orthodoxy as Chancellor (see p.49) his government only aggravated Scotland's economic plight, a situation, one suspects, not fully appreciated because of the drift of front-benchers away from

Scottish seats (with only one exception, no premier, chancellor, or foreign secretary sat for a Scottish seat between 1922 and 1963, although five had done so between 1900 and 1922). Scotland's relative political instability (the Unionists kept a consistent hold on only 45 per cent of Scottish seats, 1918–39, compared with 65 per cent in the English Midlands) was probably a factor here, though Scottish businessmen were equally reluctant to go into parliament. Unionist MPs were not distinguished, and the majority of them tended to be drawn from groups — like advocates and landowners — remote from Scotland's economic and social problems. But there were a few exceptions, and fortunately one of them played a key rôle in the Scottish Office for many of the inter-war years: Walter Elliot.

Elliot, the son of a wealthy auctioneer, and the only 'professional' Fellow of the Royal Society ever to become a Cabinet minister, had been a Fabian while at Glasgow University (one of a brilliant generation which had included James Maxton, Tom Johnston, and James Bridie). He entered parliament in 1918 — 'Will stand, which party?' had been his (apocryphal) response to nomination — and while in office became associated with collectivist, if somewhat paternalist, social reform. He was no nationalist but, as Under-Secretary for Scotland, 1923–9, was largely instrumental in securing two major changes in Scottish administration: the reorganization of Scottish central administration and the Local Government Act of 1929.

The first measure, carried through in 1928, converted the system of nominated boards, only indirectly responsible to parliament, into orthodox civil service departments on the lines of the Scottish Education Department. This was criticized by William Adamson, the former Secretary under Labour, for subordinating Scottish administration to Whitehall 'to a far greater extent than has ever been the case', but in fact it coincided with a physical decentralization of government from Whitehall. By 1936 1,333 out of 1,416 civil servants working for the Scottish departments were based in St Andrew's House, the new government headquarters in Edinburgh, planned in 1929 and built, to the design of T.S. Tait, between 1932 and 1936. But the departments of agriculture, education, and health, and the Scottish Office, were only linked by their responsibility to the Secretary of State. Effective co-ordination still had to be achieved.

Much more drastic was the Local Government Act of 1929, from which stemmed much of the nationalist agitation of the 1930s. Without the usual preliminary of a royal commission, and going far beyond the changes carried out by Neville Chamberlain in England, it swept away the parish councils, the Local Education Authorities, and many of the powers of the smaller burghs. The new system consisted of 4 counties of cities, 20 'large burghs' (over 20,000 inhabitants), and 31 county councils which divided between them the responsibility for most local authority services; 171 'small burghs' retained limited public health and housing powers, and in the 'landward areas' of counties somewhat nominal 'district councils' got what was left. The historic Scottish parish was now a religious and registration area: nothing more.

The Nemesis of Labour

The act attracted vociferous opposition from Scottish local author-ities, from the infant National Party, and from Labour, which pledged itself to repeal it. MacDonald's failure to do so, after he formed his 1929 administration, was the first pratfall in a troubled and ultimately disastrous ministry. Labour had gained strength after the General Strike, but not unity. In the ILP Maxton had supplanted Allen and attempted to win the party to an alliance with industrial militants; but this caused a divergence with the Glasgow grass-roots which Dollan cultivated so zealously. Some of the party's more convinced home-rulers, like R.E. Muirhead and C.M. Grieve, moved to the Nationalists. Wheatley, its one real statesman, who might have brought unity, was out of action, in the toils of an expensive and embarrassing lawsuit. MacDonald excluded him from his government. Ill, embittered, and extreme, he flayed Jimmy Thomas's inept attempts to cope with unemployment. Then, worn out, he died in May 1930.

The alternative policies were by now coming not from Clydeside but from Birmingham, where the Scotsman Allan Young was Sir Oswald Mosley's economic adviser. Would Wheatley have supported them, had he lived? Tom Johnston, who succeeded Thomas in March 1930, was certainly sympathetic to many of Mosley's Keynesian ideas, but, echoing Scottish Labour's rejection of Lloyd George's 'Yellow Book' proposals, swung *Forward* against the old enemies — bankers and tariff reformers.

Among the moderates, whose moralistic socialism co-existed, increasingly unhappily, with classical economics, this had logic, when expounded by the Chancellor Philip Snowden's articulate Scots lieu-tenant, Willie Graham: in exporting areas, tariffs meant retaliation and further unemployment. Until October 1929 MacDonald's policy of tariff reduction and disarmament made sense to most Scots Labour

MPs, but after the Crash, they could only demand the preservation of welfare benefits. Adamson, the Secretary of State, and Graham, resolute as Snowden against MacDonald's stumbling approaches to protectionism, were all found, in Labour's last Cabinet division on 23 August 1931, in the minority of nine voting against expenditure cuts. *Forward* went into the November election urging 'Shot and Shell against Bread Taxes', but it turned out to be 1906 in reverse. In Scotland only seven Labour MPs survived.

The National Government

MacDonald's appeal seems to have had some influence in swinging Scotland round to supporting the National Government. Whereas in Wales Labour still held a majority of seats, in Scotland the party collapsed. The effective co-ordination of Liberal and Unionist voting meant that a 2:1 majority in votes was transformed into a 6:1 majority in seats. Their huge majority did not benefit the National parties much. In September 1932, when the government negotiated the Ottawa agreements, and broke with the tradition of free trade, its Liberal supporters split. Sinclair, who had been Secretary of State, went into opposition with four of his colleagues. His successor, Sir Godfrey Collins, commanded the National Liberal remainder in Scotland. Wrangles continued in the Scottish Liberal Federation until 1935, when the 'Nationals' were expelled — henceforth becoming virtually indistinguishable from the Unionists. As for the latter, the unexpected size of the victory actually made their MPs even less representative of Scottish business than they had been in the 1920s.

This, however, was a disadvantage to Scotland rather than a benefit to Labour, which made no headway in by-elections and only a qualified recovery to 20 seats in 1935, and was plagued by a bitter feud with its old component, the ILP. Although when it disaffiliated from the Labour Party in 1932, the ILP claimed four of the seven surviving MPs, most of its Scottish members remained loyal to the idea of affiliation, and later that year set up the Scottish Socialist Party. Dollan was its effective leader and it took with it most of the ILP's 127 Scottish branches. ILP membership fell by 75 per cent, and far-left infiltration rapidly destroyed its organization in all but a few seats.

The Communist Party succeeded it as the representative of the far left — but not without difficulty. On instructions from Moscow, it had changed its line in 1928, turned on the Labour Party, and supported breakaway trade unions. On the whole this led to its increasing isolation, save in a few areas like the 'Little Moscows' of the Vale of Leven and Clydebank. Only in Fife, where William Gallacher engineered a breakaway from the Mineworkers' Union called the United Mineworkers of Scotland, was it successful. Gallacher beat the lacklustre William Adamson, Labour's former Secretary of State, in the 1935 election, but by that time, under the threat of fascism, the Communist line had changed once again.

The events of 1931, and the subsequent splits, did great damage to the left. In the 1920s Scots Labour MPs wielded strong influence in the parliamentary party; between 1931 and 1935 this momentum was lost. Successful policy initiatives thereafter tended to come from the south, particularly after Labour won the London County Council in 1934 and established a socialist laboratory on parliament's doorstep. The Scottish Socialist Party was dogged by legal battles over who should control the property of the ILP branches that affiliated to it, and expired in 1940, probably to the relief of Transport House, which did not like the left-wing company it kept. The Peace Pledge Union and the Left Book Club thrived, but not among Labour's economically parched grass roots, where the Co-operatives steadily declined. Returning to Fife in 1936, Jennie Lee, now married to Aneurin Bevan, found herself asking, 'Why were all the finest people I knew in the grip of a kind of spiritual paralysis? Where was all the vigour, the belligerancy, the robust certainties that had characterized the labour movement as I remembered it in my teens and early twenties?'

III   Consensus Nationalism 1935–1950

NPS to SNP

Nineteen thirty-five confirmed the Unionists in power. Labour had been checked; the Liberals were disintegrating, the Communists a tiny minority, and the Nationalists marginal if picturesque. But nationalism went on to provide a unifying theme. The condition of Scotland had got relatively worse, raising problems for government and opportunities for the opposition. This issue didn't upset the dominance of the two parties, but their manipulation of it gave a distinctive tone to Scottish politics.

Political nationalism was garrulous — we know more about it than about the parties for which 90 per cent of Scots actually voted — but more significant than its low membership and few votes would imply. The National Party of Scotland, founded on 23 June 1928, largely by intellectuals of the Scottish Renaissance (see p.131) and former ILP activists, gained some 5,000 members by 1929 — about the same as the Scottish ILP. Its leaders, however, had to cope with a hostile environment and internal divisions over strategy. By 1929 voters had settled into a new two-party structure, and were reluctant to budge. Given events in Europe, nationalism was a dubious ideology. So, was the NPS to compete with Labour as a radical force, or try to enter the vacuum created by the collapse of Liberalism?

The NPS — largely run by the ex-ILP members John MacCormick and Roland Muirhead — struck out on radical lines. To little purpose. In 1929 it gained an average of less than 5 per cent in two contests. In 1931, this grew to 10 per cent in five contests, but in subsequent by-elections improved little. MacCormick, increasingly dominant, now switched tack, trying to attract dissident Unionists (at this stage much encouraged by the activities of Lord Beaverbrook and his new *Scottish Daily Express*) and former Liberals. Some of these had just launched, in September 1932, the Scottish Self-Government Party, when a disastrous by-election result in East Fife in February 1933 (Eric Linklater polled only 3.6 per cent among a menagerie of fringe candidates, partly conjured up by Beaverbrook at his most impish) moved MacCormick to purge the NPS of its fundamentalists (May 1933), and (November 1933) back the Scottish party leader Sir Alexander MacEwen (1875–1941) at the Kilmarnock by-election. MacEwen polled 16.9 per cent, and in April 1934 the parties amalgamated, largely on Scottish party terms, to form the Scottish National Party. Afterwards, however, membership fell steeply, to only 2,000 in 1939. There were some promising by-election results, but the 1935 vote showed no improvement on 1931.

The Right

National grievances were, however, present, even among the government parties, foreshadowed by the formation of the Scottish National Development Council in 1930. In 1932 MacDonald himself reverted to his earliest convictions by suggesting some measure of Scottish home rule. Scottish Unionist opinion quickly repudiated this in a series of meetings and manifestos in 1932-3, but pressed for administrative devolution and special economic measures, a demand which underlay the creation of the Scottish Special Area Commissioner (see p.50), the Scottish Economic Committee, and the Gilmour Committee on Scottish administration, together with the interventionist policy of

Walter Elliot, Secretary of State 1936 − 8.

Elliot was conscious of the need to legitimate the Unionists as a party of moderate, statist reform, one that could both incorporate the Liberal tradition and attract the working class. Despite 1931, there were still deficiencies in both areas. Many Unionists remained bitterly distrustful of the Liberals. As a future Secretary of State, James Stuart, wrote: 'I do not think I have ever suffered or enjoyed the friendship of a Liberal. I regard this as fortunate for they form a race apart, sitting on the fence and incapable of deciding whether to jump down on one side or the other'. A century's enmity could not easily be overcome.

One of its products had been the identification of the Unionist party with militant protestantism. Until the 1920s officials of the Orange Lodges had sat on the Scottish Council. Sometime before 1930 this link was dropped. Because the Liberals had to be courted instead? Because the Orangemen were less deferential than they ought to have been − witness the actions of some of them in supporting the General Strike? Certainly, it seems too easy to equate protestant militancy with Unionism, then or subsequently. One of the first things that the Lanarkshire migrants to Corby after 1932 set up was an Orange Lodge; by 1960 there were six, but Corby Council had yet to elect a single non-Labour member. Although in the 1950s Catholics voted disproportionately for Labour, the protestant vote still split roughly on the British average. Orangeism was probably more cultural than political.

That Unionism could not count automatically on protestant support was shown by the rise of a distinctively right-wing movement in the 1930s — the Scottish Protestant League in Glasgow, and Protestant Action in Edinburgh. The first had four councillors in Glasgow by 1934; and the second became in 1936 the second-largest party in Edinburgh, with 31 per cent of the vote, returning a maximum of nine councillors. This movement has been well documented by Dr Tom Gallagher. The rise in the poll it caused — of 50 per cent in Edinburgh in 1936 — has some similarities to the SNP's municipal impact in the 1960s (see p. 148). It had some vaguely fascist overtones — it directed propaganda equally against Unionist landlords and Catholic control of the Labour Party, and its Edinburgh leader, an ex-serviceman called Cormack, claimed to have a bodyguard and an armoured car — but it seems to have had no real connection with grievances stemming from economic hardship. It did better in prosperous Edinburgh than in Glasgow at the worst point of the depression, and in fact waned in the west as it grew in the east. Even in Edinburgh, it broke up in the late 1930s. Apart from it, the radical right was absent. Although several of Mosley's closest confidants were Scottish — Charles Raven Thompson, Dr Robert Forgan, and John Scanlon, all of whom had a left-wing background — and some Conservative MPs voiced pro-Hitler sentiments, the only time Mosleyite candidates stood, in 1937 municipal elections, they were humiliated.

In May 1938 Neville Chamberlain moved Elliot from the Scottish Office to the Ministry of Health. In October he reluctantly supported Chamberlain over the Munich agreements with Hitler, thus sealing his fate in 1940. Churchill dropped him, and he never held office again. The loss to Scotland of the only first-rank British statesman who identified himself with Scottish issues was a severe one, and it was particularly acute for the Unionists, who were just beginning to lose ground to Labour. In terms of Westminster performance Labour had scarcely deserved this, but they were making up a lot of ground in local government. They captured Glasgow in 1933, Motherwell and Clydebank in 1934, Dundee in 1936, and Falkirk in 1937, and made steady progress in the industrial counties. This was to create a new and powerful Labour interest, and one that Elliot at the Scottish Office had actually encouraged by increasing housing and educational programmes, which redounded to the credit of the local authorities.

The Popular Front

On the eve of war this was, however, somewhat masked by a revival of home-rule agitation on the left. Tom Johnston became in 1935 Labour's Scottish affairs spokesman and, while shifting politically to the centre and towards administrative rather than legislative devolution, he continued to encourage agitation for home rule, through groups like the London Scots' Self-Government Committee. This body, run by a couple of energetic journalists, had made the not surprising discovery that it was easier to influence Scottish affairs in London than in Edinburgh, and organized an imaginative range of meetings and pamphlets which at least gave the impression that the Labour leadership, up to and including Clement Attlee himself, favoured Scots self-government. Various things helped this, not least the Popular Front policy adopted by the Communist Party in 1935. Casting around for common causes with socialists and liberals, and worried at its own tiny Scottish membership (2,815 in December 1938) it adopted nationalism. Where it went, the stage army of the Popular Front followed; not only Ritchie Calder and J.B.S. Haldane but

Krishna Menon and Jawaharlal Nehru addressed meetings organized by self-government groups, while on May Day 1938 the Communists paraded in tartan, carrying banners of Bruce and Wallace, Burns, Calgacus and (rather oddly, in view of his high toryism) R.L. Stevenson.

Popular Front activities extended further, as the international situation worsened. Scots companies fought in Spain in the ranks of the International Brigade, sustaining heavy casualties, and in December 1938 one of the most important assaults on the policy of the Chamberlain government was mounted when the Duchess of Atholl resigned her Perthshire seat to contest it as an independent backed by the Popular Front. She lost, but only narrowly. Despite the seeming imminence of war, inter-party nationalism continued to bubble away, encouraged by MacCormick, who also tried to stifle neutralist and pacifist activity within the SNP. There was to be a great convention to launch an all-party campaign for home rule in September 1939. There was war instead: 'imperialist war' to such Communists as still remained in the party, and the fundamentalist nationalists who joined them in opposing it.

Labour policy-making proceeded, meanwhile, on two levels. We already know, from chapter 2, which was the more significant. The Dalton enquiry of 1937, and Dalton's translation to the Board of Trade in 1942, was to lay the foundation of the Direction of Industry Act of 1945, on which a generation of Labour prescriptions were based. This was, however, a success secured in the corridors of power. Overtly, Labour was to show a much more nationalist front in the Scotland of World War II.

World War II

The war both boosted Labour's political recovery and helped reinforce the apparent distinctiveness of Scottish planning and economic policies, in response to widely articulated and cross-party demands, and the surprising amount of success enjoyed by the SNP. After February 1941 the desire for change was personified by Tom Johnston, whom Churchill appointed Secretary of State.

In contrast to World War I, industrial relations were tranquil; Johnston considered the loss of only 0.07 per cent of work-days on Clydeside through strikes as adequately laying the ghost of 'the Red Clyde'. But Ministry of Information surveys showed a high level of dissatisfaction with the way the war was being run, verging even on disloyalty; these were moreover borne out by vociferous criticism by MPs both of left and right and by the success of the SNP towards the end of the war. In July 1943 Sir John Reith recorded a conversation with Johnston:

> He is very bothered by Bevin and other English ministers who do things affecting Scotland without consulting him. He thinks there is a great danger of Scottish nationalism coming up, and a sort of *Sinn Fein* movement as he called it. The Lord Justice Clerk [Lord Cooper] had said in a letter that if he left off being a judge and went back to politics, he would be a Nationalist.

In terms of its past performance, and its political history during the war, the SNP did well. It got 37 per cent of the vote at the Argyll by-election in April 1940, and although its home rule and independence wings split bitterly in June 1942, John MacCormick going off to form Scottish Convention, it went on to poll 41 per cent at Kirkcaldy in February 1944 and to win Motherwell in April 1945. It took on in Scotland many of the radicalizing functions of Common Wealth, although CW, whose Scottish representative was David Cleghorn Thomson (see p.128), had one of its first notable successes when Tom Wintringham nearly won North Midlothian in February 1943. He included home rule on his platform. So too did Sir John Boyd Orr, returned in April 1945 as an independent for the Scottish Universities. Such pressure was astutely managed by Johnston to get increased autonomy for the Scottish Office.

Johnston's *Memories* invest this process with rather more symmetry than it seems to have had. He wrote that he demanded from Churchill a Council of State, composed of all living ex-Secretaries, to vet all proposed Scottish legislation. If the council approved it, the Cabinet was to press parliament to legislate with minimum delay. It was to be advised by a body representative of Scottish business, trade union, and local authority opinion, and Scottish MPs were to meet regularly in Edinburgh. It was in fact over six months before the Council met, and then its remit was confined to post-war problems, while the Scottish Council on Industry, the larger body, was independently convened by Johnston on 2 February 1942. There were a couple of meetings of MPs in Edinburgh, which were not successful. That the Council of State shifted to concentrate on wartime administration was largely the result of a forcible intervention by Elliot in December 1941, arguing that post-war reconstruction could not be divorced from attracting wartime industry. Thereafter the Council met regularly until May 1943. The parallel Scottish Council on Industry was not the fully-fledged development commission for which James Bowie and the Scottish Economic Committee had pressed, but it countervailed the *laissez-faire* attitudes of the central office of the Board of Trade, strengthened its local representatives, and gave comprehensive backing to efforts to attract industry and plan the economy. Around it Johnston set up a proliferation of specialist committees − ultimately totalling 32 − investigating subjects as diverse as hill sheep farming and the teaching of citizenship in schools. Substantial practical gains were registered: Scotland received a full and varied quota of war industries; a committee under Lord Cooper cut through the Gordian knot of environmental and vested interests which had throttled the Caledonian Power Bill before the war, enabling Johnston to set up the publicly-owned North of Scotland Hydro-Electric Board; the public sector in medicine was extended; the Scottish Office gained planning powers; and planning groups for the major Scottish regions were set up well in advance of legislation.

Was all this a move towards formal devolution which Johnston's successors betrayed? Not really. Johnston disliked London government, but preferred efficient administration to 'partisan political strife'. His Scottish success, moreover, coincided with the capture of the 'commanding heights' of Whitehall by moderate collectivists − which Paul Addison has seen as a crucial component of Labour's 1945 victory − and didn't come long after Labour's own capture of major Scottish local authorities. The political system that resulted − a form of 'government by consultation' − both incorporated municipal Labour and guaranteed the key policies that sustained it: low-rent council housing, and denominational schools. It was confirmed by Labour's sweeping victory in the 1945 election, dispelling (for the time being) the nationalist apparition, and reducing the Unionists from 42 seats to 30.

Johnston left politics in 1945, subsequently becoming head of the Scottish Tourist Board, the Scottish Forestry Commissioners, and, in 1948, of the Hydro Board. In 1946 the Scottish labour movement lost, by death, two other major figures. One represented a body that, because of his activities, had steadily grown in influence; the other's political party virtually died with him.

The STUC

William Elger had become General Secretary of the Scottish Trades Union Congress in 1922. He found a small and rather decrepit body, dating back to 1897, which differed from the British TUC in including trades councils as well as unions. Many of these unions, however, were local craft associations, with a declining membership. If it were to survive it would have to establish its independent status. Elger's first survey of unionism revealed in 1942 that only about one-third of the Scottish workforce (*c*.500,000) was unionized, and of this number only 290,659 were affiliated to the STUC. In Elger's words, there was 'no Trade Union Movement as distinct from Unions'; the relatively non-militant east was actually better unionized than the 'wild red West'; and the traditional Scottish unions were atrophying in decaying industrial sectors. There were, for example, 11 independent Scottish unions in textiles, against 4 English ones, but in growing sectors like public employment English unions had a monopoly. Elger concentrated on building up a Scottish 'movement' by winning over sceptical English unions to affiliation, even at the cost of amalgamations between them and Scottish unions. By 1939 he could look back on a 33.8 per cent increase in affiliated membership while the labour force rose by only 10 per cent (the British TUC's affiliates rose over this period by only 7.5 per cent), and a position in which the STUC had become a respectable part of the government's consultation framework.

This was not achieved without opposition, particularly from the trades councils, in which Communists of the National Minority Movement were firmly entrenched and occasionally exercised control. Their initiatives to secure backing for the National Unemployed Workmen's Movement were sustained but unsuccessful, as were their attempts to dissuade the STUC from co-operating with its 'class enemies' like Lithgow and Bilsland by joining the Scottish Economic Committee in 1936. An executive member, C.W. Gallie of the National Union of Railwaymen, put the central option confronting the STUC succinctly: 'Were they to sit quietly by until they ushered in Socialism and found themselves the possessors of a bunch of derelict industries?

This was virtually to become a text for the STUC's subsequent policy. Although firmly in a minority in the SEC, on the creation of its successor, the Scottish Council in 1942, the STUC had its position further strengthened, and its consultative role was enhanced by the post-war Labour government.

The Post-war Left

The other death was that of Jimmie Maxton. For the House of Commons his lank, unkempt figure, wit and humanity symbolized the 'decency' and moral passion of the left, the spirit of the 'Red Clyde' glowering out of its mists in Lavery's famous portrait. Not surprisingly, the ILP had for a time that other thorny moralist, George Orwell, as a member. But as a party it had long since collapsed. In 1938 its MPs had negotiated to rejoin Labour, but Maxton's pacifism would not accept Labour's conversion to rearmament. When he died, its two remaining members soon took the Labour whip. Campbell Stephen died in 1948, and the Unionists won his seat. John McGovern, the ILP's most violent and undisciplined MP, moved sharply to the right and ended his career as an exhibit on Moral Rearmament platforms, testifying to the evils of Communism.

Paradoxically, the victory of 1945 seemed to end Labour's golden age. Its personalities were dead or had retreated to the fringes. The local party structure, with its newspapers, choirs, theatre groups, and cycling clubs, had largely collapsed. In the 1950s there were probably not more than 500 regular Labour activists in the whole of Glasgow. This was not unwelcome to local councillors who wanted a quiet life, and whose financial probity was not always above criticism — there was a particularly embarrassing sequence of corruption trials in Glasgow in the late 1930s and early 1940s which made Johnston threaten to rule the place with commissioners. Nor did it really disturb party organizers cast in the mould of Sir Patrick Dollan, Arthur Woodburn, and William Marshall, who concentrated on organization and discipline at the expense of participation and ideas. The time of the 'wee hard men' had come.

Electoral success compensated Labour for such afflictions. It was not so with the Liberals. Their decline continued inexorably. Sir Archibald Sinclair was an effective air minister in the wartime coalition, but took little interest in Scottish affairs, rarely attending the Council of State. He lost Caithness in 1945, and Dingle Foot lost the party's other Scottish seat at Dundee. 'The old fire of Liberalism, which had burned so ardently during the great days of the Midlothian campaign, was now almost extinct', noted Alison Readman after attending an Edinburgh meeting addressed by the party's most notable MP, William Beveridge. Despite an energetic campaign in 1950, there was little recovery. The party gained two seats — though one of these was Jo Grimond's in Orkney and Shetland — and lost 30 deposits. Need the collapse have been so great? Possibly not, as after the war liberalism of a sort had a remarkable revival.

The Covenant Movement

While secretary of the SNP before the war, John MacCormick had courted the Liberals. In 1937 he negotiated a pact with Lady Glen-Coats allowing his party a free run in 12 constituencies of its own choice, and after leaving the SNP he stood as a Liberal in Inverness in 1945. Meanwhile his 'Scottish Convention' — backed by some authoritative names from outside political nationalism such as Sir John Boyd Orr, Naomi Mitchison, and Professor John MacMurray, and expertly serviced in its economic intelligence by James Porteous, who had been Assistant Secretary of the Scottish Economic Committee — carried on steady pro-home-rule propaganda with a view to organizing a convention on the lines of the one aborted in 1939. In 1947 such a gathering took place, with 600 delegates, broadly representative of the churches, local government, the Co-operatives, and liberal opinion in general. The following year its second meeting approved a Covenant demanding home rule within a federal system, and at the third meeting, in October 1949, attended by 1,200 delegates, this was ceremonially signed. Subsequently it gained two million signatures. But the general elections of 1950 and 1951 supervened without any home-rule intervention. This was disastrous: by the time MacCormick had produced a continuing organization, the impetus had passed. The fact that many of its opponents gave aid to the Covenant movement prejudiced Labour against it from the beginning. In December 1947 MacCormick had stood against Labour at Paisley as a 'National' candidate. Paisley had a traditionally high Liberal vote, but by accepting Unionist support he alienated the Liberals. Ultimately he polled 20,668 against Labour's 25,000, and Labour never forgot it.

Labour's Response

Attlee's first choice as Secretary of State, Joe Westwood, who had been Johnston's Under-Secretary, proved a failure and was sacked in October 1947. Arthur Woodburn succeeded him. As Secretary of the Scottish Council of the party he had given guarded endorsement to home rule during the war. He now rejected it, but used the growing support for Scottish Convention — 'a kind of smouldering pile that might suddenly break through the party loyalties and become a formidable national movement' — to persuade the Cabinet to create a Scottish Economic Conference and to widen the scope of the Scottish Grand Committee. For over 40 years it had been restricted to the committee stages of non-controversial Scottish Bills; it could now consider them in principle at second reading — if the House as a whole approved — and debate the Scottish estimates. This still proved insufficient to halt the growth of Scottish Convention, or the intention of the Unionists to exploit what they saw as a protest against the centralization of the Labour government's nationalization policies. 'I should never adopt the view', Churchill told Edinburgh electors during the 1950 campaign, 'that Scotland should be forced into the serfdom of socialism as a result of a vote in the House of Commons'. After the election Attlee removed Woodburn and replaced him with Hector McNeil, a figure more in the Elliot mould who had done well as a junior minister at the Foreign Office. But he had little time to prove himself; on 26 October 1951 Labour went out of office.

Nineteen fifty was not to be the last time that a Unionist leader would play around with the rhetoric of nationalism, fairly unscrupulously. In fact the Unionists recovered little from the setback of 1945, although they were to do better in 1951. As a party they seemed increasingly remote from Scottish reality, their MPs increasingly drawn from the landed, agricultural, and professional classes, and they lacked Labour's connection to municipal politics, in which the right wing was still represented by local 'Progressive' or 'Moderate' parties. Yet possibly their reasons for being at Westminster were more rational than anyone else's. Wartime and post-war reform in agriculture had created a powerful interest which required this central representation. Labour took far longer to exploit its Westminster position.

IV A Part of the Whole? 1950–1964

The 1950s were tranquil. The romantic episode of the snatching of the Stone of Destiny from Westminster Abbey in 1950 — in which MacCormick was involved — proved to be the swansong of the Covenant movement. On coming to power in 1951 the Conservatives set up the Balfour Commission into Scottish affairs, but removed home rule from its remit; the result was to be a modest increase in the powers of the Scottish Office, which took over responsibility for electricity in 1954 and roads in 1956. In the Indian summer of the heavy industries, the country was enjoying a stability otherwise absent for nearly half a century, and the Unionists did well, in 1955 getting an absolute majority of the Scottish vote, as well as Scottish MPs. This was partly through beating Labour at its own game. James Stuart, the aristocratic Secretary of State, got on well with Labour MPs, exceeded Labour's public housing programme by over a third, and at last secured substantial transport investment – with the Forth Road Bridge and Glasgow railway electrification. But this masked a failure to tackle the fundamental economic and social problems of the country.

During the icy years of 'Austerity' Labour had lost Glasgow and other big local authorities (a gradual process as only a third of councillors were elected each year). In the early 1950s it won them back, and then held them for 15 years, but its parliamentary presence was not effective. McNeil had moved to the right, and virtually left politics for business; his successor, Tom Fraser, though an able administrator, was unaggressive. Scottish political quiescence may have been deceptive, but it coincided with the development of 'behaviourist' political sociology, derived from American practice. This supposed a growing degree of British 'political homogeneity' – with voters increasingly conditioned by 'common' factors like social class, and 'consumerist' choices between the respective parties pushing out sectional and regional issues. Scotland seemed part of the whole.

In the later 1950s the economic situation worsened, and the labour movement got more aggressive, partly because of mighty upheavals in the Communist Party. Still subject to 'Cold War' proscriptions, the Communists had retained many of their wartime recruits and in the early 1950s had about 10,000 members in Scotland, a quarter of the party's UK total. Although electorally unsuccessful – Gallacher had lost West Fife in 1950 – its members were harder-working and better-briefed on the Scottish economy, and more corruption-resistant, than their Labour equivalents. Then, in 1955 and 1956 Kruschev's denunciation of Stalin and the Russian invasion of Hungary forced many intellectuals and activists to leave the party. One result was the New Left movement which grew up around the universities, contributing to developments as diverse as the folk-song revival and the Campaign for Nuclear Disarmament; another was Labour's acquisition of several hundred competent and radical activists. (In 1965, for example, the President, Secretary, and Vice-President of Edinburgh City Labour Party were all ex-Communists.) The result energized the left, although whether those who had followed the fiats of the Kremlin for decades could also provide imagination and open-mindedness was another matter.

This was also reflected in trade unionism. The STUC continued to grow faster than the TUC. Between 1939 and 1969 its affiliated membership increased by 128 per cent compared with 93 per cent. Elger's policy of collaboration with the Scottish Council and the Scottish Office had been continued by his successor, George Middleton, and the STUC, as 'honest broker' to incoming companies, ensured that non-union shops met union rates of pay and conditions. It, and many of the trades councils, were strongly anti-Communist until the mid 50s but ex-Communists steadily pushed it leftwards, and it developed links with unions in eastern Europe. This shift was accelerated by economic deterioration after 1958, but Middleton was able to turn it to the STUC's advantage by using it as a political bargaining counter. He built up close relations with Harold Macmillan, with him played a considerable part both in directing industries northwards and in creating a regional planning consensus. The increasing influence of the left also meant the return of home rule, traditionally backed by the Communists, to the STUC's programme in 1969, but the importance of this should not be exaggerated: union pressure had always been directed at equalizing Scottish and English wage-rates. The possibility of regional wage-bargaining, a central feature of German devolution, was always rejected. Whatever their declarations to the contrary, the unions were unionist.

Between 1958 and 1959 Scottish unemployment doubled. 'You've never had it so good' did not awake sympathetic echoes in the north that October, and Labour won four Unionist seats. Although Macmillan and his Scottish Secretary John Maclay subsequently exerted themselves to establish new industry, to introduce the concept of economic planning, and to reorganize the Scottish administrative machine to cope with these developments, they were frustrated by other aspects of their own government's programme, such as the drastic railway cuts of the Beeching programme and the run-down of the coal industry. Although it commanded widespread support in Scotland, the generalizations of the Toothill Report (1961) were not infallible, but scarcely had Maclay accepted its recommendations, and announced in March 1962 the creation of the Scottish Development Department (taking over planning and housing from the Department of Health, and roads, electricity, and local government from the Home Department) as its administrative embodiment, then he vanished in Macmillan's July purge. His inexperienced successor,

Michael Noble, had not only to face incessant attacks from the Labour benches, after March 1963 well co-ordinated by William Ross, but increasing indiscipline in his own ranks.

As rural Unionism had established itself more as an interest group than a political force, it was vulnerable to a rise in the political temperature. In the early 1960s the Liberal revival began to supply this. The party's fortunes had stayed low during the 1950s, although a popular candidate, like the broadcaster and former Rugby internationalist John M. Bannerman, could still produce the occasional good result. But under· the charismatic, if somewhat olympian, leadership of Jo Grimond, after 1957, it began to show its teeth. As a result, indiscipline and individual protests on the Unionist back benches grew, until Scottish debates tended to become a sort of martyrdom for ministers. Labour, too, was pressed — in April 1961 Bannerman ran them very close at Paisley — but a series of by-election setbacks seemed to promise Unionist humiliation in the approaching general election. In this respect at least the 'evolution' of Sir Alec Douglas-Home in October 1963, after Macmillan's enforced retirement, served Unionism well. Under a somewhat antique exterior, Home had all the unsentimental realism of his class, and spoke the language of the agricultural interest. This language proved all but untranslatable to the political correspondents who followed his election campaign in Kinross and West Perth, but it helped secure him a triumph.

All things considered, the Unionists did not do too badly in 1964. Labour gained three seats from them (much less of a swing than in the north of England) and the Liberals gained three, also coming second in another eight. The Scottish National Party, an almost imperceptible presence in Scottish elections during the 1950s, but which had come second to Labour in the West Lothian by-election of February 1962, performed poorly, giving little indication of the trouble that it was subsequently to cause the main parties only a couple of years later. But a closer look at the SNP would show an accession of membership, money, and organizational ability, under the imaginative leadership of William Wolfe and Ian MacDonald, while on the Liberal side there was a growing divergence between its Scottish support and its British aims. The Liberal successes showed that a strong Scottish radicalism still subsisted beneath the two-party system, of which the idea of home rule was an important component. Yet Grimond, and his successors, still fundamentally looked to the south, and to the notion (apparently demonstrated at Orpington in March 1962) that they would prosper by ministering to the discontents of the English suburbs. Their failure to concentrate on a Scottish programme (a repetition of Sinclair's mistake in the 1930s) was subsequently to imperil them, just as Labour was to be hoist by the expectations of planning and social welfare it had created.

V *Dramatis Personae*

Twentieth-century Scottish politicians have not had a good press: observers have often contrasted the social irrelevance of the Unionist gentry and lawyers and the inarticulacy of Labour with the front-benchers of the pre-World War I period. But the latter's 'fortnight once a year' attentions were only possible when the role of government was limited. When this changed, and Scotland got more politically unstable, the front-benchers left. (In 1910 over half of Scottish MPs lived in England; by 1979 less than 10 per cent.) The Unionist response had some logic: their MPs represented first business and then, as economic autonomy declined, and they lost urban seats, the politically significant interest of agriculture. Labour's declining prestige was not due to the party becoming more proletarian, though it suffered from the southward shift of trade union authority. In 1922 its MPs were dominated by miners' agents; in 1964 by local councillors. More than a third of its MPs were 'middle class' in 1922, two-thirds in 1964. Its waning influence probably resulted from two factors. After 1945 the Labour party was centrally controlled by a small but very well-organized Oxford-educated élite, which (with a five times better chance of office than non-Oxford MPs) never made up less than a third of most Cabinets. Secondly, the growth of Scottish government both absorbed Scottish MPs, and created conventions which barred them from 'British' portfolios in areas devolved to the Secretary of State, such as education or housing.

The press also assaulted Scottish MPs for their silence in parliament. This was unfair. While they spoke less on non-Scottish subjects, they worked hard within the Scottish committees (further ones were added in 1957 and 1962) and on questions to ministers. Questions to the Secretary roughly quadrupled between 1924 and 1962. These not only reflected his increased powers but population distribution as well. In 1924 (when there were 34 Labour MPs) nearly two thirds of questions concerned the Highlands. Between 1960 and 1964 Labour made Scottish question-time, with every enquiry wired-up to supplementaries, a distinctive and deadly tactic.

The personnel of local authorities was similar, but their status was even lower. Until the mid 1970s the independent right survived, in 'Progressive' or 'Moderate' parties, while independents ran most county and district councils. After 1929 local hegemony shifted from gentry and minister to businessmen and retailers in the smaller towns, but this was outweighed by the increasing domination of permanent officials – medical officers, surveyors, directors of education. In the towns the representation of capital shifted from manufacturing to trade; and, after 1945, as housebuilding and redevelopment increased, to the construction industry. Labour representatives tended to be lower-middle rather than working class: small business-men, union officials, and housewives. Both sides were inhibited by the fact that the 'state sector middle class' – teachers, civil servants, council employees – was banned from local office until 1974. The exclusion of a group which provided about 20 per cent of Labour MPs in the 1960s unquestionably harmed Labour in particular – as did the fact that many working-class councillors were employees of council contractors, who thus reinforced their interest.

Twenty per cent of Edinburgh councillors in 1960 were women. Their local government rôle grew, but their parliamentary rôle stagnated. At no time were there more than five women MPs (6 per cent) and after 1983 there were only two – although in terms of numbers elected (13.5 per cent of UK women MPs) and years served (11.7 compared with 11.1 UK average) Scotland's record was actually a little better than its machismo image, and the trade unions' persistent neglect of women's issues, would suggest. But Scandinavian countries had, by the 1960s, over 20 per cent of women MPs, and this example probably had some influence on the prominent rôle of women in the SNP, where they made up 3 out of 13 MPs, 1967–79.

By 1964 'St Andrew's House' had indeed become 'Dublin Castle', with 7,000 civil servants under its sway, and was the terminus of most enquiries and appeals, not only from MPs but from councillors. It developed a dynamic of its own, particularly in environmental, educational, and economic planning after 1960, culminating in the Toothill Report. John Mackintosh and others accused it of subservience to Whitehall, yet against Whitehall's secrecy and lack of professional specialism, St Andrew's House's more problem-orientated structure made it potentially more flexible and imaginative. Still, while not an Oxbridge fief – only about 20 per cent of its senior staff were from Oxbridge, compared with over 50 per cent in Whitehall – had it the planning and economic skills that its expanded

commitments demanded? Scottish administration has yet to be anato-
mized, but its heads tended to be directly drawn from the Scottish
universities, and hence to reflect both their deficiencies in the social
sciences and the constricting social solidarity of the Edinburgh professions. Only in the 1970s, for instance, did it receive an adequate
economic intelligence department, under Gavin McCrone.

Two biographies, moreover, provide a worrying insight into the
development of this secretive institution. John Highton became Permanent Under-Secretary under Elliot in 1936. Working class in background (his brother was Chairman of Glasgow Trades Council) he
organized unemployment investigations and adult education in his
spare time, and was well placed to give administrative shape to Elliot's
innovations. Tragically, he died after only a few months in office.
George Pottinger, a dynamic figure of the 1960s, whom many
expected to become Permanent Under-Secretary, cultivated an
impressive upper-class lifestyle. At his trial in 1975 it was found that,
for years, he had been in the pay of the corrupt Yorkshire architect
John Poulson, to the tune of £30,000, entanglements of which his
colleagues and superiors were unaware. Highton was the sort of
administrator the Scottish Office needed. Pottinger, perhaps, was led
to his downfall by his aspirations towards the Edinburgh upper-class
values that prevailed instead. Were such values relevant to a modern
administration?

As Scots MPs — especially the Labour members — were fairly
homogeneous, it seems surprising that a 'Scottish interest' took until
the 1960s to emerge. Lack of leadership seems critical. In Max
Weber's formulation 'imperative co-ordination' — the acceptance of
common goals and discipline — comes, pending an organized
bureaucracy, from a 'charismatic leader'. Parnell was such a figure in
Irish politics in 1880s, linking peasantry, local leaders, Church, exile
politicians, and MPs. The machinery he helped create survived his fall
in 1890. Tom Ellis and David Lloyd George, who might have done the
same for Wales, weakened Welsh nationalism by their co-option into
UK politics. There was no parallel to either in Scotland: the
Clydesiders did not attempt to lead Scottish MPs in the 1920s; there
was hardly anyone to lead in the 1930s, and although Johnston came
close to the Weberian pattern in 1941–5, he chose not to develop a
political movement.

What inhibited leadership? The constraints of Scottish working-
class consciousness (see p. 86)? A relatively open entry into the
southern élite, which drew the politically and administratively able

away — particularly between the wars? Certainly, for those who stayed, law, local government, education, and the Church offered secure and reasonably influential niches, while MPs who tried to build up a party following in Scotland as well as at Westminster ran risks. Elliot and Johnston lived beyond 65, but William Graham, Hector McNeil, and John Mackintosh died in their 40s; Wheatley, Maxton, Keir Hardie, Noel Skelton, and John MacCormick at around 60. Stress-based ailments terminated or damaged enough careers to suggest that the peripatetic life damaged party politics — particularly on the left — more than the other power-bases of Scottish society.

For the traditional institutions had their own élites, too. The reunited Church now eschewed party politics, but it still pronounced on political issues. Although two UF ministers — Campbell Stephen and James Barr — were prominent Labour MPs, they dissented from Church unity, and no ministers have followed them into parliament. The lawyers showed their solidarity in 1931, when the Lord Advocate, Craigie Aitchison, the Solicitor-General, and most of the Advocates Depute left Labour to join the National Government. Yet Labour still loved a lawyer; in 1936 another advocate, Robert Gibson, was chairman of its Scottish executive. Finally, after 1918, educational politics intensified to the point of impenetrability, with the incorporation of the Catholic schools, the shifting of the SED to Edinburgh, the education authority experiment, central salary negotiations, and the growing unionization of the teaching profession.

Did party majorities matter more than leaders? Probably not. Tom Johnston, leading the minority party in World War II, was a success; the Liberal Secretaries of World War I, with huge majorities, were flops. In our own day, Labour's 11-seat majority was not sufficient to counter Bruce Millan's distinctly anaesthetic effect on the devolution debate. The Secretary of State's position was surely critical. Until 1964, when his Welsh counterpart was created, he was unique in his control over a wide range of government functions and patronage. But was he party manager, administrative reformer, or national leader? The first rôle — the line of least resistance? — was taken by the weakest. The second, pioneered by Elliot as Under-Secretary in the 1920s, meant co-operating with local authorities and creating an administrative cadre. Elliot's precedent was followed *de facto* by Collins, Johnston, Woodburn, McNeil, and Maclay, and as a matter of principle by William Ross. The result was usually a consensus in favour of collectivist reform. But Johnston and Ross also encouraged a specifically Scottish will towards change: a difficult situation to master if, once expectations had been raised, the political machine failed to deliver the goods.

Finally, Labour in particular had to supply an ideological substitute for élite solidarity. Practically all the Unionist Secretaries were drawn from, or had married into, the Scottish landed and commercial establishment. They knew fairly well how to serve its needs. In the case of the best of them, Walter Elliot, there was also an intellectual input, the residue of pre-1914 'civic consciousness'. Hence the liveliness of his collaboration with its professional representatives, such as Boyd Orr or Grierson. Until 1941 Labour lacked a socialist concept of Scottish government (Adamson exemplified right-wing trade unionism at its dimmest) or an explicit power-base. Johnston, Dollan, and Elger created this base, but its essential pragmatism ruled out further ideological development, not only towards home rule, but virtually in any direction that might challenge the power-brokers in local government and the unions. This sterility meant that, when its plans turned sour in the late 1960s, Labour was peculiarly vulnerable to the challenge of the SNP.

5

Mass Media: High Culture
1922–1964

I

In the National Museum in Helsinki are three great stained-glass windows: Ethnography; Philology; History. These sum up the attempt of nineteenth-century Finnish liberals to give their nationalism an intellectual basis, by concentrating on the customs, language, and common experience of their people, on the whole still peasants. This implied, of course, a process of selection; the whole thing could pass for an exercise in intellectual hegemony. Different in aim, though not, possibly, in actual outcome, was the 'great tradition' of British intellectuals invoking 'culture' as 'the great hope in our present difficulties' — the intention of Carlyle, Mill, Ruskin, Arnold, and so on being to combat tendencies towards materialistic, capitalist, and class-divided democracy by positing the goal of cultural excellence as a 'common pursuit'.

Scotland cannot quite be fitted into either tradition, although expatriate Scots largely formulated the second. It had long ceased to be a peasant society, but its popular culture was still quite distinct from that of England. Yet this culture, and the position of the intellectuals within it, was the result of the coincidence of a particularly dramatic industrial impact with an intellectual ambivalence towards cultural nationalism, and an effective transference of political nationality — not necessarily to Westminster. In the changed circumstances of the twentieth century the national model exerted its pull, but it was countered by this other experience. The result was to be an intellectual dialectic — the 'Scottish Renaissance' — of enormous quality and interest, although its linkage with politics and popular culture remained as complex and unsatisfactory as ever.

117

II Popular Culture and the Impact of War

Working-class culture, before 1914, was deeply divided: between rural and urban, between respectable and rough, between Catholic and Protestant, between men and women. In the country literary culture was limited: James Littlejohn found in *Westrigg* in the late 1940s that its staples were still the Bible and Burns. Long working hours meant that the same was probably the case elsewhere, though folk song survived in the 'bothies' of the north-east and among tinkers and fisher-folk. But this oral tradition had difficulties in the machine shop and the mine, leaving the male industrial worker with the choice between respectability and roughness, meaning drink. The first meant 'improvement', through the Churches, adult education, or the labour movement. Although sustained by philanthropy and local government, 'improvement' had to struggle against inimical living and working conditions.

Roughness underlined the sheer unpleasantness of working-class life. Football, the 'bevvy', the sluggish Sunday — these were emotional escapes rather than a form of socialization. There was no elaborate pub society, such as Brian Harrison has described in England. In Scotland the architectural magnificence of pubs was strictly proportionate to the drinkers' income. Instead, devoutness and drink were frequent doppelgangers, among Catholic and Free Churchman alike. Spirit drinking — as in Scandinavia — and 'wee haufs' helped overcome foul weather and draughts (for a majority of Scots workers probably spent most of their time in the open), and tiny crowded houses. If the result was a certain social inadequacy, then it would have been much worse but for the women. They created a home-life and a sort of community-politics, even if only through policing by gossip. They stayed away from drink and crime, saved, organized their families, read. They were a coiled spring.

War broke up many of these divisions. Although it breached religious sanctions, it also gained some of the objects of the temperance movement, as liquor control and stringent licensing cut heavy drinking. There had been 1 pub to every 424 Scots in 1900; by 1955 there would be only 1 to 806. In the same period drunkenness convictions declined tenfold to 2.6 to every 1,000 people. Both as cause and consequence of this more cash was spent on other recreations. Women's wartime gains meant that their exclusion from leisure was no longer possible, while along with the Liberal hegemony there departed much of the power of the churchgoing middle class to control the weekend. Catholics were notoriously flexible about the Sabbath, and so was the internal combustion engine. In 1910 only 21 Sunday trains had run on the Caledonian Railway, but buses operated regularly on Sunday, and motorists drove whenever they liked. Bus tours — for sport, sightseeing, or drinking — car trips to country tea-rooms, the growth of mountaineering and hiking, gave urban Scotland access to recreations previously confined to the well-off or determinedly secular.

III Outlets: Sport

If sport of various sorts dominated Scottish leisure time, there was good reason for this. With a large land area relative to population, Scotland had been, next to Switzerland, 'the playground of Europe' in the nineteenth century. A sportive ethos had been created, even if it was initially a socially restrictive one. It is worth looking at it in some detail.

We can begin by dividing it into three main areas: leisure-class activities, mainly field sports; spectator sports; and participant sports. The first were in theory participant sports, but they were much more important as economic activities, and as indicating social boundaries. A vast amount of rural Scotland was devoted to grouse-moors and deer forests. They were an important part of the Highland economy, an even more important hindrance to its development, and an essential ingredient of Scottish upper-class life. Yachting involved more of the middle classes, and was definitely of some benefit to the boatyards of the Clyde. If the middle classes fished a lot, they seem to have gone shooting infrequently, and hunted rarely if at all. But, to judge by *Scottish Biographies* (1938), participation in sport seems to have been, in Scotland much more than in England, a badge of social respectability. Thirty-seven per cent of a random sample of entries played golf, 17.5 per cent fished. Only 2 per cent and 1 per cent admitted to an interest in music or art. But then, only 1 per cent said they followed football.

For most Scotsmen, sport meant football. Watching and discussing it took up much of the weekend, and it filled a third of the popular press. Save in the Borders, Rugby Union was middle class. Cricket was less so, but mainly confined to the east coast. Shinty never took on outside the Highlands — unlike in Ireland, there was no nationalist attempt to promote 'Scottish' sports. Yet football was politically important: it defined class, gender, religion, and nationality, and

E

ritualized and contained all of these. The period 1920−39, years of potential social upheaval, was its golden age. It was almost a paradigm of the Scottish situation: its skilled artisans were paid by little local oligarchies, or cleared off to richer fields in the south. The internationals with England, 12 out of 20 won by the Scottish David, were often the only time the best players represented their country, and all the more symbolic for that. Only with the onslaught of television did gates start to fall − by over 30 per cent, 1955−65. For George Blake in *The Shipbuilders* (1935) the crowd at 'ra gemme' − drink, swearing, and all − stood for the values of the skilled workers: decadence was represented by the new greyhound tracks, dedicated purely to the cause of easy money.

The politics of football between the wars are a curious business, anyway. The middle classes, the Churches, government encouraged football playing as an antidote to the demoralization caused by unemployment. But the same classes made social boundaries more rigid by imposing rugby on many senior secondary schools. They may have seen the enemy as commercialism − football pools became commonplace in working-class homes in the 1930s − and their goal may have been the 'democratic game' of the Borders, but the headmasters forgot that rugby needs grass if it is not to be murderous, while football simply needs a ball. So football tended to become an affirmation of working-class solidarity against 'improvement'. The aristocracy was little troubled by such scruples, and was appropriately rewarded. The fifth Earl of Rosebery was popular in Scotland despite his racehorses, his son because of them, although off-course gambling was not made legal until 1969.

Other participatory sports expanded, admitted women, but remained otherwise more class-bound, because of expense. Bowls and pigeon-racing remained symbols of artisan worth. Tennis, like curling in winter, spread from the upper to the middle class. With the help of municipal courses, golf filtered further down, although the golf club remained a major centre of middle-class socializing. Only in the 1960s did sailing and winter sports cease to be the preserve of the well-off, but rowing and amateur athletics, out of the same stable as the Boys' Brigade and YMCA, involved all classes. Aptly enough, Scotland's greatest runner of the inter-war years, Eric Liddell, forfeited an Olympic gold medal in 1924 by refusing to run on a Sunday. Swimming, in heated baths which were a by-product of the public health movement, was probably the most democratic participatory sport, and one in which Motherwell, in particular, did well.

IV Outlets: Indoor Entertainment

Enthusiasm for sport was a blow struck against a malign climate. Indoor entertainment, and the cinema in particular, had technology as well as unemployment on its side; it offered warm and reasonably harmless refuge from drink and overcrowding. Theatres and music halls either withered or blossomed into this new life. Glasgow's 14 fell to 9 in 1940, though some of her sentimental singers and alarmingly ethnic comedians put up a strong fight. The winter pantomimes of such as Tommy Lorne and Will Fyffe virtually merged into their summer seasons at holiday resorts. But by 1929, when talkies arrived, Glasgow had 127 cinemas. Large burghs had three or four apiece by the 1940s, and even the smallest towns would boast one, sometimes in bizarre conversions, like a former church in Melrose and a brewhouse in Kelso. Even the wilds were reached by the travelling projectors of the Highlands and Islands Film Service. To the Scots the movies were magic. In 1950 Glasgow people went on average 51 times a year, and Scots as a whole 36 times, while the English paid only 28 visits.

Reports on Scottish youth dwelt on the evils of 'corruption by Holly-wood'. Certainly, Scottish cinemagoers were more likely to be corrupted from across the Atlantic than from England. They disliked British films save where these dealt with Scottish themes. On the other hand there seems to have been a positive commitment to film culture, with a film society showing continental films in Glasgow in 1929, and an 'art' cinema, the Cosmo, opening in 1939.

Almost more important, and like the cinema a 'mixed' activity, was 'The Dancing', which gripped Scotland in the 1920s and only died with the ballroom style in the 1960s. Young men in their 'paraffin' — three-piece suits and slicked-down hair — and girls would flock, up to six nights a week, to huge dance halls. Glasgow had 30; in some you could dance for six hours for sixpence. Liquor was banned and there wasn't much sex around; the stress was on skill and style — a classy evening out for the poor and unemployed. Some dance halls were the scene of clashes between Glasgow gangs, graphically described in MacArthur and Long's *No Mean City* (1934), but there's a curious innocence about the fact that the toughest gang leader would only dance with men. The halls were in the main fiercely respectable, and Glasgow dancing was by World War II the best in Britain.

V Outlets: Literacy and its Uses

At the time of the 1872 Education Act 14 per cent more Scots children than English children were at school. This factor still affected popular culture a couple of generations later. The Scots had accustomed themselves to literacy, endowed it, and organized for it. Public esteem was reflected in library provision, while popular spread was facilitated by a disproportionate number of booksellers and newsagents, and a thriving demotic literature.

Libraries had been a feature of town and country alike during industrialization, and they were rapidly expanded in the early twentieth century by donations and state action. Carnegie presented whole buildings and their contents to the larger towns in the 1890s and 1900s, while J. & P. Coats gave every school in the country a collection of classic works (religion carefully excluded). Finally the education act of 1918 made school libraries part of the county system, and enlarged them. Dunbartonshire, for example, started with a private endowment at Helensburgh, gained early in the century two Carnegie libraries at Dumbarton and Clydebank and a municipal one at Kirkintilloch, and after 1918 added 90 branches in schools and eventually a travelling van. Libraries were a prudent investment. Between the wars they were a refuge for the unemployed, leafing through papers (with the racing pages pasted over) in the relative warmth. Utilization figures must therefore be treated with caution as evidence of literary awareness. But Scots were certainly devoted readers by British standards; by 1960 Edinburgh held the record for books borrowed per head per annum: 13.

The Scots read newspapers avidly; despite a lower standard of living, and consequent reduction in advertising revenue, their purchases were comparable with the rest of Britain in 1936. Probably, in the central belt, they were actually higher: Glasgow was until 1957 the only city outside London with three evening papers. The rise of the Sundays was even more remarkable. There had been none in 1913, but by 1949 the *Sunday Post* claimed one of the most saturated markets in the world. Lack of advertising obviously hit magazines, but even here the Scots established an export ascendancy, with the products of Thomson and Leng, the 'Dundee Press'.

The newspapers that Scotland read were avowedly Scottish in tone, and became more so as the *Daily Herald* declined and the *Daily Mail* set up a Scottish edition. But the pattern of ownership had changed radically in the 1920s. English firms rapidly took over mass-circulation papers, although Outrams of Glasgow, Findlays of Edinburgh, and Thomson and Leng still survived. Only Outram's *Glasgow Herald* and Findlay's *Scotsman* were in any sense quality papers, with authoritative correspondents and reviewers and full political coverage; the others were dominated by local issues and sport. When Beaverbrook's Glasgow incursion of 1928 caused a circulation war, 'human interest', crime, and sport gained his *Scottish Daily Express* the upper hand, although Scotsmen – George Malcolm Thomson, John Gordon, John Junor – acted as senior counsellors at the Aitken court.

In 1900 T.W.H. Crosland assaulted Scots literary men in *The Unspeakable Scot* for reducing all literature to journalism. The remarkable research of Dr William Donaldson has indeed shown how central journalism was to Scots literature from the mid-nineteenth century on, with the weekly provincial press a conduit of radical politics and popular enlightenment. By 1990 however, there was some loss of publishing nerve. Although Scots firms — chiefly Collins, Blackie, and Nelson — produced a disproportionate number of British books, they tended to specialize in theology and reprints (which frequently ended up anyway as Sunday School prizes). The only firms with an interest in publishing contemporary Scots authors were the rather staid concerns of Oliver and Boyd and Blackwoods. A notable southward shift in the 1880s had coincided with the creation of the modern 'literary industry' of agents, publicity, and

Table 5.1: Scottish daily newspaper ownership, 1920-1992

	1920		1940		1992	
	number of papers	owners	number of papers	owners	number of papers	owners
Glasgow	5	all S	7	4S 3E	4	2S 2MN
Edinburgh	3	all S	4	2S 2E	2	2MN
Aberdeen	4	all S	2	2E	2	2MN
Dundee	4	all S	2	2S	2	2S
Paisley / Greenock	2	all S	2	2S	2	1S 1MN
Sundays	2	all S	1	1S	4	1S 3 MN
total:	20	20 S	19	11S 8E	15	4S 2E 9MN

(S = Scottish-owned; E = English-owned; MN = Multinational)

Table 5.2: Scottish newspaper readership, 1935 and 1949

	1935		1949	
	Scotland	UK	Scotland	UK
No. of papers taken per family per day	1.5	1.5	0.66	0.70
No. of Sunday papers per family	1.1	1.7	2.26	1.9
No. of magazines per family per week			0.9	1.07

Source: M. Abrams, *The Home Market* (1950)

commercialism. And only one kind of Scottish literature was able to exploit this market.

They key figure was Sir William Robertson Nicoll, and the chosen instrument Hodder and Stoughton. Nicoll provided a bridge between the perfervid polemic of the mid-Victorian and the London literary industry with the British Weekly (1886) and the Bookman) (1891); he drew on the techniques of Scottish industry and the products of educa tion; he brought women in, with the significantly titled Woman at Home (also in 1891). Thirty years later, in *Hugh Selwyn Mauberly*, Ezra Pound would refer to him as 'Dr Dundas'. This was apt. Nicoll ran a new gravy train of patronage − literary, this time − to the south. His school of 'Kailyard' writers established the market for the 'Scottish story' and made aspirant authors only too aware of the riches it could provide.

The Kailyard developed beyond the Scottish parish. In the twentieth century it is better to define it as a literature whose content was established by market analysis. It was targeted not only on the Scots but on the emigrant community and a general middle-class readership which wanted to be reassured that, in an age of increasing social alienation and class-polarization, community identity was still possible. Poliitically it was midly reformist: Mrs Burnett Smith ('Annie S. Swan'), Nicoll's henchperson, was a prominent Scottish suffragist, the Liberal Party's first woman candidate, and a founder of the SNP. It may be unfair to endorse MacDiarmid's opinion that the anti-Kailyard novels of George Douglas Brown and James Macdougall Hay, *The House with the Green Shutters* (1900) and *Gillespie* (1913), were 'the same thing disguised as its opposite', but fairly soon even this genre had been swallowed by it, in the novels of Jane Duncan and A.J. Cronin. In the twentieth century the Kailyard strain changed and expanded into a somewhat disproportionate Scots presence in general readership light fiction, from adventure stories through historical novels to animal tales and hospital romances. Behind Alastair MacLean, Nigel Tranter, Mary Stewart, Dorothy Dunnett, Gavin Maxwell, James Herriot, and Lucilla Andrews might have been the shadowy lineaments of Stevenson, Scott, Dr John Brown, and Mrs Oliphant, but what mattered was the literary machinery that Nicoll and his friends had set up. As time went on, it drew on its more prole tarian wing, the Dundee press, which sustained the same values but salted them with older and less respectable popular fictional tradi tions. In *The Uses of Literacy* (1957) Richard Hoggart noticed how, along with detailed and faithful renderings of working-class life,

Dundee women's magazines specialized in serials in which the path of true love was splashed with quite a lot of blood, but James Cameron, a distinguished graduate of Thomson and Leng, recollected the strictness of the rules: drawings could show slit throats but not bare knees.

Patterns of Scottish leisure had thus changed to cope with increased income, changing relationships between the sexes, and increased (if not always intended) free time. They were both more individually- and more socially-oriented than those of England. Popular literature was at a premium in a country of small houses, where it at least offered a range of individual options. The alternative was organized social activity, provided municipally or commercially. The commercial structure was partly Scottish-owned, as in football, but was also, like many inter-war enterprises, increasingly dominated by large-scale English-run concerns.

Scotland was weak in family activities: gardening, for instance, increased, but not to the same extent as in England with her lower-density housing developments. Coarse fishing never became, as in the south, the most important participatory sport. Those who lived in the country, or could afford it, caught trout; the rivers and canals in the industrial areas were too polluted for roach or bream to survive. Hobbies requiring house-room, like model engineering, woodworking, motor car maintenance, and 'do-it-yourself' projects, were virtually ruled out. Educational reports commented on the inadequacy of Scottish girls as cooks and dressmakers, citing the same reasons. The growth of domestic science classes in the schools was a response. In the long run such factors probably had some part in the decline of skill within the Scottish working class. The state provided no countervailing resources, as technical education remained miserably inadequate, and voluntary working-class education — through the Workers' Educational Association in its early years and the Marxist National Council of Labour Colleges — was geared to political militancy and workshop organization rather than to acquiring new techniques or 'the full rich life'.

VI Uplift and Improvement

Although the expansion and diversification of popular entertainment certainly mitigated the tensions of the depression, it was not planned to do so. However, explicit attempts were made, by voluntary bodies and the state, to direct recreational activities in specific directions. These reflected the waning of traditional institutions of social co-operation, new technological possibilities, and new client groups.

The main diminution was of religious fervour. Although this had yet to register in terms of Church membership (see p.83), and the Churches still took a leading rôle in many of the developments to be surveyed, the primacy of 'controversial divinity' had vanished. Instead, the churches developed their social organizations, and some bodies traditionally connected with them provided paradigms for more secular developments.

The Freemason style, for instance, expanded significantly. Masonry had always been important in Scotland, with about 25 per cent of lodges in Britain and about 10 per cent of adult males as members. One of the few areas of interclass mixing, it was supplemented in the inter-war period by ex-servicemen's organizations, most notably the British Legion. Such bodies could have become — as in France or Germany — intensely political. Instead the Legion, founded under the headship of Earl Haig in 1921, provided a combination of social activities, quasi-masonic ritual, and religious involvement which made it a conservative and mildly nationalist presence. Analogous groups like Rotary — an American import which brought together the 'leaders' of local trade and industry, and established itself very strongly in Scotland from 1912 on — provided such 'non-political' (and by implication, conservative) bodies with a 'general staff'.

Unlike masonry, the British Legion and Rotary accommodated women — though at arm's length in separate and subordinate women's organizations. A similar logic had led to the creation in 1918 of the Scottish Women's Rural Institutes. The Board of Agriculture had set them up to increase participation in the war effort, and they expanded after the war until most parishes had branches. Like the Legion, their values were conservative and mildly nationalist. In fact they helped on its way a major Kailyard revival, the Community Drama movement, whose annual festival swelled from 35 competitors in 1926 to over 1,000 in 1936. The artistic standards of such groups were not high: their demand for 'kitchen comedies' ruined play-wrights, like the pacifist miner Joe Corrie, who had something serious to say, but until television arrived they remained an important element of Scottish popular culture.

In another area of activity the Churches were still successful. In Scotland there were no national youth organizations like the Czech Sokol or the Irish Fianna, although the socialist nationalist John Kinloch did persevere with Clan Scotland, and the Scottish Youth Hostel movement, formed after the German model in 1931, had much of nationalism about it in its early days. But the real growth was in the

Scouts and the Boys' Brigade. Both were founded before 1914 but only really expanded in the inter-war years, when they also added parallel girls' organizations. Of the two, the 'BBs' were the more urban and proletarian — all you needed was a white belt and a pillbox hat, instead of the Scouts' expensive bushveldt paraphernalia — and even more than the Scouts, they were tied to the Churches. BBs would be shocked to hear of Socialist Sunday Schools (in Glasgow, naturally) where Jesus didn't feature but humanist hymns by such as Edward Carpenter were sung. Not to much effect. Socialist Sunday Schools declined along with the ILP, and the Co-operative's Woodcraft Folk could never really compete with bugles and woggles. God had all the best tunes.

The failure of the political culture was also glaringly evident in the weakness of 'serious journalism' — this despite, or possibly because of, the important positions held by Scots in British political journalism, such as James Margach, Robert Carvel, or Alastair Hetherington. Scotland sustained no regular Unionist or Liberal magazines, and those of the left, once so promising, steadily declined, although *Forward* and *Plebs* of the National Council of Labour Colleges limped on until the 1960s. It took individualists — John Wheatley, James Leatham, Guy Aldred — to run socialist papers, and these usually died with them. By contrast, the nationalist *Scots Independent* has lasted since 1926.

As might be expected, 'institutional journals' flourished, but at the cost of parochialism. The Kirk had the monthly *Life and Work*, the Catholics the weekly *Glasgow Observer*, law the *Scots Law Times*, teachers the *Scottish Educational Journal*. In contrast to these, and to the situation in Wales and Ireland, attempts at a national critical review were usually failures, although there was usually a hopeful newcomer around to pick up the guttering torch. Between 1926 and 1934 William Power edited *The Scots Observer*, a well-meaning if clumsy vehicle for the literary revival; in 1934 the SNDC took over the fight with *Scotland*, which closed down during the war but performed respectably in the 1950s and 1960s. The left-wing Scottish Reconstruction Committee tried its hand with *New Scot* (1945–50), the Saltire Society with the *Saltire Review* and *New Saltire* (1954–64), but the formula was never found to raise circulation beyond a few thousand. Dundee's *Scots Magazine* (founded 1739) with a dependable mixture of anecdote, local coverage, and a huge exile sale, and Outram's somewhat classier *Scottish Field*, proved incomparably more successful.

Scottish cultural developments had depended on patronage, and a consequence of the depression and the southward migration of capital was that business patronage declined. Edinburgh University, for instance, received no endowments on the scale of the pre-war gifts of the Usher and MacEwan families. State grants were increased following the formation of the University Grants Committee in 1918 but, as noted earlier (see p.78), they simply ensured that the situation didn't deteriorate further. But State action did ensure a major improvement in research facilities. Following the 1918 Education Act a Scottish Central Library was set up in 1921 to co-ordinate local activities, and in the same year the creation of a National Library began. It got its act in 1925 and took over the 750,000 volumes of the Advocates' Library. In 1936 its building, to the design of Reginald Fairlie, was started on George IV Bridge, Edinburgh. Because of the war, it took 20 years to complete. After 1956 Scottish researchers had the most convenient and efficient copyright library in Britain, but its earlier absence was sadly missed.

If the state in this way encouraged a national cultural movement, its other major action was much more ambiguous. Radio began in Scotland in March 1923 under the private British Broadcasting Company. Three years later it was transformed into a public corporation. Ten years later it reached over 40 per cent of Scots homes. In charge of both was John Reith, apostle *par excellence* of uplift and improvement, yet at the same time the architect of an extremely centralized organization. Although the BBC set up a Scottish Region, its autonomy was limited; promising attempts to marry its aims to those of the literary renaissance by David Cleghorn Thomson and Moray MacLaren ended in frustration. Ultimately, under the regime of the Rev. Melville Dinwiddie (1933−57) the BBC in Scotland became a by-word for puritanical parochialism. Many of its early staff stayed in post much longer than Dinwiddie. No one would grudge those gentle Uncles and Aunties the right to become national institutions, but not at the expense of a broadcasting service that could have done so much more to cope with Scotland's social and cultural problems. The Scottish BBC was in fact a paradigm of the fate of regional organizations within otherwise highly-centralized UK bodies. The nominated Broadcasting Council was selected to represent the Scottish establishment, and it tended to concur with an equally conservative local executive. If talented radicals could be got rid of by promoting them to positions at the centre, who would complain, least of all at Broadcasting House?

VII The Scottish Renaissance

A provincial culture, distinct from that of England for various reasons, rather than superior to it. An acute awareness among Scottish intellectuals of the power of parochialism and the mediocrity of its cultural values; a sense of attraction to and revulsion against the metropolis. These factors appear to be constant throughout our period. But they were made explicit by the sudden efflorescence of the Scottish Renaissance in the 1920s and, despite its subsequent setbacks, this continued to sustain, and ultimately strengthen, a sense of a distinct national intellect.

World War I had not, in itself, stimulated Scottish literature, if the work of the two Anglo-Scottish front-line poets C.H. Sorley and E.A. Mackintosh be excepted, although a Scots-Canadian medical officer, John MacCrae, did create one unforgettable symbol, in the lines,

> In Flanders fields the poppies blow
> Among the crosses, row on row

while at Craiglockhart Sanatorium in Edinburgh an enlightened psychiatrist stimulated two battle-scarred officers to publish their poetry — Siegfried Sassoon and Wilfred Owen. Popular literature had done its bit, with the novels of 'Ian Hay' (*The First Hundred Thousand* and its sequels) and the saga of *Spud Tamson*, Glasgow 'ned' turned war hero proved (we have Harry McShane's word for it) a very effective recruiting tract. John Buchan, possibly the most energetic war reporter and propagandist, loaded Richard Hannay with symbolism and sent him off to the Red Clyde, among other places, in *Mr Standfast* (1918). The result was not very convincing. The tragic impact of the war had to wait for a decade and a half to be commemorated, in Grassic Gibbon's *Sunset Song* (1932).

But before society had readjusted itself, the upheavals, not merely of the war but of revolution and cultural radicalism, gained an articulate and aggressive voice. Christopher Murray Grieve, 'Hugh MacDiarmid', son of a Langholm postman, had been a socialist journalist in 1914. He saw service in Salonika and France, but the war, as such, scarcely registered on him. He used his time abroad to devour the literature and recent history of Europe and then turned on Scotland a mind grown international. As a literary editor his first anthology, *Northern Numbers* (1920), was respectful to older literati like Buchan and Neil Munro; his third series dropped them and adopted a radical tone, at once nationalist and revolutionary. Behind this lay the impact of the Irish war of independence (1919–21), the onset of the depression, and the influence of John Maclean. Although James Connolly, a Scot by birth, had been *Forward*'s Irish correspondent, the constitutional left had ignored the Irish Rising. Now, after his sacrifice, Connolly's aim seemed to have succeeded. Poets and socialists had together pulled their country away from the English connection. Yeats became a senator and was awarded the Nobel prize, and in 1922 James Joyce published *Ulysses*, assaulting the preconceived limits of the English language. To MacDiarmid, already associated with the radical *New Age* group, a centrifuge seemed to be at work; the hegemony of English, as well as of the Empire, was collapsing. The parochialism of Scottish literary life would have to be destroyed. 'Dunbar, not Burns!', 'Not Traditions – Precedents!' were the watchwords of his *Scottish Chapbook* (1922), and he went on to lay down to the teachers of Scotland, between 1925 and 1927, the standards that a new Scottish culture would have to achieve to gain international acceptance.

Thus far he resembled the great 'political' critics of nineteenth-century European literature – Carlyle, Belinsky, Brandes – but he also punched his message home with poetry of rare muscle and skill:

> O Scotland is
> The barren fig
> Up, carles, up
> And round it jig!
> A miracle's
> Oor only chance.
> Up, carles, up
> And let us dance!

By 1925 the French critic Denis Saurat was writing of the 'Scottish Renaissance', a term which MacDiarmid instantly appropriated. For his aims were not simply the achievement of a national literature akin to that of Norway or Ireland, but something consonant with Scotland's experience – an achievement on a world scale.

Controversy and contradiction governed MacDiarmid's philosophy. He would confront the debased vernacular with the abstracted rationality of the Scots forced abroad by the absence of a genuinely national culture. His aim was a perpetual unrest, 'a Caledonian antisyzygy' (a phrase borrowed from Professor Gregory Smith's

Scottish Literature of 1919). There were other nationalist patrons, like William Power or Ruari Erskine of Mar, who had nurtured any and every shoot of Scots literary ability. MacDiarmid was prepared to flay as well as encourage. Confessedly anti-English, he was also prepared to be equally anti-Scottish, where the enemy was smugness and complacency. This verse is cut into his tombstone:

> I'll hae nae hauf-way hoose, but aye be whaur
> Extremes meet — it's the only way I ken
> To dodge the curst conceit o' bein' right
> That damns the vast majority o' men.

MacDiarmid could still have been an isolated figure — there were plenty of gloomy precedents among nineteenth-century literary nationalists — but his self-confident initiative coincided with growing doubts among publicists, home rulers, and scholars not just about the Scottish economy but about the survival of nationality in face of the political centralization induced by the war, and also with a remarkable flowering of literary talent. The foundation of Scottish PEN (1926) and the National Party of Scotland (1928) were possibly the key literary–political events, but the decade 1924–34 also saw MacDiarmid's 'A Drunk Man Looks at the Thistle' and his first and second 'Hymns to Lenin', the first novels of Neil Gunn, George Blake, Eric Linklater, Fionn MacColla, and Naomi Mitchison, the critical writing of Edwin Muir and the early plays of James Bridie. And then, between 1932 and 1934, hammered straight on to a typewriter in a few weeks out of a short life, Lewis Grassic Gibbon's Mearns trilogy, later to be known as *A Scots Quair*.

What unified these, besides a degree of literary success which, if modest by British standards, was unprecedented in Scotland, and a general identification of literature with nationality? MacDiarmid wrote in 'The Kulturkampf: to William Power' (1935) that:

> No man can state the truth of Scotland,
> But he can establish some sort of relation
> Between his truth and the absolute. . . .

> Artists cannot be taken out of their own times and places
> To be shown around — just as the beauty of a tree
> Cannot be made visible by uprooting the tree;
> Here, they were shown together with their country.

The sense of finding a voice in Scotland, as well as for Scotland, was crucial. Besides the war and the wounds it had dealt, besides resentment at the failure of home rule and the failings of political parties, there was also a rebellion against parental authority, a discovery that sex could be talked about, even enjoyed, a sheer desire to write because no other means of communication and protest were available, much as women had used novel-writing to break their social isolation a century before. In this sense the achievement of the renaissance was personal rather than social or national. But an escape from the formula that had been Scotland did not necessarily mean a commitment to MacDiarmid's vision of a nation regenerated through the reconstruction of the old Scots tongue and political militancy. MacDiarmid had seen the recovery of Lallans as both democratic and nationalistic, but after the collapse of the General Strike in 1926 (see p.94) he moved to a position both more intransigent and more aristocratic, invoking scientific supermen just as Carlyle, his model in so many respects, had invoked Cromwell and Frederick the Great.

After 1930 MacDiarmid rarely wrote in Lallans, but the relevance of his work was shortly to be dramatized by the extraordinary achievement of Grassic Gibbon's trilogy. Like MacDiarmid, who was eight years older, Gibbon was an autodidact who had knocked around in journalism and the more boring parts of the services, all the time grasping for some great scientific world-view, and then fused his ideas, under intense pressure, onto the experience of Scotland. The result — *Sunset Song, Cloud Howe,* and *Grey Granite* — like MacDiarmid's 'Drunk Man' combines the sweep of historical change — the transition from rural to urban, the impact of the General Strike, the collapse of the Labour government — with the grip of individuals' struggles with one another, with society, or with the land itself, for their own identity.

Gibbon was ambiguous about nationalism, although his use of the Scots tongue amply proved its vitality. Yet the impact of the *Quair* seems ultimately ambiguous, even elegiac. Chris Guthrie, its central figure, returns to farm her father's Aberdeenshire croft, and dies. Her son, Ewan, leads a hunger march south to London. The old rural life ends, the industrial struggle begins. And yet in Gibbon it is the rural life that seems real, and the industrial episodes two-dimensional by contrast. Much the same can be said of MacDiarmid. The absorbing interest in nature, in character, demonstrated in the symbolism with which he invested his home landscape of Langholm, co-exists awkwardly with his 'scientific materialism' and dogmatic and sometimes inhumane politics. In 1936 Edwin Muir courted — and got — MacDiarmid's wrath by arguing, in *Scott and Scotland*, that the vernacular had no future. His premises were actually the same as MacDiarmid's: English was a foreign language, in which the Scots had never really been articulate. Muir's only remedy was a systematic linguistic assimilation. Given the achievements of MacDiarmid and Gibbon, this may seem tactless, but Muir had hit at a weak point. The greatest triumphs of the renaissance still failed to penetrate to the real matter of Scotland. The society that Gunn or MacColla or Mac-Diarmid or Gibbon celebrated was marginal to the urban life that the mass of the people now lived. Even the Kailyard had managed to make the transition which writers of much greater talent had failed to do.

The Scottish renaissance's failure to supply 'the great bourgeois novel' — anything comparable with the triumphs of Mann, Musil, Proust, and Joyce — was not its own fault. As Doris Lessing has pointed out, partly because Britain did not go through, or even seriously attempt, the centralizing process of state-formation in the nineteenth century, the essentially provincial attitudes of the gentry remained too strong for too long. Further, in Scotland, the tradition of the skilled craftsman, passing from the crofter to the weaver and the engineer, and safeguarded by the essentially 'planned' nature of the transition to industrialization, kept alive a range of attitudes that were never wholly of industrial mass-society. When, in *Grey Granite* (1934), Chris Guthrie rounds on an unemployed man: 'My class? It was digging its living in sweat while yours lay down with a whine in the dirt', she is speaking for more than the tradition of the Mearns peasants — for a series of now-vanishing skills which even when found in the engine-shops had more in common with those of the miller, blacksmith, and ploughman than with those of the assembly-line operative. Although MacDiarmid asked in his 'Second Hymn to Lenin'

> Are my poems spoken in the factories and fields
> In the streets o' town?
> Gin they're no, then I'm failin' to dae
> What I ocht to ha' dune

his ambition for his own poetry was rarely realized, and in fact was only intermittently held. The ordinary people still read the Dundee Press and went to Burns Suppers, while MacDiarmid's later poetry grew more cerebral and elitist: 'a sound like talking to God' was not something everyone could hear.

By 1936 the renaissance was over, and MacDiarmid an embittered exile in Shetland. Those whom it had stimulated to write continued to write — the best novels of Gunn, the Gaelic poetry of Sorley MacLean and George Campbell Hay, were still to come. But they were no longer part of a movement. Scottish *political* nationalism, as if in reaction to the word's increasingly unpleasant European connotations, was moderate, centrist, and not very effective, and, despite the founding of the Saltire Society in 1935 and some patronage from Elliot as Secretary of State, the revival did not move out of literature into other fields. It had been as paradoxical a development as MacDiarmid had wished for. It was about Scotland, yet would it have succeeded without the support of Anglo-Scots and London publishers and critics who took up its writers when they might have been ignored in the north? Without the advocacy of Ivor Brown, the Leavises, or T.S. Eliot? It was about politics, but these were infinitely varied. MacDiarmid wrote great socialist poetry — 'The Ballad of the General Strike' — in the same year that he prefaced *Albyn, or the Future of the Scots* with texts from Barres and Maurras, the pillars of the French right. Grassic Gibbon may have based the plot of *Sunset Song* on Frenssen's *Jorn Uhl* (1900), a German classic of the 'blood and soil' school favoured by the Third Reich — which also responded enthusiastically to the peasant society depicted by Eric Linklater and Neil Gunn. Both were blameless democrats, yet Linklater, Compton Mackenzie, and above all James Bridie represented an ironic, convivial Toryism, rather in the style of *Noctes Ambrosiana*, far removed from the Marxism of MacDiarmid and Gibbon. Oddest of all, it showed men — particularly Gunn and Gibbon — writing with sensitivity about women, while their pub society still kept women on the sidelines. The best women writers, Rebecca West and Naomi Mitchison, still went south. But, just as the one fully-aware person in 'The Drunk Man' is the poet's wife, the personnel of the renaissance frequently had to be kept together by the quiet civil servant Helen Cruikshank, poet and secretary of Scottish PEN. It was good sense for a later woman writer, Muriel Spark, to capture the spirit of 1930s Edinburgh in an opinion-ated Miss Jean Brodie, dabbling in authoritarian European politics, but at the time getting her 'set' to think for themselves.

Linked to the renaissance had come another characteristic activity of nineteenth-century nationalism — the compilation of a linguistic dictionary. Here, in fact, was a classic instance of transferred nation-ality, as the apotheosis of standard English, the *Oxford English Dictionary*, was the creation of one 'lad o' pairts', Sir James Murray, and was carried on by another, Sir William Craigie. In the 1920s Craigie returned to Scottish themes, and set about the creation of a *Dictionary of the Older Scottish Tongue*. MacDiarmid hailed this as a major reinforcement of the literary revival, a conviction confirmed by the fact that when Craigie circulated the imperial outposts of tartan nationalism, Burns Clubs and Caledonian Societies, he got only two replies to 500 letters, both refusing to help. The dictionary compilers divided into two. Craigie's first volume came out in 1931 and is still underway; the (post-1707) *Scottish National Dictionary* appeared between 1931 and 1975.

Yet a renaissance on a Florentine scale, which transforms an entire culture, requires patronage provided by economic growth, or political institutions that encourage the artists involved. Scotland's Medicis, if they had not moved south, were preoccupied with not going bankrupt. The money was not around to encourage the art forms that needed it. The literary renaissance came cheap; funds of an altogether different order were needed for theatre, music, or architecture.

VIII Architecture and Art

Architecture and design, what Ruskin called 'the greater arts of life', are crucial instances. In the 1890s Charles Rennie Mackintosh had laid down the principles of a modern Scottish architecture, combining the vernacular − 'as indigenous to our country as our wild flowers, our family names, our customs, or our political constitution' − and the functional. But his aims were confounded by the economic decline in building in Edwardian Scotland, and by 1914 many of the best Scottish architects had gone south or, like Mackintosh himself, given up. There was to be no recovery after the war, Major building was effectively restricted to council houses and schools, and most of this work went to the rather unimaginative architects' departments of the local authorities. There was a reaction. In 1932 the nationalist Robert Hurd restated Mackintosh's case, armed with examples of what architects could do in small nations like Finland and Czechoslovakia. One of this emerged the Saltire Society, and the movement for better town planning. Under Walter Elliot, the state also emerged as a major patron, with Thomas Tait's St Andrew's House (1935−9) and the £11m. project of the Empire Exhibition, which Tait supervised and which also involved the young Basil Spence and Jack Coia. The effects of this long innurition, however, were to be tragically apparent when large-scale building again took place in the 1960s, and a respectable number of good modern buildings were literally overshadowed by disasters like the destruction of Edinburgh's George Square and the multi-storey housing programme. In design the situation was, if anything, worse. As the Scottish Economic Committee's enquiry into light industry in 1937 found, there was a tradition of expensive hand-crafted work in textiles, furniture, and glass, but, below that, design standards were awful. The manufacturers who tried to remedy this were few, though the textile magnate Alastair Morton, patron of Picasso and Braque, deserves honourable mention. Conscious action over design education, of the sort that enabled Scandinavian countries to compensate for high prices through high-standard mass-produced goods, was almost totally lacking.

If Scottish architecture was disadvantaged by the absence of great patrons, Scottish art was constrained by already having adapted itself to a middle-class clientele. In contrast to mid-nineteenth-century painters like MacWhirter and Faed, engraved versions of whose senti-mental studies of Scottish country life and scenes from Burns could be found on countless artisan walls beside samplers and family photo-graphs, the 'Glasgow Boys' of the 1880s and their successors, the 'Scottish Colourists' — E.A. Peploe, F.C.B. Cadell, and Leslie Hunter — produced moderately-priced oils, water colours, and etchings for a middle-class public, represented by private buyers and the developing municipal collections. These collections, run by gifted connoisseurs like Sir James Caw and T.J. Honeyman, deserved their high reputation, but the indigenous art they patronized was domestic in scale and socially unadventurous. Scottish art may have avoided the worst ramps of the international 'art market', but public art like murals was non-existent and the innovators — Alan Davie, Robert Colquhoun and Robert MacBryde, Eduardo Paolozzi — got out. If Tretchikov's green ladies had taken over in living rooms from 'Burns's Meeting with Highland Mary', where was the improvement in that? Even photography, potentially the most radical art form and one that nineteenth-century Scotland had helped create, rarely escaped from the seductions of a photogenic landscape. Fine work was done in Scot-land by the Londoner Jim Jarché and the American Paul Strand, but not by the Scots themselves.

IX Theatre and Music

As with art and architecture, so with theatre and music? In both the latter cases twentieth-century economic problems complicated a situation in which the Calvinist ethos had scarcely encouraged such art forms. That nineteenth-century Scotland had managed to sustain some dramatic activity and a modest musical revival was remarkable enough, given the puritanism of the Kirk and the total absence of the institutions of religious music-making which had sustained the great achievements in England of Parry, Stanford, Elgar, Vaughan Williams, and Holst. But just as touring repertory companies survived by sticking to tried formulas and the classics — the radicalism of Alfred Wareing's Glasgow Repertory Company, 1909–14, which premiered Chekhov in Britain, was late and short-lived — Scots music also played safe. The Scottish Orchestra had been founded in 1891. Until 1959 it never had a Scots conductor — although its direction included at various times Walter Susskind and Sir John Barbirolli — and its programmes included little music by Scots composers. MacDiarmid never hesitated to criticize this, though music was scarcely his strong suit, and to advocate the songs of his friend and collaborator Francis George Scott, and the sort of national musical revival associated with Bartók and Kodaly in Hungary. This involved the systematic recovery of the folk-song tradition, and its use in musical education as well as composition. The problem was that this activity had already been pre-empted by a variation on the Kailyard. Following on the rise of pipe-band music in the nineteenth century, Mrs Kennedy-Fraser and Hugh Roberton had made Gaelic song into an undemanding if attractive middlebrow taste.

Another model of national cultural sponsorship was provided by the Irish Free State, which in 1924 made the Abbey Theatre in Dublin the first subsidized theatre in the English-speaking world. The Scottish National Players (1922–34) were directly influenced by the Irish example, but hamstrung by lack of funds, although they gave the young Tyrone Guthrie his first chance as a director and produced in 1928 the first play of Osborne Henry Mavor or 'James Bridie'. Both men rapidly advanced to a British reputation, as did many of the actors from another Scottish independent venture, the left-wing Glasgow Unity Theatre (1938–47). During World War II, however, there were two important developments. Bridie and others set up the Glasgow Citizens' Theatre, and Bridie was nominated by the Scottish Council of State, on the recommendation of Elliot, his closest friend, to the Council for the Encouragement of Music and the Arts (CEMA), the forerunner of the Arts Council and of a programme of systematic state funding.

The result of this was something that no one could have foreseen:

the Edinburgh Festival. It was not secured by any Scottish initiative but by the owner and manager of Glyndebourne, John Christie and Rudolf Bing, who saw that after the ravages of the war there was no chance of Glyndebourne, Munich, or Salzburg mounting their festivals for several years. They lighted almost by chance on Edinburgh and on a sympathetic Lord Provost, Sir John Falconer, and Corporation, Arts Council, and a public appeal got £60,000 together. In 1947 Edinburgh found itself hosting Bruno Walter, Szigeti, Alec Guinness, Margot Fonteyn, Barbirolli, and Kathleen Ferrier. The Festival's artistic success was never in doubt. Whether the host would accept the transplant was another matter. But the romantic tartanry of the Military Tattoo on the Castle Esplanade attracted mass enthusiasm, while the rediscovery and presentation by Robert Kemp and Tyrone Guthrie of Sir David Lyndesay's renaissance morality, *The Thrie Estaites*, in the spectacular setting of the Church's Assembly Hall, showed that Scottish theatre had now the skill and talent to rise to this challenge.

The Festival took time to permeate Scottish life. Even in the 1960s, to defend it in the Edinburgh City Labour Party was like publicly kicking an old-age pensioner. But gradually it helped break up Scottish middle-class philistinism, and led directly to a great expansion in musical activity, which culminated in the launch of Scottish Opera in 1960, under the direction of the Scottish National Orchestra's first Scots-born conductor, Sir Alexander Gibson. If there was still little Scottish music in its repertoire, this was the result of the fashionable obscurity of modern Scottish composers, not of their absence. That the examples of Bartók and Kodaly were ignored by such as Thea Musgrave and Iain Hamilton was doubly unfortunate, as the post-war period saw, through the work of men like Norman Buchan and Hamish Henderson, the revifying of the folk-song tradition. Apart from the fact that interest in it tended to outcrop in the same radical milieu, it is difficult to explain why Edinburgh, and the Royal High School in particular, became the nursery of some of the best jazz talent in Britain, including Sandy Brown, Al Fairweather, and Stan Greig. But, in the late 1940s, it did.

X Bohemia or Utopia? Literature, Cinema, Television

Royal High was also, through its English master, Hector MacIver, one of the centres of a literary bohemia in which the spirit of the renaissance still fermented away. 'The view from Regent Road', MacIver's pupil Karl Miller has written, 'towards the planes and declivities of the sleeping Lothians, took in a landscape which was far from benighted, a hinterland where contributing poets and pamphleteers lay in their suburbs and country cottages'. MacDiarmid had written to Roland Muirhead in 1928 that it would be 20 years before his aims would be understood. He was accurate to within a few years. In the 1950s came international recognition, academic honours, and the republication of his poems in accessible editions. At the same time, Scotland also saw a rich poetic output: the ironic, contemplative voice of Norman MacCaig, the austere Orcadian threnodies of George Mackay Brown, the robust bar-room Lallans of Robert Garioch and Sydney Goodsir Smith; Edwin Morgan, the Glasgow Marinetti, actually applauding the planning earthquake that had hit the place, Derick Thomson and Iain Crichton Smith carrying on Sorley MacLean's revival of the Gaelic lyric. Scottish poetry was almost a surrogate politics, with parties and manifestos — a romantic world, maybe, but more interesting and possibly also more realistic than the self-conscious flat-footedness of the English 'Movement'.

Yet MacDiarmid's self-questioning 'Are my poems spoken . . .' was as much an epitome of the Scottish predicament in the 1960s, as Yeats's 'We had fed the heart with fantasies, The heart's grown brutal with the fare' was to prove relevant to Ireland. The renaissance had remained an intellectual preoccupation. In the 1920s it had wilfully distanced itself from the main developments in popular entertainment. In the 1950s there had been another revolution in the media, but its consequence was to be a continuation of this isolation.

A powerful prosecution case can surely be mounted against the renaissance. MacDiarmid aimed at national regeneration, but his methods were those of the nineteenth century, or even more antique forms of pamphlet literature and 'flyting'. He totally ignored the impact of film and broadcasting. Would matters have been different, one wonders, if Compton Mackenzie's attempt to make him edit a critical magazine on broadcasting — *Vox* — in 1929 had succeeded? If this had worked, could his influence have been swung beside that of the other great Scots cultural innovator of the period — John Grierson?

Like MacDiarmid, Grierson had had his outlook changed by the Russian revolution. He had a vision of a new society in which film — exemplified for him by the work of Eisenstein, Pudovkin, and Vertov — became the great public educator, the link between intellectual and people. Much of this was held in common with Reith, and indeed was drawn from that stock of Hegelian ideas of social improvement which floated about the Scottish universities before 1914. But Grierson viewed the media itself as a revolutionary force. 'The imaginative treatment of reality' — his definition of documentary — implied destroying the traditional boundary between culture and society.

Grierson's achievements in the 1920s and 1930s were protean. He travelled to Russia, and publicized the work of Russian directors, even impressing the arch-reactionary Rudyard Kipling. Walter Elliot got him to set up the Empire Marketing Board Films Department in 1927, which brought him to Scotland to film *Drifters*, the first classic of British documentary, in 1929. It was about the only film he made by himself: his main aim was to teach, and there were few British directors whom he did not influence. Before he left for Canada in 1939 to create the Film Board of Canada, probably that country's most distinguished cultural contribution this century, he had helped reorientate British films towards the realistic treatment of social issues.

His influence was not lost on Scotland. Walter Elliot got his help in setting up Films of Scotland in 1938, and a growing number of directors came to make films that, even when comedies or dramas, dealt realistically with the problems and attitudes of contemporary Scotland. Michael Powell's *The Edge of the World* was the first of a distinguished line of films — John Baxter's *The Shipbuilders* (1945) from George Blake's novel, Alexander MacKendrick's *Whisky Galore* (1945), Powell's *I know where I'm going* (1945), MacKendrick's *The Maggie* (1953), and Philip Leacock's *The Brave don't Cry* (1952). As evidence of intellectual attempts to grasp the 'condition of Scotland question' such films can bear comparison with the poems and novels that preceded them. *The Maggie* — the duel between puffer captain and American millionaire — can be analysed as a pessimistic parable of the establishment of American industry in Scotland, for example. But the problem was that films, like any new industry derived from electrics, were firmly based in the south. Like MacDiarmid, Grierson's training was Hegelian. He believed that a change of consciousness was the effective victory. But economics were even less favourable to a genuine Scottish film industry than they were to the renaissance.

Like MacDiarmid, Grierson was fundamentally a product of the Scottish artisan class, and required the sustenance of a national base. After his Canadian triumphs he returned to Scotland, and to frustration. The cinema itself was proving mortal. Television started in Scotland in 1952. In that year there were 41,000 sets; a decade later there were 1,119,000. The number of cinemas was halved, and visits dropped to 10 per person per annum. In 1953 'the box' got a big boost from the Coronation; in the following year the BBC was challenged by Independent Television. In Scotland Reithianism clung on hard, and the Canadian Roy Thomson, who had just taken over the *Scotsman*, had to battle hard to get support for Scottish Television. Two years after its foundation in 1955 he could describe it as 'a licence to print money'. It was certainly not a cultural ornament. It allowed Grierson to present documentaries, but not to make them, and its drama and current affairs work was poor. With only 5 million viewers to beam advertising at, STV was much worse off than, say, Granada in Manchester, and Granada it was that got the ablest Scots documentary makers for its *World in Action*, just as the BBC, in its successful counter-attack, was able to use many of the best Scottish producers and actors — again, all too often, in the south. Yet STV did establish a Scottish identity of a sort, with a great expansion of sports coverage and local news. Both of these were relatively inexpensive to produce, but they provided career opportunities for those ambitious to make a Scottish reputation, and they provided a fertile ground for nationalist publicity to grow in. Thus, although literary life in Scotland in the 1960s was unprecedentedly lively, and MacDiarmid was able to say, in retrospect, that 'one of the main aims of my *Contemporary Scottish Studies* has now been realized — the recognition that anything that purports to be a contribution to Scottish literature must be judged by the standards applied to literature in all other civilized countries', the renaissance's successors now had to cope with two Kailyards, one traditional and one electronic.

6

Future Deferred? Scotland since 1964

I

Two contradictory themes inevitably affect this chapter: the waywardness of political nationalism, lurching in manic-depressive spasms from dramatic success to humiliating setback. Did the failure of devolution arise from misinterpreted politics? Was the 'Scottish dimension' itself unreal — only an opportunist revulsion from the deterioration of the British state? Did this only mask accelerated integration, producing a politics incapable of constructive constitutional action, no matter how much high-minded prompting it received?

The 1980s looked superficially like the 1920s, with high unemployment reinforcing unimaginative Labour loyalties. Yet beneath this were trends which were not volatile: support for independence steadily grew. It had been only 9 per cent when first polled in 1945, and stuck around 20 per cent in the 1970s. In the early 1990s it was vying with devolution as the favourite option, hovering around the 35 per cent mark, and much of this support was coming from the Labour ranks. Scottish intellectuals, moreover, no longer regarded a Scottish commitment as a turning away from the 'real world'. The problem of being Scots, like that of being Catalan or Czech, was now seen as being important in a Europe that was rejecting the established ideologies of capitalism or communism in favour of the protection of individual liberties, community participation, and the natural environment — although such enlightenment was still constrained by the strictures of the Scottish class system.

II 'The White Heat of Technology'

Volatility was scarcely apparent in 1964. Labour was confident that 'planning' and 'technology' would settle the fundamental problem of economic decline. This prescription in fact differed little from Macmillan's initiatives, but it was comfortably remote from Labour's bitter debates on nationalization in 1959−60 and, as presented by its new leader, Harold Wilson, it appeared a dynamic alternative to the 'stop-go' cycles and Venetian intrigues of the Conservatives' last years. Wilsonian 'technocracy' may have had even less to do with science than with socialism, but in Scotland this was not immediately apparent: the Toothill Report and STUC collaboration had already given planning consensus backing. But the Unionists were penalized by continuing threats to railways and collieries, and the leadership of Sir Alec Douglas-Home, however welcome in the counties, seemed a provocation in the housing schemes. For Scottish Labour MPs, on the whole on the right of the party, 'planning' was magic. Labour's 15-seat majority in Scotland clinched their shaky 7-seat grasp on office.

In *Signposts for Scotland* (1962) Labour had ignored home rule but, besides increases in housing, health, and welfare programmes, promised new development bodies. The chief of these was the Highlands and Islands Development Board, funded by block grant, which William Ross, the new Secretary of State, carried in 1965. The Unionists described it as 'undiluted Marxism'. Unwisely, as after the 1966 election most Highland constituencies were in Labour or Liberal hands. Labour also set up, in Scotland as well as in the other British regions, economic planning boards and councils which were supposed to co-operate with the new Department of Economic Affairs in formulating and executing the *National Plan*. This emerged in October 1965, forecasting a 3.8 per cent annual growth rate between then and 1970.

The *Plan* was never at any time a detailed strategy; after the deflation of July 1966 it was not even a pious hope. The regional bodies were failures. They started without trained staffs; by the time they got them the policy had dissolved. But in Scotland the new Scottish Development Department was to hand, and provided a Regional Development Division. So the *Plan for Scotland* which Ross presented in January 1966 was much more detailed and specific than any of the English regional responses. It echoed Toothill's stress on new industries, but it also linked employment growth to social expenditure. Housing, hospitals, roads, and schools − building these would both improve the infrastructure and create more jobs than were being lost in the old industries. The resulting spending power would attract the service and consumer goods industries which Scotland lacked. So enquiries began into Scotland's major social problems, while local teams advised on physical planning not only in the main industrial areas but in the north-east and borders, with their endemic problem of depopulation.

For a time there was a near-euphoric atmosphere in higher education and the social sciences — among a minority, true, but one which was now growing, in the post-Robbins period, and was taking on the tasks for which it had pleaded 30 years earlier. Professionals were replacing the gentry and the businessmen on public boards and advisory committees; departments of geography, economics, town planning, and social work were expanding. So much are the social sciences in Scotland the product of the mid 1960s that for years it has been difficult to stand back, survey the period, and see how little was actually achieved.

The crucial problems were not intrinsically Scottish. Could planning be successful when the state lacked firm control of investment institutions and sterling remained an international reserve currency? And when, as yet, there was no cadre of senior civil servants committed to it? In Germany the success of the 'social market' economy had still depended on tight control of banking, and the devolution of detailed planning to Land governments; in France highly-centralized planning was carried out by the meritocracy produced by the Hautes Écoles in Paris. But in Britain the only effective instrument open to government was the management of demand, and as the Fulton Commission found in 1968, the administrative class of the civil service was still biased against professional and technical expertise.

Scotland faced the consequences of both dislocations. With an economy still disproportionately dependent on capital goods industries or, as far as new industries were concerned, on public expenditure, she was slow to respond to injections of cash into the British economy, while acutely sensitive to deflationary measures. Moreover Labour's enthusiasm for government-sponsored amalgamations within the private sector, as well as nationalization, further increased the external control of the Scots economy, without promising any more sympathetic understanding of its problems. Finally, the executants of planning were themselves inexperienced, finding a way over new and treacherous ground, and subject to the lures of well-heeled and unscrupulous pressure groups.

So, despite the fact that public expenditure per head in Scotland was 20 per cent over the British norm by the late 1960s, and that most of this excess was due to investment assistance, the fundamental problems of the economy still persisted. Some remarkable progress had been made in industrial attraction, notably the expansion of the electronics industry from 7,500 jobs in 1959 to 30,000 in 1969 — three times the growth foreseen by Toothill — yet the situation of the heavy industries continued to deteriorate. Shipbuilding and engineering took with them into the shadows, moreover, satellite industries — optics, hydraulics, control mechanisms — whose record as innovators had been high in the post-war period, when the marine stabilizer, fibreglass, and the steam catapult had originated in Scotland. Although publicity stressed that educational resources had induced American electronics concerns to move to Scotland, their record in utilizing these was bad. Although American firms as a whole employed 87,730 in 1973, they had taken on only 250 graduates between 1965 and 1969. Economic control, research, and development was concentrated, as never before, in England or overseas, and so far the government had made no attempt to create Scottish institutions that would countervail this drift.

This meant that detailed regional planning in Scotland was from the start distorted: stressing the areas that the Scottish Office itself could handle, such as roads and housing. The regional plans both lacked sociological depth and, following the Buchanan Report of 1963, were over-influenced by American land use/transportation planning techniques. In the context of using state expenditure to manage private consumption, these assumed that (1) the state, by building roads and public housing, injected resources directly into the economy, and (2) it regulated the economy by controlling private housing and motoring through mortgage and hire-purchase rates. A fashionable application of Keynesian principles, whether this was an appropriate solution to Scotland's industrial and social problems was another matter. Carried out, such plans disrupted existing industries and communities and undermined the public transport on which most people depended. In 1966 Glasgow had only 1 car to 11 people, compared with 1 to 4 in Surrey, yet the city's urban motorway plans were among the most ambitious in Britain. Even before the fuel crisis in 1973 official thinking had moved away from the Buchanan formula, but by then the damage done to Glasgow was past help. Road and urban renewal schemes had resulted in the closure or relocation away from the city of much local industry, and unprecedented numbers of people had been moved into the new and unproven experiment of high-rise housing. Always more conservative and subject to influence by environmentalist groups, Edinburgh had shelved a motorway scheme in 1969, but by the time such caution became the new orthodoxy, tens of millions which could have been used for environmental improvement or industrial investment had been squandered.

Many of these schemes were based on shaky political foundations. Local government was antique; the income and status of Scots councillors low even by British standards. Moreover, party control over council activities was sketchy, especially in the west and in Labour-controlled wards where councillors frequently regarded active local parties with an unfriendly eye. Corruption was a fact (see p.81); in the late 1960s it was serious enough; but the sheer failure to apply any political perspective to 'planning' went far beyond this, and was largely the responsibility of Labour, as the traditional Scots majority party. Labour responded badly to criticism. Although the natural party of the planners and social scientists, it was all too clearly subject to Michels' 'iron law of oligarchy' — centralized, authoritarian, equally suspicious of socialist 'theoreticians' and of the Scottish 'capitalist' press. If Ross and the party secretary William Marshall quarantined their more articulate critics like John Mackintosh — the leading authority on cabinet government — the local party hierarchies were scarcely more flexible, and such attitudes encouraged press and public alike to view the advance of the SNP with indulgence.

By 1968 'planning' was in disarray — and worse. Deflation checked regional assistance expenditure, while unemployment increased beyond 1961 levels. Investigations that had been commissioned into social problems, such as the 1967 report by Professor Barry Cullingworth, *Scotland's Older Housing*, were exposing conditions that the government could do little about — and thus making effective propaganda for its critics. Despite Labour's many worthwhile initiatives — the Scots Law Commission (1965), and the Social Work (Scotland) Act (1967), the new town of Irvine (1969), the appointment of the Wheatley Commission on local government (1965) — the central economic failure imposed a mounting penalty. Paradoxically, even Labour's successes accelerated its undoing: rehousing, the uprooting of old communities and old relationships, overspill, new industries and new towns were creating a less settled working class which was tempted to explore a new politics.

III The March of the Nats

Labour won the March 1966 election convincingly, returning 46 Scottish MPs. Then trouble started. A seamen's strike, causing much disruption in the Scottish islands, was ineptly handled. A run on the pound provoked a battle in the cabinet between the expansionism of the DEA and the orthodoxy of the Exchequer, which the latter won:

expenditure was cut, planning effectively killed. Unemployment started to increase. The right wing and Liberals made gains in the May municipal elections, then in July Gwynfor Evans struck the first blow for nationalism by winning Carmarthen for Plaid Cymru.

Within two years the government's Scottish political problem was to change to one of 'coping with the Nats'. Most of its supporters saw this as fudging the main issue: the growth of the Scottish National Party vote was simply a protest against the government's non-socialist economic policies. To a minority it was more complex: a reflection of the remoteness and inadequacy of Scottish politics, as well as of a persistent national consciousness. But there was no dodging the fact (or compelling fantasy) that the SNP had in eight years grown from 2,000 to perhaps 100,000 members.

This had not come out of the blue. The Scottish situation favoured third party growth, if not a repetition of the Convention movement of the 1940s. The Unionists were too deeply tied to agriculture (although they were beginning at last to become aware of this), and their re-adoption of the name 'Conservative' in 1965 scarcely helped them in the following year. But what of the Liberals? In 1965 David Steel added Roxburgh to the three constituencies captured in 1964, and in 1966 they took West Aberdeenshire.

The trouble was that, as in the West Country and Wales, this revival reflected the radical tradition as well as the problems of remote areas. For the leadership, these successes were overshadowed by the lure of the English centre, especially after 1962, when opinion polls briefly put the Liberals ahead of the 'big two'. Though a fickle fellow, 'Orpington Man' showed up often enough to divert the attention of Grimond, and after 1967 Jeremy Thorpe, from Scottish policies. The division was replicated in Scotland itself. In the major towns, outside Greenock and Paisley, activists tended to be disproportionately English, remote from the working class, and vague although sympathetic on Scottish issues. This was often more than could be said of Liberalism in the northern isles or the Borders, which was much more conscious of region than of nation. At any rate, after some fumbling negotiations in 1964 the Liberals kept their distance from the SNP, so the latter inherited many of the mainly liberal impulses which had gone into Scottish Convention, although it retained its Sinn Fein-like programme of full independence through a withdrawal from Westminster once it had captured a majority of seats. Unlike Convention, it was also determined to contest elections − and election results largely sustained, and ultimately betrayed it.

No government ever regarded by-elections with quite the awe of the Wilson administration of 1964–70. At first its life depended on them, but after 1966 their huge fluctuations rocked a premier whose sensitivity seemed to outweigh his grasp of strategy. And Scotland, with a gaggle of elderly Labour MPs, was particularly at risk. On 9 March 1967, at Glasgow Pollok, the SNP candidate got 28 per cent, and Labour lost the seat. In the May local elections the SNP poll rose from 4.4 to 18.4 per cent. In the same month Tom Fraser left his safe Hamilton seat for the chairmanship of the Hydro Board. In the course of a long campaign Labour demonstrated all its organizational failings, while the economic situation got worse and devaluation became inevitable. On 2 November the articulate SNP candidate, Mrs Winifred Ewing, turned a 16,000 Labour majority into an SNP one of 1,799. Next May the Nationalist vote at the local elections rose to 30 per cent.

Two main analyses quickly emerged in the Cabinet. The first saw the SNP as a protest which had either to be endured or combated (according to the left) with 'socialist policies'. The second saw the SNP, along with the huge fluctuations in British local elections, as evidence that the balance of central and local government had to be recast. Paradoxically, the 'territorial' ministers — Ross and the Welsh Secretary, George Thomas — took the first view, while English departmental ministers, notably Richard Crossman, took the second.

Studies of the SNP, its voters and activists — and before long there were many — could be made to back either interpretation. It was plainly drawing into politics, in both capacities, people whom the parties had hitherto failed to involve. Votes at municipal elections rose sharply in 1967 and 1968, and much SNP support, particularly in the big towns, seemed to come from previous non-voters within the working class, whose patriotism had rested at the football level until tapped by SNP propaganda. The new nationalist councillors likewise had little previous political experience. Only about 40 per cent of a representative sample had been members of the SNP for more than three years, and only 13.5 per cent had been members of other parties. All of this — and the subsequent inept performance of many of the SNP councillors — bore out the 'protest vote' interpretation. Yet the SNP vote showed a more consistent pattern in new towns, and in country areas of the east of Scotland, and the general demand for a greater measure of home rule was being echoed, not simply by the Church of Scotland and the STUC, but by bodies as diverse as the May Day Manifesto Group from the New Left, and, most disturbingly, the

Conservative party. The Scottish Unionist conference had called for devolution in 1967, and in the following May Edward Heath set up a Committee of respectable churchmen, constitutionalists, and ex-ministers, under Sir Alec Douglas-Home, which reported positively in March 1970. Heath's own subsequent record of inaction, and Home's well-timed repudiation of devolution just before the 1979 referendum, cast valid doubt on the party's actual commitment, but it probably played a key role in prompting Wilson to set up a Royal Commission on the Constitution in December 1968.

The Labour government's move from hostility to an apparent open mind about home rule helped to check its decline in Scotland, while the SNP ran into internal problems. It had acted as a focus for a range of discontents; it now found it difficult to formulate positive policies that would not lead to it being identified in conventional left — right terms. Its 1969 conference showed a division between a 'social-demo-crat' wing around Wolfe, and a more traditionalist 'independence first' wing around Arthur Donaldson, whom Wolfe defeated for the Chairmanship. The poor performance of its councillors was embar-rassing, and its repeated claims that Scotland was being over-taxed were authoritatively combated by Dr Gavin McCrone who, in *Scotland's Future: The Economics of Nationalism* (1969), calculated that Scotland still remained indebted to England in the tune of £56m. — £93m. per annum. In October 1968 Labour did well in a by-election at Glasgow Gorbals, where the large Catholic vote refused to swing to the SNP; in May 1969 the SNP's municipal vote fell to 20 per cent, and in the South Ayrshire election they did no better against Labour's aggressively unionist candidate, Jim Sillars. Membership was falling, some of the activities of the 'heid-bangers' of fundamentalist nationalism proved worrying, given developments in Ulster. All things considered, the SNP did well to take 11.4 per cent of the vote and get one MP elected in June 1970. After this election the Conservatives had a UK majority of 30, but they had made only three gains in Scotland, only one from Labour. With only 38 per cent of the popular vote Heath's new Secretary of State, Gordon Campbell, was even more exposed than John Maclay had been in 1959.

IV Labour and Industry

Scotland's 'balance of payments' deficit reflected the rapid growth of public expenditure, especially on industry: in 1964 £15m. had been thus spent; by 1973 £192.3m. — in real terms a 900 per cent increase.

Scotland had by then absorbed about a third of the cash available under the Local Employment Act (1964), Regional Employment Premiums, and shipbuilding subsidies — 9.3 per cent of the British labour force got 15 per cent of government industrial expenditure and agricultural subsidies and 17 per cent of UK cash for roads. Only Edinburgh and Leith were left out of the 'Scottish development area'. Besides this, government also pushed major enterprises northward. The Unionists 'persuaded' a pulp and paper mill to locate at Fort William in 1964; in 1968 Labour got an aluminium smelter established at Invergordon. Not without protest from its employees, the Post Office (later National) Savings Bank was shifted to Glasgow in 1968, and, more amicably, the headquarters of the Forestry Commission (which did most of its business in Scotland anyway) was moved from Basingstoke to Edinburgh in 1978. After a troubled start, the Highlands and Islands Development Board, whose budget had grown to £4m. per annum by 1973, provided useful and flexible finance for local industry, tourism, and transport, and brought Scotland abreast of local development strategies in other countries with remote and underpopulated regions. Yet — was this strategy working? Manufacturing wages certainly improved: 91 per cent of the UK average in 1961, they were 96.6 per cent in 1971. Yet the labour force fell. Male workers fell by 6 per cent, and a 6 per cent rise in women workers still left an overall decline of 1.75 per cent. Unemployment rose from 3.1 to 5.8 per cent, its relationship to the UK figure changed only imperceptibly, and annual emigration in the 1960s actually increased by 16 per cent on the previous decade. In fact, although £641m. had been spent between 1966 and 1971 in creating 105,000 jobs, in the same five years 156,000 had been lost, mainly from heavy industry and agriculture. Mines and farms, traditionally labour-intensive, made up half this figure, yet, besides these 'structural' changes, technological innovation was inducing sweeping increases in productivity, the full consequences of which even union leaders were only dimly aware. The first container terminal in Britain, for instance, was opened at Grangemouth in 1968; within a decade general cargo handling had dwindled away; the main Glasgow docks had been filled in and the dock labour force decimated. By the 1970s, too, 65 per cent of the coal mined in Scotland's dozen or so remaining collieries was being conveyed by automatically loading and discharging bulk trains to the hoppers of four huge power stations. Over £150m. investment in BP's oil refinery and petro-chemical complex at Grangemouth had yielded less than 2,000 jobs. Even in industries where employment in the late

60s had seemingly stabilized – like steel and shipbuilding – rumours of rationalization and contraction were by 1970 becoming more insistent.

Behind this lay, moreover, far-reaching changes in company control. The Wilson government, as well as nationalizing iron and steel, sponsored extensive industrial amalgamation. Anthony Wedgwood Benn, the minister of technology, was particularly enthusiastic, seconded by businessmen and trade unionists seeking specific advantages – such as a monopoly position, or a national wages structure. As swiftly as in the early 1920s control shifted southward, or abroad. Scots ownership still prevailed among small firms, but external control increased with size, until by 1977 only 3 out of the top 10 Scottish industrial employers were Scots-controlled.

Even before Peugeot took over Chrysler in 1978 the Scottish-owned sector in manufacturing industry had dropped to 41 per cent of employment. Forty per cent was controlled from England, 15 per cent from North America, and 1.5 per cent from the EEC. Paradoxically, government money for job-creation – over £6,000 per job in the average case – often seen d to reduce employment, through new technology and rationalization. Moreover, as trade-union pressure had made up wage differentials, an important incentive to move north had been lost. Although Scottish financial institutions remained healthy, Scottish industrial capitalism was now of only marginal importance. Old-fashioned tycoons like Lithgow and Bilsland had retained a paternalist sense of obligation, which led to developments like the Scottish Council. This was unlikely to be replicated in the boardrooms of the City of London and Los Angeles.

The economics of some of the new transplants soon looked shaky. The vehicle factories at Linwood and Bathgate were, by 1970, operating at barely 50 per cent capacity. One reason was bad industrial relations, partly due to the difficulty of adapting a hitherto skilled workforce to the numbing discipline of the assembly line; another was the failure of ancillary trades to come north. If 20 per cent of the parts entering Linwood were Scottish this was a success, since the West Midlands' economies of scale kept the average cost of an English part down to £0.096, against £0.246 for the same part made in Scotland. But even when manufacturing was successfully transplanted, the 'generative' elements of the parent companies – research and development, organization, corporate planning, marketing – rarely shifted from the south. In 1972 Scotland came ninth out of 10 British regions in research and development expenditure, and government research allocated to Scotland, 1964–73, was only 5.1 per cent of the British total.

V Society and Culture

Labour's 'modernization' goals were only partly economic, however, and the limited progress made was partly masked by the social and cultural changes initiated or encouraged by the government, which altered traditional institutions and social life on a scale unparalleled since the nineteenth century, or even, in some cases, since the Reformation.

Education

Education was an important route to equality in social democratic theory, and a reinforcement of economic diversification. Encouraged by inspectors and some teachers, reform was under way before 1964. The institution of O-levels meant an increase in candidates from 17,175 in 1961 to 83,805 in 1967. Fifteen per cent more were staying on to 16, although the leaving age was not raised until 1973. Following Labour policy, Ross instructed local authorities to reorganize secondary education on comprehensive lines. In comparison to England the transition was fairly painless: by 1974 98 per cent of pupils were in comprehensives, against under 50 per cent in England. Overall, the size of schools increased, and their numbers fell. In 1947 171,193 secondary pupils attended 1,037 schools; in 1974 over 400,000 attended 439.

At the same time both the primary and secondary curricula were reformed, following a working party report of 1955 and the Brunton Report of 1963, which stressed vocationally-centred studies for non-academic pupils. Both reforms were contentious, but tended to be drowned out by the clamour of the profession itself, as it debated its reorganization after 1966 under a General Teaching Council for Scotland.

Partly to provide teachers, partly to supply the troops of the technological revolution, higher education expanded. Following the Robbins Report of 1963 the great technical colleges of Glasgow and Edinburgh received charters in 1964 and 1966, as did Queen's College, Dundee, in 1967. A new university at Stirling opened in 1968. Student numbers doubled to 33,000 between 1960 and 1969, although their percentage of the British total slightly decreased, from 16 to

15 per cent. The government also opened three education colleges, at Falkirk, Hamilton, and Ayr, in 1964—5 and, largely through the Industrial Training Act (a Conservative measure of 1964) dramatically expanded technical colleges, which had over 80,000 full-time, day, or block release students by 1970.

Yet was expansion enough or in time? Could the school really check Scottish social inadequacies? The Advisory Committee Report of 1947 had placed the school in the front line against 'a barely literate populace, debased by vulgarisms and corrupted by Hollywood'. The language was inapposite for the 1960s, yet the less didactic new curricula actually stressed parental involvement, at a time when television and working mothers were changing the structure of Scots families. Was such innovation not, therefore, more likely to benefit the middle class? Moreover, innovation spared two disquieting aspects of Scots education — religious schools and corporal punishment. If education was now to centre on the child in the community, why divide it into two communities? If education was to be a partnership, why retain this savage sanction? Catholic schools may have protected their position by a judicious scepticism about the new methods: this appealed to many non-Catholic teachers, but the political problem remained; although Labour preferred to ignore it. Corporal punishment answered the challenge of the bully, but it also preserved an esteem-system in which he and his values of 'toughness' survived. So, despite all the expenditure on them, many potential sixth-formers were by 1970 leaving the comprehensives to take qualifications in the more adult atmosphere of further education colleges.

The teaching profession, over 52,000-strong in 1973, had grown by 60 per cent in 20 years. Counting universities and further education, teachers now outnumbered all but three groups of manufacturing workers, yet despite strong unionization they were remote from the working class and internally divided. Graduates (mainly male) declined from 46 to 39 per cent, increasing tension with largely female non-graduates. A profession 66 per cent female remained as subject to male hegemony as skilled engineering had been before World War I.

There was, moreover, little unity between it and the anglicized staff of the universities, and tensions grew in the 1970s as it looked likely that 'British' universities would remain aloof from 'Scottish' education. These were aggravated by the fact that the first largish generation of Scots postgraduates confronted a less-than-inspiring, but tenured, university establishment, recruited in the fat years of the mid 60s.

Housing

Housing was an ostensible success story. Between 1960 and 1970 completions rose from 28,500 to 43,100, roughly double the rate of demolitions. Surviving smaller or older houses now tended to be occupied by young couples or single people. Yet Cullingworth pointed out in 1967 that a third of Scottish families were living in 'inadequate' accommodation, and much of this was steadily deteriorating into slums.

Rent control and low council rents meant that private landlords could never undertake renewal, and although Cullingworth suggested that private rents could be subsidized by grants to landlords, a Labour government would never wear this. Owner-occupation in large old tenements involved difficult modernization problems, let alone rising mortgage rates. That left co-operatives or associations, or council policies of renewal rather than demolition. By 1970 both were being pursued, but progress was slow.

As private tenants (21 per cent in 1977) dwindled, owner-occupiers (26 per cent) and council tenants (53 per cent) grew. In industrial burghs such as Motherwell over 80 per cent of households rented from councils. But St Andrew's House gained more central control over rents, which in 1967–8 moved to more realistic levels — and brought a bonus to the SNP in local elections. Problems of housing management, however, also increased, mainly involving 'anti-social families', slum-clearance schemes of the 1930s and 1950s which now required total renewal, and the future of many multi-storey blocks scarcely 10 years old. Leaving aside design problems, like the Glasgow blocks with lifts too small for coffins and stretchers, these had required sophisticated technology, regulated heating, and regular maintenance. They didn't always get it. If heating was switched off, because of rising charges or falling income, condensation and mould appeared; if lifts broke down, families and pensioners were stranded 200 feet up. By 1980 several ambitious projects, such as Edinburgh's 18-storey Martello Court, were actually uninhabitable.

Housing didn't show Labour at its most imaginative. Low-rent policies had narrowed its municipal constituency while the lack of alternatives to council housing tied improvements too closely to government expenditure, which deflationary policies were reducing. Wholesale clearance destroyed communities; building contract awards and house allocations led to periodic corruption charges. The losses of 1966–8 cut some of the dead wood out of the councils and enabled some improvement in the early 1970s. Not before time: a survey based on the 1971 census showed that Scotland had 77.5 per cent of Britain's 5 per cent of 'worst areas' for social deprivation. Ironically, the reformers were frequently Labour councillors who were neither tenants nor working class.

Religion, Sex, and Drink

In 1960 almost 70 per cent of Scots over 14 were claimed as church members, compared with around 23 per cent in England and over 90 per cent in Ireland. But that year was the Church of Scotland's peak, and after 1970 the Catholics, too, started to decline. Television and Sunday entertainment obviously took their toll of marginal Christians, but there was also a more fundamental lapse in belief among the 'serious' middle class — albeit a century after the same development in England. The attitude of, say, students and teachers to religion was not malignant: they simply transferred their commitment to other social or political organizations. Whether these provided adequate compensation was another question.

Among professions with a strong sense of local position — such as law or banking — church membership remained strong, but its grip on the lower middle and working classes, which had survived the 1950s largely due to church extension programmes, could not cope with the social changes and population movements of the 1960s. As it became more middle class its politics moved to the right, and in the 1970s it trod an uneasy path between a rather diffuse ecumenicalism and the revival of fundamentalism which had gripped Protestant America. As for the Catholic hierarchy, the election in 1979 of a conservative, populist pope came as a welcome reinforcement of its own position. Both Churches seemed to have halted their concessions to secularism, but it remained to be seen how effective a conservative restatement of dogma would prove.

Religious decline was bound up with upheavals in family and personal relationships. The marriage rate increased, but for many couples it was now a second attempt. Divorces rose by 400 per cent between 1961 and 1974, although subsequent simplification, by transfer from the Court of Session to the Sheriff Courts in 1977, did not lead to a further escalation. Family size fell to nearer the English norm, and numbers of single-parent families rose. People talked more about sex. In the case of the Churches they seemed sometimes to talk of nothing else. It certainly posed a challenge to their traditional puritanism, but not one which they came out of particularly well.

Rational concession certainly did not appear to pay dividends: the Church of Scotland accepted divorce reform, abortion, and state provision of contraception; its numbers fell faster than those of the Roman Catholics, whose leaders resolutely opposed all three. Whether rank and file Catholics did so is another matter: their attitude to contraception, for instance, seems to have been much the same as that of the Free Church to drink.

On drink, the puritan case was more straightforward. Scots spending per capita on alcohol, 89 per cent of the UK level in 1955, rose to 109 per cent by 1970. Why? Because of more affluence? More consumers? Fewer abstainers? Or a combination of all three? Licensing hours had been extended, women were accepted in most pubs, young people were no strangers to drink. Had the 'dour drinkers of Scotland' vanished? The Clayson Report of 1975 thought that drink could now become a civilized accompaniment to life, and opening times were extended to a Continental pattern in 1978. Scots alcoholism ran at five times the UK rate; and smoking levels were destructively high, but most pubs now offered cheap and good food; Scots football supporters sobered up and were even counted a droll attraction by the continentals; spending on drink fell back to 102 per cent of UK levels in 1990, when only 36 per cent of the male population smoked, compared with 51 per cent in 1980. A wholly healthy Scotland? Not quite. Drug addiction rose from 90 addicts notified in 1980 to 525 in 1990, and provided an environment for the spread of Aids.

The Arts

Intellectual life in the 1960s and 1970s was lively — for a minority. Although the commercial theatre was now all but extinct, experiment thrived at the Traverse and the Citizens and on the Festival Fringe. It even became less remote from the pubs and housing schemes, as John McGrath's 7:84 Company, the indescribable talents of Billy Connolly, and the work of such as James MacTaggart, Eddie Boyd, Roddy Macmillan, and Peter MacDougall for television gave it a greater demotic edge. Sir Alexander Gibson, appointed conductor of the Scottish National Orchestra in 1959, helped set up Scottish Opera in 1963, and by 1980 the country's musical life was richer — and internationally more respected — than it had ever been before. The annual pollination of the Edinburgh Festival had borne rich fruit, as had the help of local authorities and government. Scotland's share of the Arts Council budget had dropped from 8.4 per cent to 6.3 per cent between 1948 and 1963. Under Jennie Lee, now Wilson's arts minister, it climbed back to 11.4 per cent by 1970, extending subsidies to painting, literature, Gaelic culture, and folk music.

MacDiarmid lived on until 1978 as an honoured if wayward national institution, alternately courtly and infuriating. 'He'll charm old ladies on to the mantelpiece/And leave them there' as Norman MacCaig put it. He outlived most of the other writers of the Renaissance, but there was a talented succession. Poetry and the short story thrived in the quality papers and the little magazines, and the novels of the time, if not immediately appreciated, showed a determined effort to come to terms with the traumas wrought by Calvinism and industrialisation on the Scottish psyche. J.D. Scott's *The End of an Old Song* (1954) ended with his anti-hero burning his ancestral castle down. One retrospective image of Scotland was thus destroyed, but with it also the 'high road to England'. Writers like James Kennaway, Robin Jenkins and William MacIlvanney saw something moulding in the Scots experience – not necessarily positive, but not to be ignored. At the same time George Mackay Brown and Iain Crichton Smith were articulating the distinctive experiences of Norse and Gaelic Scotland, and Muriel Spark and (on stage) Cecil Taylor the continuing, fricative argument of Scot and Jew.

At the time this activity was underestimated, not least by the present writer. It took a determined increase in Scottish publishing activity, particularly in history writing, reviewing, and reprinting, in the 1970s and 1980s, to display the liveliness of the post-Renaissance literary output. Perhaps, in retrospect, bogeyman Knox loomed too darkly, and there was too enthusiastic a dash to the psychiatrist's couch. R.D. Laing and Aaron Esterson may have worked in London, but Karl Miller was not alone in connecting their perceptions about the social origins of schizophrenia with their native land, home of the Justified Sinner and Jekyll and Hyde. Miller himself, out of Hector MacIver's Royal High School by Leavis's Cambridge, contributed to the plethora of analyses that followed the rise of the SNP and was responsible for the Marxist philosopher Tom Nairn's first bout with nationalism. Within a few years Nairn's *The Break-Up of Britain* (1977) had become the central text of a new and unsentimental intellectual nationalism. Overall, the 'lads o'pairts' seemed, at least mentally, to be returning home, and there was a shift from the imaginative to the analytical; work by Scots and about Scotland, in history, politics, and economics, was as distinguished as anything since the eighteenth century.

In the 1970s everyone, seemingly, talked politics. A few, like Neal Ascherson, were worried that there didn't appear to have been the sort of literary movement that nationalism ought to gestate. Rather too many big publishing names closed down or moved south – Nelsons, Oliver and Boyd, Collins – and native literary and political reviews still tended to have short lives. *Scottish International* was good while it lasted (1966-74); Edinburgh students nurtured their valuable *New Edinburgh Review* and added *Cencrastus* at a timely moment, when many were overcome by post-Referendum *accidie*. *Radical Scotland* (1982-91) invented the 'Doomsday Scenario' and helped change the language of 'respectable' Scottish political discourse. By the 1980s the quality papers, edited now by the sons of 'renaissance' men – Arnold Kemp on the *Herald* and Magnus Linklater on the *Scotsman* – could hold their own with anything coming from London; and the BBC and 'independent' broadcasting were showing initiative and a European sense. 'Work as if you were in the early days of a better nation', was the injunction of Alasdair Gray, from whose *Lanark* (1982) there seemed to flood out the pent-up experience of the country from the Reformation onwards. Happily, his advice was taken.

VI Conservatives, Ships and Oil

After six years of Wilsonian ductility, the new Conservative government seemed to know where it was going. It took up the principles of the Wheatley Report of 1969 and in 1973 reorganized Scottish local government, creating nine regions with powers over planning, transport, social work, and education, and 53 districts, mainly dealing with housing. Joint bodies supervised the police, but health services were placed under separate nominated authorities in the following year. Such sweeping changes implied that Edward Heath had ceased to toy with devolution, and although the Scottish Office acquired an Economic Planning Department in 1973, its authority slipped back.

Energy was not however the same as effectiveness, and Heath, pledged to 'roll back' Labour's interventionism, soon ran into a crisis in shipbuilding. The rescue of Fairfield's in 1965 had shown that the industry badly required government investment. It received it somewhat haphazardly. After the Geddes Report of 1966 Labour reorganized Clyde shipbuilding in two groups: Scott Lithgow, based on Greenock and Port Glasgow, and Upper Clyde, based on Clydebank, Linthouse, and Govan. In the latter case management and unions vied with one another in exploiting the settlement, its economics became chaotic, and in late 1970s, as losses on pre-reorganization contracts mounted, some of Heath's most doctrinaire ministers demanded near-total closure. But, by the time UCS reeled into receivership in June 1971, the government's policy had already been changed, and it had nationalized the bankrupt Rolls-Royce. It now had to suffer a reverse on the Clyde, in the full glare of publicity.

The workers at the threatened John Brown's yard started a 'work-in' on 30 July. Led by two articulate Communist shop stewards, Jimmie Airlie and Jimmie Reid, they captured the attention of the media, and raised almost £250,000 and considerable public support. The government shifted its policy to retain and re-invest in two of the UCS yards, while Brown's was, after dramatic transatlantic negotiations, taken over by the Marathon Engineering Company of Texas for oil-rig building.

No one came out of the UCS affair with much credit. The 'work-in' was merely a publicity coup. There was no industrial reorganization. A sequel in 1975−6, when the new owners of the *Scottish Daily Express* shifted printing to Manchester, and its workers attempted, with government assistance, to produce the *Scottish Daily News*, was disastrous. But UCS highlighted one problem of industrial reconstruction. 'Old' nationalized industries, like railways, electricity, or coal, could draw on long traditions of state involvement or municipal enterprise. Could reorganization of manufacturing industry be achieved not only without this, but by remote control from London? Opinion − among civil servants and on the left − was beginning to shift away from centralized planning towards greater regional autonomy.

But there was a powerful counter-current, of which Marathon was a portent. By 1973 oil exploration had moved to the fore, and almost 90 per cent of the equipment for it had to be imported. To blame with hindsight is easy, but could the consequences of the Yom Kippur War of November 1973 − the Arabs' use of their economic muscle, the six-fold increase in the price of crude oil − not have been forecast? Well, to some extent yes. An oil famine was in prospect from 1967, when exploration off Scotland started; early in 1973, by suspending oil import quotas, the USA forecast substantial price increases. Government could have explored some preliminary options; instead, its reactions were hasty and brought Scotland little benefit.

North Sea oil exploration began off Holland in 1959. Gas was discovered off East Anglia and pumped ashore in 1965, and in 1970 the first commercial 'Scottish' field − the Forties − was located. This was to come on stream in 1977, the whole project yielding 13m. tons annually by 1980. Only in 1973, however, did government and business really take an interest. The southward shift of control, post-nationalist boredom with Scottish affairs, an apparent slackening in the Scottish Office, may all have played a part. Thereafter the hyper-activity of politicians simply concealed the fact that they could do little to control either the rate of oil extraction or the distribution of oil-related contracts. The sooner the fields were on stream, the better for the balance of payments — even if this meant surrendering to the Americans' command of the appropriate technology.

Apart from Marathon's products, exploration rigs were nearly all built abroad, as were supply vessels. The only important construction in Scotland was of production platforms, vast steel or concrete structures which had to be assembled near the fields. Heath quickly secured construction sites, bruising a few environmentalists. But although seven were prepared only five were used, and all but one of these were in areas remote from the job-starved upper Clyde. As a result they got an unstable workforce. Their Yukon-like atmosphere, or the garish and inflationary affluence that hit the north-east, was no compensation for the missed opportunities of industrial development.

As if anticipating such haphazard 'planning', the SNP launched in September 1972 its own well-articulated campaign: 'It's Scotland's Oil'. Besides the Middle East, several events thrust it into the foreground. The MP for Govan died, and Labour seemed determined to repeat the Hamilton scenario. The report of the Kilbrandon Commission on the Constitution appeared a week before polling day in early November. Labour found it 'at first glance totally unacceptable'. The SNP won.

VII To the Referendum

The weakness and opportunism of the major British political parties underlay the subsequent constitutional crisis, which lasted until the referendum and election of 1979. In the election of February 1974, called amid the chaos caused by the miner's strike and 30-hour week, Heath lost 16 seats and Labour gained 3, but the main swing was to third parties. In England the Liberals went up from 13.6 to 24.2 per cent; in Scotland the SNP from 11.4 to 21.9 per cent. Labour, which formed a minority government, had a manifesto rich in socialist rhetoric, but little chance (or even, in the Cabinet, inclination) to do much about it. But it was now challenged in 10 Scottish seats by the SNP, which had added six Conservative and one Labour seat to the one it held after 1970. Harold Wilson, expecting an election any week, had to act on Kilbrandon, both to conciliate centrist opinion and secure his Scottish flank. The rest of 1974 was to present the actors and the scenario of a complex and ultimately disastrous drama.

Devolution divided Labour in Scotland. Its Scottish executive, having voted in favour on 10 March, threw out the government's pro-devolution green paper on 22 June. The Cabinet and Transport House invoked the big unions which, at a special Scottish conference on 18 August, brought the Scots to heel. Just in time. Labour went into the 10 October election committed to a somewhat nebulous Scottish Assembly. Such manoeuvres probably encouraged rather than checked the SNP vote; in October, while Plaid Cymru's vote declined slightly, the SNP's rose to over 30 per cent. It captured another four seats, and now challenged Labour in 35 out of its 41 while, at the height of the oil excitement, its oil policy attracted enough attention to suggest that a Scottish breakaway would not disappoint international financial institutions — although on reflection the move of capital into Scotland probably increased external control rather than the opposite. In some areas like retailing and the press (see p. 123) the devolution clamour concealed the fact that not simply English but multinational firms had made important inroads.

Several factors dominated the subsequent scene. In Scotland some socialists enthused over devolution in publications like the *Red Paper* of May 1975. They were given some support by the creation in 1975 of the Scottish Development Agency, which reversed the Dalton approach (at least in principle) and restored much regional autonomy. But a reaction had already set in. In May 1974 the first elections for the new regional and district authorities had produced several huge Labour majorities in Strathclyde, Central, Lothian, and Fife, with a strong interest in establishing and upholding their power; and distaste for devolution still existed, not only at the Scottish grass-roots but among English MPs and the Cabinet itself. This struck directly at the drafting of the White Paper, and a battle — in contrast to 1967—8, now between pro-devolution territorial ministers and hostile English departmental ministers — delayed its appearance until late in 1975.

The White Paper was essentially a Whitehall creation and showed a successful resistance by ministers and civil servants to the concession of any significant degree of autonomy to the Assembly. In this way it cut across the historical evolution of the Scottish Office and prevented a logical division of its responsibilities. Housing was devolved, but mort-gages — and so private housing policy — withheld. Education went north, but not universities; infrastructure planning — including the new SDA — but not economic planning; transport, but not railways; law, but not courts or judges; local government, but not police. The Secretary of State still retained substantial powers: over agriculture, fisheries, most of law and order, electricity, large areas of economic policy. He stayed in the Cabinet, but also had quasi-Viceregal powers vis à vis the 142-seat Assembly. He would appoint its executive and adjudicate on whether its enactments were within its '*vires*' or not. Scotland would continue to send 71 MPs to Westminster.

Our Changing Democracy satisfied only such groups as had been forced into action: the Labour establishment, Whitehall, the unions. In Scotland it was generally condemned. Pro- and anti-devolutionists alike argued that its concessions could only be a first stage. Hostility among business groups, local authorities, and some unions increased, the spirits of the 'Antis' having received a fillip by the results of the EEC referendum of 5 June. In this a co-ordinated campaign by the pro-Europeans against a disunited and mutually-hostile anti side, dominated by Labour and the SNP, converted a January poll of 29 per cent pro-EEC and 45 per cent anti, to 58.4 per cent and 41.6 per cent. On a low poll (61.7 per cent) Labour and SNP could not mobilize their vote: an encouraging sign should there be a referendum on devolution.

In the shadow of the White Paper, the devolutionist left made the first tactical mistake. Early in 1976 Jim Sillars and various associates, mainly journalists, created the Scottish Labour Party. 'The Magic Party' — socialist and devolutionist — proved for a short time remarkably popular: it attracted about 900 members, comparable to about 25 per cent of regular Labour activists, but it also drew in left-wing sects, without gaining a 'bottom' in the trade unions. As a result, Sillars presided, ineffectively, over a party consumed by clashes between middle-class ideologues. The SLP episode was a disaster for devolution: it isolated its most eloquent left-winger, and gravely weakened the cause within Labour.

Nor was it aided by Harold Wilson's sudden resignation in April 1976. James Callaghan, his successor, replaced both Ross and Lord Crowther-Hunt, Wilson's constitutional expert, and Ross's successor, Bruce Millan, a competent administrator, fatally lacked his public personality. Difficulties soon mounted. The Scotland and Wales Bill, tabled on 13 December by Michael Foot, was literally incomprehensible, as it did not transfer sovereignty but abstracted powers from existing legislation. It was, morever, evident that the Conservatives, since February 1975 under Mrs Thatcher, were prepared to exploit to the full the divisions that existed between the Cabinet and the unenthusiastic Labour back-benchers and the discontent of the Liberals, who had ostentatiously not been squared by any offer of proportional representation. In committee the bill sank into a quagmire of 350 amendments, from which Foot's concession of a referendum could not extricate it. An attempt to force a 'guillotine' on 22 February 1977 failed by 29 votes.

There was little reaction in Scotland: no demonstrations, no riots. The SNP went ahead to 36 per cent in the opinion polls, but the hiatus pending a new bill being tabled, on 4 November, proved critical. The steam had gone out of the issue. Nationalism expressed itself in a notable coolness towards the Jubilee celebrations of June 1977, and became a fascinating topic for intellectuals, but it did not affect the Scots electorate like unemployment – the consequence of Labour's tight monetary policy – which advanced from 3.6 per cent in 1974 to 7.6 per cent in 1978. While John Smith, a Labour advocate, piloted the new bill through the House, Scottish MPs sat silent. Only the hostile were vociferous, although they were partly mollified by a clause which made the ultimate enactment of the bill depend on over 40 per cent of the Scots electorate voting 'Yes'. During this gap, on 13 July, John Mackintosh, one of its most convinced proponents, died, aged only 48. The Assembly might have given him the chance of high office that the Labour Party had continually denied him; his eloquence was certainly needed to save it.

In Scottish politics, the bill seemed, however, to have paid off. While English by-elections were disastrous for Labour, in Scotland it easily beat off the SNP challenge – even in Hamilton (1978 was not a good year for extremes of patriotism, being dominated by Scotland's appalling performance in the World Cup). But trouble was on its way, in the shape of the same trade-union power that had secured devolution in 1974. The unions, like Scottish nationalism, had their price, and in 1978 it came due. In October, perhaps encouraged by such election successes, Callaghan postponed a general election until after the referendum, and shortly afterwards announced a rigid pay policy. The result was catastrophic, for him, as well as for devolution.

In October 1978 the Whitehall élite seemed to have squared the union magnates and the nationalists – if each of these groups could command its forces. By February 1979 union discipline had collapsed. A tide of badly organized strikes coupled with the worst winter since 1947 aided the Conservatives while demonstrating working-class disunity. The intricate compromises Whitehall had written into the Devolution Bill offered no easy solutions, to this, or Scotland's growing economic problem. And Labour and the SNP again failed to mobilize their vote. Both had minorities who hoped that devolution would fail, and the imaginative ideas for deploying the devolved powers canvassed by the young and mainly middle-class supporters of the Assembly were almost drowned out by the well-heeled 'Scotland says No' campaign's constant harping on the themes of expense, bureaucracy, and disruption, echoed loudly by the *Scottish Daily Express*, whose new owner, Victor (Lord) Matthews, ditched Beaverbrook's cherished home rule in the interests of Conservative policy.

On 1 March, Referendum day, 63.63 per cent of the electorate turned out to vote. The highest poll was 67 per cent in the Borders, the most hostile mainland region; the lowest was 49.4 per cent in the SNP-held Western Isles, which voted 'Yes'. These two were almost an epitome of the whole. The Labour heartlands — Strathclyde, Central, and Fife — ensured a 'Yes' majority, but only Highland joined them. Lothian was only just 'Yes', Tayside only just 'No'. The main Liberal or Nationalist areas — Borders, Grampian, Orkney, and Shetland — were all hostile. The Assembly won, but only by 32.85 to 30.78 per cent, 7.15 per cent short of the 40 per cent hurdle.

Before the referendum, nationalist and radical socialist intellectuals had preached the doom of social democracy. Between January and May 1979 doom occurred: its devolution compromise was destroyed: by unions demanding an end to wages policy, by Scots local government magnates clinging on to their own authority, by an antique but incredibly tough landowning class — represented by the two Old Etonians who did more damage than anyone else to devolution, Tam Dalyell and Lord Home — and by the Nationalists themselves. It was the SNP MPs who ended a less than distinguished parliamentary presence by rejecting Callaghan's offer of all-party talks and tabling the vote of no-confidence that on 28 March brought his government down. In the election on 3 May Labour took its revenge and removed the threat to most of its seats, while the SNP saw its vote fall to 18 per cent and lost (albeit usually by narrow margins) 9 of its 11 seats, 8 to the Conservatives. But Labour's Scottish success was over-shadowed by its shattering defeat south of the border.

VIII 'We in Scotland'

'Instant post-industrialisation'

The 1980s was to be an extraordinary decade, but the Scots did not enter on it with hope. Nor, if the election of 1992 were its terminus, did they leave it with their expectations much altered. Throughout the world an economic neo-liberalism which claimed descent from the Scottish enlightenment was knocking over command economies and social democracies. Some expatriate Scots – Andrew Neil of the *Sunday Times*, Dr Madsen Pirie of the Adam Smith Institute, Professor Norman Stone – were implicated, at least in the publicity offensive that accompanied this. Yet the ideology itself found little echo in Scotland. When Mrs Thatcher travelled to Edinburgh to instruct the Kirk in morality in 1988 she was received no more than civilly. Two years later the extravagant use of the regal 'we in Scotland' in a hard-fought interview with Kirsty Wark seemed to indicate that *hubris* was imminent. On 22 November 1990 it struck.

Mrs Thatcher often came north. Why? Scots regarded her with dislike, occasionally with loathing; a Scottish Conservative memo in 1987 recommended a period of prime ministerial indifference. Yet Scotland figured in the ideology of this 'absolute bourgeois'. Thatcher's relationship with the English establishment was ambiguous: deferential to the crown, effectively neutral in religion, grinding out honours as no premier had done since the war. In Scotland, she perhaps believed, her values could come into their own. The poll tax was born of a Scot, Douglas Mason; and her most drastic (and in England, most unpopular) venture into institutional reform followed the appointment of a Highland Calvinist, John MacKay, as Lord Chancellor.

Thatcher believed rational Scots ought to appreciate her classical economics, and was distressed (though not disarmed) when they didn't. But she had a further reason for observing Scotland; the country was keeping her in business. The fuel trade surplus, from North Sea oil, bankrolled her 'achievements', reaching a peak of £6 billion in 1985, or about 8 per cent of the balance of payments. Initially, this did Scotland little good. The high petro-pound, coupled with the 'sado-monetarism' of a tight money supply, helped induce one of the worst recessions ever, which carried away much of the industry expensively induced to settle in Scotland in the 1960s and 1970s, such as the Corpach pulp mill, the Invergordon aluminium smelter, and the motor vehicle plants at Linwood and Bathgate. Industrial closures and unemployment were implicitly deployed by government – along with measures curbing trade union autonomy – to discipline the labour force: with some success. The question of 'who runs the country' was settled in the government's favour: definitively by the long-drawn-out miners' strike of 1984-5.

In the government's favour, perhaps; but in favour of *Scottish* businessmen? Between 1985 and 1986 a spate of takeovers in a swelling share market transferred £2.4 billion out of £4.7 billion of Scottish manufacturing capital to London control. By 1990 the traditional industries had dwindled to only two shipyards on the Clyde, one colliery at Longannet, and the threatened steelworks complex around Ravenscraig. Mechanical engineering output alone slumped by 28 per cent between 1979-85. The Silicon Glen phenomenon, instead of achieving the 'critical mass' which would generate high value-added concerns, obeyed the policies of the multinationals which controlled it and slowed up; textiles and whisky were in trouble; and manufacturing (including energy production) was down to less than 30 per cent of GNP, employment dropping from 605,000 in 1979 to 412,000 in 1986, and investment falling by two-fifths, from £561 to £339 million.

Government ministers spoke consolingly of the fact that Scottish workers exported more per capita than the Japanese, and to some economists the shift to services was inevitable. In the 1980s 'services' became an overloaded grab-bag, packing in everything from computer software to selling hamburgers. (In 1989 Ronald McDonald probably mattered more than Adam Smith in projecting Western values to Eastern Europe). But while Baden-Württemberg still had manufacturing running at over 40 per cent of GNP in 1987, and 'microcapitalism', sponsored by powerful regional authorities, had revitalised the textile and clothing industries of central Italy, even oil could not prevent a reduced manufacturing sector putting the country increasingly in deficit with the rest of the UK, whose own balance of payments plunged ever deeper into the red. Attempts to check this by raising interest rates could only make a bad situation worse.

The stock market crash of October 1987 was followed not by a slump but by an extraordinary comsumption and property boom, fed by the government. But by mid-1988 a trade deficit, stemming directly from the shrinkage of manufacturing, forced a drastic correction and, soon, a long-drawn-out recession. In this Scotland – for the first time – suffered proportionately less than the south of England. Unemployment peaked at 15.6 per cent in 1985 (UK: 11.8 per cent); it fell to 8.1 per cent in 1990 (UK: 5.8 per cent) but in recession rose to only 9.2 per cent in December 1991. The UK figure was 9.0 per cent. Scotland's wages fell further below UK levels (from 99 per cent in 1980 to 93.5 per cent in 1990) but Wales was more successful in using this differential to attract new investment.

'There is no such thing ...'

This mitigation wasn't due to the oil business, in the doldrums with a collapse in world prices – from $40 a barrel in 1980 to $14.5 in 1986, ironically just after the peak year of North Sea production. The downside to a neo-liberal economic policy which transferred resources to the wealthy (which the latter promptly invested abroad!) was infrastructural deterioration. Unplanned, unregulated London had become an expensive, inconvenient and unreliable business centre; its house prices were exorbitant; travel to work a torture. To one sympathetic commentator, Anthony Hilton of the *Evening Standard*, the circumstances surrounding the takeover of Distillers by Guinness in 1986 could only suggest that, in the City, 'dishonesty has become institutionalised'. Against this, infrastructural investment in Scotland – in transport, communications, banking – seemed to have paid off. Comparisons by Walter Henderson showed the highest output of graduates *per capita* in Europe. Edinburgh and Glasgow – the European Culture Capital in 1990 – were consistently rated among the top European cities, and a growing agglomeration of high-grade and science-based service industries were attracted north, not to speak of 'white settlers' who exchanged expensive south-eastern property for its cheaper Scottish equivalent, and lived in part on the proceeds. This in-migration even caused an upward blip in the population figures towards the end of the decade.

There seemed, however, little acceptance within the Scottish bourgeoisie of the Conservative ideal of a privatised, acquisitive 'lifestyle'. This existed, certainly – in the boutiques and posh restaurants of Edinburgh and the 'merchant city' of Glasgow – but it was combated by doctrines of social 'fairness' and frustrated nationalism, which meant that doctors, bankers and lawyers espoused principles unthinkable among equivalent groups in the south. Were these Michael Frayn's 'herbivores .... with eyes full of sorrow for less fortunate creatures, though not usually ceasing to eat the grass'? Possibly. Not only unemployment – in some places affecting the third generation – but a deliberate government policy, modelled on Reagan's America, of forcing down wages and substituting part-time for full-time work, seemed aimed at that third of the population which struggled to survive on or below the poverty line. Although the state sector in housing fell from 54 per cent of tenancies in 1979 to 40 per cent in 1990, thanks to concessionary sales to tenants, the limits of privatisation were reached when tenants simply could not afford to become owners. The grim system-built suburbs of East German towns in 1990, after the Wall fell, still seemed somewhat better endowed – with piped central heating, fast, subsidised trams, cheap grocery stores, community centres and kindergartens – than Castlemilk or Craigmillar.

'Pure capitalism, or pure communism?' a Thatcher adviser was supposed to have remarked on encountering the pullulating black economy of a Glasgow housing scheme. Such precarious enterprise, even if collapsing at the edges into crime, drink, drugs and despair, held some areas together in ways unthinkable in the 1930s. Yet the ligatures of Adam Ferguson's 'society' still bound: if a potential big league capitalist emerged, 'a neighbour picked up a phone'. Did the 'makers, movers and menders' of Alasdair Gray's *Lanark* exist in embryo, a market structure on a collectivist base? Or was it enough, as Gray wrote in his 'Postscript' to Agnes Owen's *Gentlemen of the West* (1986), to survive, threaten no one, and try to be articulate on behalf of folk with low incomes? 'Mac is typical of a huge piece of Britain. Conservatives can draw soothing morals from his existence. I hope they will not.'

Party Pieces

Transforming a capacity for 'getting by' into the competitive culture of Thatcherism was by definition difficult, and further hampered by an electoral system which favoured the Conservatives in England and did the opposite in Scotland. In a four-party system, with the Liberals and SNP getting together around a third of the vote, the Conservatives captured few seats, proportionate to their vote; so did the SNP. The opposite was the case for Labour and the Liberal Democrats. Following the split in the Labour Party, the Liberal/SDP Alliance vote rose to 24.5 per cent in 1983, when their seats moved from three to eight; but in 1992, when their vote almost halved, their seats still stood at nine.

The Conservatives bore themselves cannily after their successes in 1979. George Younger, a 'wet', ex-officer and brewer, did what he could to temper the winds of orthodoxy, retained the Scottish Development Agency and established a Select Committee on Scottish Affairs – meeting occasionally in the Royal High School – yet his room for manoeuvre was checked by an increasingly ideological Whitehall and a fast-waning Scottish industrial capitalism. His successor Malcolm Rifkind, previously reckoned a liberal and devolutionist, proved pliant to London command. He acquiesced in the dismantling of regional economic policy by Lord Young, and the demoralisation and dismemberment of the SDA. Regional preferential assistance fell 34 per cent between 1986 and 1990. Rifkind also carried through the poll tax and bus deregulation and privatisation. The latter scarcely improved public transport – bus miles went up 22 per cent and passenger journeys went down 22 per cent over the decade – though it managed to produce traffic jams caused *completely by public transport*. The two electricity boards were privatised (although the nuclear generators, which supplied most of the power, remained with the state).

After 1987 the Scottish Select Committee was suspended because of conflict between Scots Labour MPs and the bored and malicious English Tories put in as makeweights. An isolated professional, in a post usually occupied by former whips and members of Scottish business dynasties, Rifkind nevertheless became vulnerable to his own party's right wing after an appalling result in 1987, when Tory MPs fell from 21 to 10. The premier installed the self-proclaimed 'Thatcher sycophant' Michael Forsyth as Scottish Chairman, and his importation of a highly ideological staff led to civil war within the party, culminating in Forsyth's removal. Not long afterwards, Rifkind played a key role in toppling Thatcher, and moved on to become first Transport and then, after April 1992, Defence Minister.

A similar professionalisation affected the other parties, the prototype being David Steel, who took over the Liberal leadership in 1976 after the fall of Jeremy Thorpe. He was followed in the SNP by Gordon Wilson in 1979, and in the Labour party by Donald Dewar in 1983. Politics seemed almost stitched up by the lawyers, but rates of recovery from 1979 were variable. The SNP plunged into intra-party right-left feuding, which claimed many victims and led to a wretched result in 1983. The Liberals acquired former right-wing Labour allies, the Social Democrats, in 1981, but their one by-election success, Roy Jenkins's capture of Glasgow Hillhead in 1982, seemed more a re-run of his hero Asquith's late flowering at Paisley in 1920. The new party gained few adherents in Scotland, and Jenkins's replacement as leader by the incalculable Dr David Owen was to bring David Steel much trouble in the 1987 campaign.

Labour suffered in 1979 the double humiliation of a defeat in the European elections; none of the left-wing parties had taken any interest in European affairs in the 1970s, and in a low poll the Conservatives took five out of the eight seats, with only two going to Labour and the Highlands seat to Mrs Winifred Ewing of the SNP. In 1984 Labour increased to five, and in 1989 removed the Conservatives altogether. Europe, in general, began to preoccupy Scottish regional authorities and pressure groups, frustrated by the negativism of Whitehall, until the concept of 'Independence in Europe', projected with typical force, brought Jim Sillars back into the Commons as SNP MP for Govan in November 1988.

Under Neil Kinnock, in Scotland a figure even less loved than Thatcher, Labour underwent a drastic 'modernisation': party like leader ditched unilateralism and Bevanite collectivism in favour of a degree of double-breasted respectability which would convert the south-eastern voter. (In 1987 Labour had only 16.8 per cent there, compared with 42 per cent in Scotland). A new generation, university-educated, and formed in the politics of the student movement, Union debates, and the Labour clubs

– John Smith, Gordon Brown, Robin Cook, Martin O'Neill – had come to the fore, not just in Scotland but in Westminster politics: the first time Scots had exercised such authority since the time of ... well ... Ramsay MacDonald.

Conventional Wisdom

MacDonald had of course started his career as a home ruler, and following the 1987 election, the theme emerged again. The Campaign for a Scottish Assembly, which had struggled to keep interest alive, secured an influential committee to draft *A Claim of Right for Scotland*, published on 6 July 1988. This proposed the summoning of a 210-strong Constitutional Convention composed of MPs, council representatives, trade unionists and the Churches, to deliberate on Scotland's constitutional future. Within a year, Labour and the Liberal Democrats had accepted membership, and the issue was given added urgency by the Govan by-election.

Then trouble started. The SNP's poll position soared after Govan and it announced it would only take part if its policy of independence in Europe were included in the referendum options. The other parties wanted a single agreed option, but the Convention's composition obviously favoured the electoral *status quo*. The SNP withdrew. The Tories announced they weren't interested and anathematised the articulate minority of the party which persisted in backing home rule.

The Convention first met in the Kirk's Assembly Hall on 30 March 1989, and its Convener, Canon Kenyon Wright, issued its report *Towards Scotland's Parliament*, in November 1990. The scheme was for a legislature with 'entrenched' powers broadly resembling those of a German *Land*, elected under a form of proportional representation and financed by 'assigned revenues' deducted from the taxes raised in Scotland. The problem was that any electorate's attention-span for matters constitutional is limited, and these conclusions, although significant for the constitutional policy of the Labour party, were mostly of interest to the political *cognoscenti*. Only in late 1991, with the sad death of the Tory party's one home ruler MP, Alick Buchanan-Smith, did a by-election victory for the Liberal Democrats, and a new, aggressive SNP leader, Alex Salmond, kick the issue back into life.

Alive it remained, throughout the long election campaign of early 1992. 'And over to Scotland, where the election agenda is completely different ...', ran the broadcasters' rubric. And then, on 9 April, hardly anything changed. Was it 1979 all over again? Against an almost wholly hostile press (a remarkable contrast with England), the underrated

Secretary of State, Ian Lang and his team, managed to hold their position (a couple of hundred votes the other way would have been a disaster) and induce their opponents to lay into one another.

One, unregarded, Tory weapon was the poll tax. It had helped dislodge an unelectable Mrs Thatcher, and prompted the most sustained campaign of civil disobedience ever seen in Scotland, when up to a third refused to pay, but Labour suffered overall from a fall in district and regional revenue, and up to 5 per cent of its voters dropped off the electoral register. The SNP gambled on signals of a Labour defeat inducing Labour voters to secede to them, but these came far too late. A one-third increase in their vote gave them no new seats, and Jim Sillars lost Govan. Although united on the constitutional issue, there was no co-operation between Labour and the Liberal Democrats. Slightly increasing their vote from 24 to 25.7 per cent – the 'white settler' influx played some part here – taking one seat from Labour and regaining Kincardine, the Conservatives had some reason for satisfaction, at least in the short term.

Yet the Conservative utopia of minimal government and choice exercised through the market, was illusory. The reality was the modulation of state monopolies into private monopolies, fitfully and ineffectively controlled, and a 'people's capitalism' which lasted only until the people had sold their shares off at a profit. Government assaults on local authority competence in areas like health and education produced a potential chaos of competing public authorities: school boards, hospital trusts, training and enterprise councils battling it out with districts and regions. The latter were, anyway, down for abolition. Effectively, this meant that more powers ended up with St Andrew's House, yet ministers resisted the far right's demand that Scottish administrative autonomy be diminished. They took over from 'British' institutions in areas like the environment and higher education. Opponents regarded the result as semi-colonial, and the Secretary of State as a governor, even a *gauleiter*. But there was nothing purposive about the situation; only irritation among the governed and irresolution in the executive.

Where were the mass protests? Occasionally the STUC and left-wing bodies could put several thousands on the streets, but there was nothing resembling the repeated, peaceful demonstrations which felled Communism in East Germany. All parties were suffering substantial membership loss, with the number of fully-paid-up less than 100,000, or 2 per cent of the population. The Tories had lost any Scottish identity beyond the sartorial *grotesquerie* of Sir Nicholas Fairbairn – nothing was left of the tradition of Walter Elliot and John Buchan – and the other parties were still trapped in a Westminster-derived confrontational style which interested few outside the initiated.

Millennial

In 1981 the first edition of this book presented a sombre view of the country, much influenced by parallels with Sicily. On the face of it, nothing much had changed eleven years later. The one articulate voice of Scottish unionism, Alan Massie, persisted in Lampedusan pessimism. Globally, and indeed in Britain, there was much to be pessimistic about. The climate deteriorated, the thinning of the ozone layer doubled Scots skin cancer cases over the decade, caesium from Chernobyl polluted the hills. Salmon-farming and oil extraction had ominous ecological consequences, and the human costs of the latter were made grimly apparent by the Piper Alpha disaster on 6 July 1988, while the anarchy of the Middle East caused the horror of Lockerbie on 21 December of that year.

Euphoria over the fall of Communist Europe in 1989-90 soon gave way to apprehension as 'new democracies' tottered into hyperinflation, ungovernability and civil conflict. The market utopia seemed as deceptive as its socialist predecessor, and doomed to be much shorter-lived. Had the time for the Scots to decide on their nationality simply come too late, when the dreams both of European union and of small nations were falling apart? But what was the alternative?

The Conservatives sought to replace social democracy's concept of welfare citizenship with their ideal of the shareholding consumer: his mortgaged house, imported car, Telecom shares, Lloyd Webber CDs and Jeffrey Archer paperbacks. Mrs Thatcher's dictum 'there is no such thing as society, only individuals and families' might have had meaning in Essex, but it didn't help solve the problems crowding in on the world, and found few takers in Scotland. In a decade which saw the monarchy, banks, City and media, undermined by folly where not by downright criminality, the losers were the traditional institutions – Tom Nairn's 'enchanted glass' of Britishness.

In late 1992, this process seemed to accelerate almost alarmingly. On 14 September, John Major, April's unexpected victor, visited Scotland to 'take stock' of the situation, or perhaps to view the new Labour leader, John Smith, in his natural habitat. He breakfasted with one lot of unionists, restating his rigidity over home rule, and assured another, the Glasgow Chamber of Commerce, that the £ sterling was safe in his hands. One day later, and the £ was down against the Deutschmark by 15%. His next visit north was on December 11-12 for the summit which concluded Britain's sticky headship of the European communities. Edinburgh launched a miniature festival, and cultural and ethnic delights almost drowned out the further disintegration of the British monarchy, and the premier's effort to prove that whatever the 'word of the year' – subsidiarity – meant in a 'regional' Europe, it meant in Britain more of the same from Westminster. Scots would disgrace themselves, in the eyes of the Secretary of State, by demonstrating in favour of autonomy. Most home rulers wearily expected that, as usual, they would disgrace themselves by *not* demonstrating. 25,000 turned out on a cold December afternoon. Alasdair Gray's gentle notion of a 'Scottish Co-operative Wholesale Republic' didn't seem a total fantasy any more ...

For all its political frustration, the 1980s in Scotland had been rich in cultural re-examinations and rediscoveries, provoked by the reaction to 1979 and the challenge of 'Scotland in Europe'. Major achievements in literary and social history – *The Literary History of Scotland, People and Society in Scotland, The Dictionary of Scottish Business Biography* were just the peaks – filled out epochs and individuals who had been at best shadowy when the present book was first drafted. The imaginative achievement of Scots novelists and dramatists – Alastair Gray, James Kelman, Liz Lochhead, John Byrne – now feeding on the life and problems of urban Scotland, complemented one of Europe's richest and most polyphonic poetics: to MacCaig, MacLean and Morgan were added the architectural statements of Ian Hamilton Finlay, the humanism of Douglas Dunn, and the busy evangelism of the Scottish Poetry Library. Scottish painting and sculpture – Stephen Conroy, Ken Currie, John Bellany, Eduardo Paolozzi – established a European reputation, following rules unheard of in London.

The old man, whose centenary fell on 11 August 1992, would have marvelled. But MacDiarmid's crystallate intellectual ambition might not have recognised the linkages – particularly in the music of the young, whether folk, rock or blues – which stretched out across the social classes to create a language of national identity which was open and experimental, not closed and autistic: a Scotland which could help tackle the problems of the world, before they overwhelmed it. If this 'popular politics' had a godfather, it was Hamish Henderson, who gave this book its title. Leave the last challenge with him:

> ... Either build for the living
> love, patience and power to absolve these tormented,
> or else choke in the folds of their black-edged
> vendetta.

A Note on Further Reading

Place of publication is London except where otherwise stated.
Coverage of recent Scottish history is so patchy that much of my reading has had to consist of work in primary sources, and some discussion of these is useful.

A   *Government Papers* available under the 30-year rule are divided between the Public Record Office (Cabinet and British Ministries) and West Register House, Edinburgh (Scottish Office); they are valuable on economic and social issues after the 1930s.

B   *Private Collections*: The National Library, Edinburgh, is particularly strong on nationalism (the Scottish Secretariat and J.A.A. Porteous papers) with smaller collections of Elliot, Johnston, and Woodburn papers; Liberal Party papers are in Edinburgh University Library; those of the Labour Party: Scottish Council in Labour Party Headquarters, London.

C   *Statistical Sources: Census Returns* are important but flawed. Occupational categories change between 1911 and 1921, the 1931 census took place at the pit of the slump, and there was not another until 1951. There were *Censuses of Production* in 1907, 1924, 1935, and 1948, subsequently becoming very frequent, but there has yet to be an adequate attempt to collate and compare the results. The same goes for the *Glasgow Herald Trade Reviews*, the *Annual Reports* (*AR*) of the Boards (later the Department) of Agriculture and Fisheries, and the Scottish Education Department, although the Scottish Economic Committee's *Scotland's Industrial Future* (Glasgow, 1939) and the Clydesdale Bank Reports (1934–9) sum up inter-war trends. *Industry and Employment in Scotland*, an annual paper after 1947, was supplemented by the twice-yearly *Digest of Scottish Statistics* (1954–71), dividing into the annual *Scottish Abstract of Statistics* and the twice-yearly *Scottish Economic Bulletin* (1971–). The SNP published a useful statistical digest in 1976, and the Scottish Council's valuable *Input – Output Table* (Edinburgh, 1977) draws on 1975–6. There is some Scottish material in B.R. Mitchell and P. Deane, *Abstract of British Historical Statistics* (2 vols., Cambridge, 1962 and 1971), A.H. Halsey, *Trends in British Society since 1900* (*TBS*) (1972) and David Butler *et al.*, *British Political Facts* (1985). *The General Election of 1950*, etc., and in F.W.S. Craig's various compilations of election results. The Unionists published a useful *Yearbook* for Scotland until 1970; this gap has been plugged by the *Yearbook of Scottish Government* (*YSG*) (Edinburgh, 1974–). The *Third Statistical Account* (*TSA*), conceived in 1943, varies wildly in quality and utility. J. Cunnison and J.B.S. Gilfillan, ed., *Glasgow* (Glasgow, 1958), is, thankfully, one of the best volumes.

D   *Bibliographies*: P.D. Hancock's *A Bibliography of Works Relating to Scotland, 1916–1950* (Edinburgh, 1959–60) has not so far been supplemented; but see also W.H. Marwick's bibliographies in the *Economic History Review* (*EcHR*) in 1952, 1963, and 1972 and C. Allen in the *YSG*; see also the Scottish Labour History Society's *Labour Records in Scotland* (1977).

E   *General Introductions and Serial Publications*: W. Ferguson, *Scotland, 1689 to the Present* (Edinburgh, 1968) and G.S. Pryde, *Scotland after 1603* (Edinburgh, 1962) draw on the good though now dated surveys of R.S. Rait and G.S. Pryde, *Scotland* (1934, 2nd edition 1954), and I. Findlay, *Scotland* (Oxford, 1945), and H.W. Meikle, ed., *Scotland* (Edinburgh, 1947). For the later period see J.G. Kellas, *The Scottish*

Political System (SPS) (1973, 1978), *Modern Scotland (MS)* (1968, 1980), and C.T. Harvie, *Scotland and Nationalism* (1977), J.N. Wolfe, ed., *Government and Nationalism in Scotland (GNS)* (Edinburgh, 1968) and G. Brown, ed., *The Red Paper on Scotland (RP)* (Edinburgh, 1975). Only one volume of *Scottish Biographies* (1938) ever appeared, otherwise see the *Dictionary of National Biography*, and *Obituaries from the The Times* and *The Times Guide to the House of Commons*. Newspapers and periodicals are mainly referred to in the text, but the *Glasgow Herald* was also indexed until 1968. *Scotland* is valuable on economic affairs in the 1950s and 1960s. *Keesing's Contemporary Archives* and *Hansard* have also been consulted.

F   *Industry*: Matters have improved a lot recently, with several important monographs and articles: Peter Payne, *Colvilles* (Oxford, 1980); John Hume and Michael Moss, *Beardmores* (1980), R.H. Campbell on the N.B. Loco in *Business History (BH)* (1978) and on the Scottish Office and the Special Areas in the *Historical Journal (HJ)* (1978). *His Rise and Fall of Scottish Industry* (Edinburgh, 1980) draws on the *Glasgow Herald Reviews*. A. Slaven, *The Economic Development of the West of Scotland, 1760–1860* (1975), amplifies *TSA Glasgow*; and see also Slaven on John Brown's, 1919–38, in *BH* (1977), and N.K. Buxton on Scottish shipbuilding, also in *BH* (1968), and on economic growth in Scotland (*EcHR*, 1980).

The World War I historian still depends on W.R. Scott and J. Cunnison, *The Industries of the Clyde Valley during the War* (Oxford, 1924) and the printed but unpublished *History of the Ministry of Munitions* (1922); A. Marwick, *The Deluge* (1966) and A.S. Milward, *The Economic Effects of the Two World Wars in Britain* (1970) set out the UK context. For the Clyde episodes see J. Hinton *The First Shop Stewards' Movement* (1973); W.J. Reader, *Weir: Architect of Air Power* (Glasgow, 1968), and *The Weir Group* (1971), H. McShane, *No Mean Fighter* (1976), W. Gallacher, *Revolt on the Clyde* (1936), *Last Memoirs* (1966), and N. MacLean Milton, *John Maclean* (1973), have to be taken with caution. E.M.H. Lloyd, *Experiments in State Control* (Oxford, 1923), has much on the textile industries and A.L. Bowley, *Prices and Wages in the UK, 1914–20* (Oxford, 1921) on incomes. H.W. Richardson *Economic Recovery in Britain, 1932–39* (1967), and B.W.E. Alford, *Depression and Recovery* (1972), sum up the debate on the inter-war economy. There was a spate of publications in the 1930s, including the Scott Report on *West Central Scotland* (1930) and the SEC's *The Highland Economy* and *Light Industries* (1938); see also the Special Area Commissioners' *Reports* (1935–9). More 'partisan' are C. Maclehose, *The Scotland of our Sons,* (Glasgow, 1936). R. Findlay, *Scotland at the Crossroads* (Edinburgh, 1937), J.A. Bowie, *The Future of Scotland* (Edinburgh, 1939). On agriculture see J.A. Symon, *Scottish Farming* (1959), D. Jones, ed., *Rural Scotland during the War* (Oxford, 1926), and A. Smith, *Joseph Duncan* (Edinburgh, 1974). On the Highlands, David Turnock, *Patterns of Highland Development* (1970), D. Thomson and I. Grimble, *The Future of the Highlands* (1968); Nigel Nicholson, *Lord of the Isles* (1965). S.G. Checkland, *Scottish Banking* (Glasgow, 1975), and M. Gaskin, *The Scottish Banks* (1965), supplant the earlier house histories. Transport coverage consists of a wealth of enthusiasts' accounts, of which John Thomas's *Regional History of the Railways of Great Britain: Scotland* (Newton Abbot, 1971) acts as introduction. See also the various regional plans and the British Association. *A Scientific Survey of S.E. Scotland* (Edinburgh, 1951).

For the post-war period, John Gollan presented an intelligent left-wing view in *Scottish Prospect* (Glasgow, 1948), and J.A.A. Porteous, *Scotland and the South* (Stirling, 1947) draws on much SEC material. A. Cairncross, ed., *The Scottish Economy (SE)* (Cambridge, 1953) is uneven (it misses out fishing and is weak on manufacturing) but still essential, as is G. McCrone, *Scotland's Economic Progress (SEP)* (1965), and T.L. Johnston *et al.*, *Structure and Growth of the Scottish Economy* (1973); for consumption patterns see G.T. Murray, *Scotland, the New Future* (Glasgow, 1973). On Scotland as a 'problem region' see McCrone, *Regional Policy in Britain* (1969), C.H. Lee, *Regional Economic Growth in the United Kingdom since the 1880s* (1971), B.E. Coates and E.M. Rawstron, *Regional Variations in Britain* (1971), and Manners *et al.*, *Regional Development in Britain* (New York, 1972). Two key Scottish Council: Development and Industry (SCDI) reports are J.N. Toothill *et al.*, *The Scottish Economy* (Edinburgh, 1961) and *Oceanspan* (Edinburgh, 1970 and 1973); in between comes the Labour government's ill-fated *A Plan for Scotland, 1965–1970* (1966), with its various regional accompaniments. For North Sea oil see D.G. Mackay and G.A. McKay, *The Political Economy of North Sea Oil* (1975), SCDI, *Oil and Scotland's Future* (Edinburgh, 1973).

G   *Society*: Halsey, *TBS*, the *TSA*, and the regional plans of the 40s and 60s contain uneven amounts of data. James Littlejohn, *Westrigg: The Sociology of a Cheviot Parish* (1964), actually a study of Eskdalemuir in the late 1940s and the early 1950s, is an important Scottish analogue to R. Frankenberg, *Communities in Britain* (1966); an urban equivalent is G. Hutton, ed., *Social Environment in Suburban Edinburgh* (York, 1975). See also the surveys of Glasgow school-leavers by T. Ferguson and J. Cunnison, *The Young Wage-Earner* (1951). *In their Early Twenties* (1956). Specific subject areas: Housing: W.M. Ballantine, *Rebuilding a Nation* (Edinburgh, 1944), Douglas Niven, *Scottish Housing* (1979), *The History of the Scottish Special Housing Association* (Edinburgh, 1978), *The Cullingworth Report* (Edinburgh, 1967), A. Sutcliffe, ed., *Multi-Storey Living* (1974). Food: Boyd Orr, *Food, Health and Income* (1936) is basic; see also D.J. Robertson 'Consumption' in *SE* and MacCrone, *SEP*, Health: R. Levitt in *The Reorganised National Health Service* (1976) has an historical introduction; see also T.T. Paterson in *SE* and the *TSA* volumes R.M. Titmuss, *Problems of Social Policy* (1950) has information on wartime developments. Unemployment and Poverty: *The Scottish Poor Law Magazine* lasted until 1929; after 1935, the *AR* of the Unemployment Assistance Board. See also Wal Hannington, *The Problem of the Distressed Areas* (1937), and, for the post-war scene, Ian Levitt, 'Poverty', in *RP*. Education: The *AR* of the Scottish Education Department; J. Scotland, *The History of Scottish Education* (1970); R.M. Knox *250 Years of Scottish Education* (Edinburgh, 1953) and *Studies in the History of Scottish Education* (1970). A.S. Neill and R.F. Mackenzie's books provide a dissenting commentary. Religion: *AR* of the Church of Scotland and various special reports, particularly *God's Will for Church and Nation* (Edinburgh, 1943); the *Scottish Catholic Yearbook*, John Highet, *The Scottish Churches* (1960); I. Henderson, *Power without Glory* (1967); clerical memoirs proliferate; the most useful is Augustus Muir, *John White* (1960).

H   *Politics and Government*: The student of twentieth-century Scottish politics has still to dovetail a few Scottish books, like Kellas, *MS* and *SPS*, and S.B. Chrimes, ed., *The General Election in Glasgow, 1950* (Glasgow, 1951), I. Budge and D.W. Urwin, *Scottish Political Behaviour* (1966) with 'national' accounts like J. Ramsden, *The Conservative Party: the Age of Balfour and Baldwin* (1978), R.E. Dowse, *Left in the Centre* (1966), Henry Pelling, *The British Communist Party* (1958), and Roy Douglas, *The History of the Liberal Party, 1895–1970* (1971). The history of the Labour Party has still to be written: R.K. Middlemass, *The Clydesiders* (1965) has been much criticized but not replaced. Ben Pimlott, *The Left in the Thirties* (Cambridge, 1977) has some Scottish material, as have two studies of *The General Strike* (both 1976), ed., respectively by Margaret Morris and Jeffrey Skelley.

Nationalism, by contrast, is almost over-written; besides Harvie, *Scotland and Nationalism*, see J. Brand, *The National Movement in Scotland* (1978), K. Webb *The Rise of Nationalism in Scotland* (1977), and Harry Hanham *Scottish Nationalism* (1968) as well as various symposia, e.g. D. Glen, ed., *Whither Scotland* (1971) and N. MacCormick, ed., *The Scottish Debate* (1970). There are any number of autobiographies (a) and memoirs (b) with Scots material. I will simply give a list of the more important names: H.H. Asquith (ab), J.M. Bannerman (b), Balfour of Burleigh (b), Winston Churchill (b), James Clunie (a), Hugh Dalton (a), Walter Elliot (b), William Gallacher (a), William Graham (b), Jo Grimond (a), Lord Home (ab), Tom Johnston (a), Jennie Lee (a), John MacCormick (a), Ramsay MacGonald (b), J. MacGovern (a), John Maclean (b), Harold Macmillan (ab), Harry McShane (a), James Maxton (b), Abe Moffat (a), Robert Munro (a), Boyd Orr (a), Lord Pentland (b), Jimmie Reid (a), John Reith (ab), Lord Rosebery (b), James Stuart (a), William Wolfe (a).

Recent political events have been covered by *The Year Book of Scottish Politics* (Edinburgh, 1975–); Henry Drucker, *Breakaway: The Scottish Labour Party* (Edinburgh, 1978), Tam Dalyell, *Devolution: The End of Britain* (1977), and A. Macartney and D. Denver, eds., *Yes or No: The Devolution Referendum* (Aberdeen, 1981).

Administration: Sir David Milne, *The Scottish Office* (1957), is still basic, supplemented valuably by Kellas, *SPS*, and Hanham in *GNS*; George Pottinger, *The Secretaries of State for Scotland, 1926–76* (Edinburgh, 1978) adds a little inside information, but see G.S. Pryde *Central and Local Government in Scotland* (1953), Scottish Home Department, *Local Government in Scotland* (1958), for the old system, and Ronald Young, *The Search for Democracy*, (Paisley, 1977) about the new.

I   *Culture*: Too many treatments are either exclusively literary or simply strings of names, but there's ample material in *TSA Edinburgh* and *Glasgow* and the essays in Meikle, *Scotland*. Interpretatively, Tom Nairn, *The Breakup of Britain* (1977) offers an important model. On the 'Kailyard' see Harvie, 'Behind the Bonnie Brier Bush' in *Proteus* 1977, as a corrective to George Blake, *Barrie and the Kailyard School* (1951); there are biographies of Nicoll, Annie S. Swan, and Barrie. MacDiarmid, *Contemporary Scottish Studies* (1927, rep. Edinburgh, 1976) is still essential reading for the earlier part of the century, supplemented by William Power, *Should Auld Acquaintance* (1937), etc. Both Kellas volumes give information on the press, supplemented by PEP, *British Newspapers* (1938), the Royal Commissions of 1948 and 1977, and the various Butler election studies. There is no Scottish equivalent of A. Mason, *British Football, a Social History* (1978). On broadcasting see the *AR* of the BBC; Asa Briggs, *The History of Broadcasting in the UK* (1961, 65, 70) has little on Scotland; R. Braddon, *Roy Thompson of Fleet Street* (1968) deals with the origins of STV. On the literary revival compare Karl Miller, ed., *Memoirs of a Modern Scotland* (1970) with D. Cleghorn Thomon, *Scotland in Quest of her Youth* (Edinburgh, 1932). Hugh MacDiarmid, *Lucky Poet* (1942) and *The Company I've Kept* (1966) yield a vast amount of undisciplined information. Duncan Glen's *Hugh MacDiarmid and the Scottish Renaissance* (Edinburgh, 1964) is solemn but valuable. There are short studies of MacDiarmid by K. Buthlay (Edinburgh, 1964), E. Morgan (1976), and R. Watson (Milton Keynes, 1976); of Grassic Gibbon by D. Young (Aberdeen 1976); of Edwin Muir by P.H. Butter (Edinburgh, 1962). George Bruce's *The Scottish Literary Revival* (1968) is a good introductory anthology.

Post-World War I architecture is not well documented outside the architectural journals, but see A. MacLaren Young and A.M. Doak, *Glasgow at a Glance* (1965), P. Nuttgens, *Reginald Fairlie* (1960), and C. MacWilliam, *Lothian* in Pevsner, ed., *Buildings of Scotland* (1979). Alan Reiach and Robert Hurd's *Building Scotland* (Edinburgh, 1944) is a seminal work of the modern movement. There are numerous monographs and catalogues on Scottish painters.

Theatre, music, and cinema: again, much periodical and ephemeral literature, and few monographs. But see D. Hutchinson, *The Modern Scottish Theatre* (Glasgow, 1977), J. Bridie, *One Way of Living* (1939), and W. Bannister, *James Bridie and his Theatre* (1955), George Bruce, *Festival in the North* (1977). For folk song see D. Buchan, *The Ballad and the Folk* (1972) and Ted Cowan, ed., *The People's Past* (Edinburgh, 1980). A useful guide to Scottish documentary is Norman Wilson, *Presenting Scotland* (Edinburgh, 1945); see also H. Forsyth Hardy's biography of *John Grierson* (1978) and Charles Barr's *Ealing Studios* (1979).

Appendix to 1987 reprint
C   *The Third Statistical Account* has resumed publication, but without the county introductions. New volumes include *Orkney, Shetland* and *Midlothian.*
E   A *Dictionary of Scottish Biography* is being organized from Stirling University, and see W. Knox, *Scottish Labour Leaders, 1920–1950* (Edinburgh, 1983) and the forthcoming *Dictionary of Scottish Business Biography.* T.C. Smout, *A Century of the Scottish People* (1986).
F   W.S. Howe, *The Dundee Textile Industries 1960–77* (Aberdeen, 1983). Tony Dickson, ed., *Capital and Class in Scotland* (Edinburgh, 1983). C. Lythe & M. Majumdar, *The Renaissance of the Scottish Economy* (1982). Richard Saville, ed., *The Economic Development of Modern Scotland 1950–80* (Edinburgh, 1985). N. Hood and S. Young, *Multinationalism in Retreat* (Edinburgh, 1982). James Grassie, *Highland Experiment* (Aberdeen, 1984).
G   *Uncharted Lives: Scottish Women's Experience, 1850–1982* (Glasgow, 1984). Bill Murray, *The Old Firm, Sectarianism, Sport and Society* (Edinburgh, 1985). Steve Bruce, *Militant Protestantism and Modern Scotland* (Edinburgh, 1986). M. Cuthbert, ed., *Government Spending in Scotland* (Edinburgh, 1982). G. Gordon and B. Dicks, *Scottish Urban History* (Aberdeen, 1983). J. Cameron, *Prisons and Punishment in Scotland* (Edinburgh, 1983). W. Humes & H. Paterson, eds, *Scottish Culture and Scottish Education* (Edinburgh, 1983). G. Brown & R. Cook, eds, *Scotland, the Real Divide* (Edinburgh, 1983). D. Hamilton, *the Healers: A History of Medicine in Scotland* (Edinburgh, 1982).
H   I.C.G. Hutchinson, *A Political History of Scotland, 1832–1924* (Edinburgh, 1986). Ian MacDougall, ed., *Militant Miners* (Edinburgh, 1982). Bernard Aspinwall, *Glasgow and the United States* (Aberdeen, 1982). Iain McLean, *The Legend of Red Clydeside* (Edinburgh, 1982). J.S. Gibson, *The Thistle and the Crown* (Edinburgh, 1985). Henry Drucker and Gordon Brown, *Devolution and Nationalism* (Edinburgh, 1982). M. Spaven, *Fortress Scotland* (1983).
I   T. Royle, *Companion to Scottish Literature* (1983). Roderick Watson, *History of Scottish Literature* (1985). Isobel Murray and Bob Tait, *Ten Modern Scottish Novels* (Aberdeen, 1985). Douglas Gifford, *Gibbon and Gunn* (Edinburgh, 1984). Colin MacArthur, *Scotch Reels: Scotland in Cinema and Television* (1982). A.E. Boutelle, *Thistle and Rose: A Study of MacDiarmid's Poetry* (1983). D. Thomson, ed., *The Companion to Gaelic Scotland* (Oxford, 1983). C.W.J. Withers, *Gaelic in Scotland, 1689–1981* (Edinburgh, 1984). D. Daiches, ed., *A Companion to Scottish Culture* (1982). Ian Campbell, *Kailyard* (Edinburgh, 1982). Rodger Knight, *Edwin Muir, an Introduction* (1982).

Appendix to 1992 reprint

C Anthony Slaven and Sidney Checkland, eds., *Dictionary of Scottish Business Biography* (Aberdeen, 1986ff.). *Third Statistical Account* now includes *Caithness, Kincardine, Sutherland* (Edinburgh, 1988).

D The annual bibliographical and research surveys in *Scottish Economic and Social History*, from 1979 on, and in the *Scottish History Review*, are very comprehensive. The *YSG* was recast as the quarterly *Scottish Affairs* in 1992.

E Ken Cargill, ed., *Scotland 2000* (Glasgow, 1987). Christian Civardi, *Ecosse* (Paris, 1991). Bernard Crick, ed., *National Identities* (Oxford, 1991). Colin Crouch and David Marquand, ed., *The New Centralism* (Oxford, 1988). Ian Donnachie *et al.*, *The Manufacture of Scottish History* (Edinburgh, 1992). Iain Finlayson, *The Scots* (Oxford, 1988). Hamish Fraser and R.J. Morris, eds., *People and Society in Scotland, 1930-1914* (Edinburgh, 1990). Hugh Kearney, *The British Isles: a History of Four Nations* (Cambridge, 1989). Michael Keating, *State and Regional Nationalism* (Hemel Hempstead, 1988). Michael Lynch, *A History of Scotland* (London, 1991). David McCrone, ed., *The Making of Scotland: Nation, Culture and Social Change* (Edinburgh, 1989). Rosalind Mitchison, ed., *Why Scottish History Matters* (Edinburgh 1991). Kenneth O. Morgan, *The People's Peace, 1945-1990* (Oxford, 1990). Tom Nairn, *The Enchanted Glass* (London, 1988). Murray G.H. Pittock, *The Rediscovery of Scotland* (London, 1991). Roland Sturm, *Nationalismmus in Schottland und Wales* (Bochum, 1981). *The Sunday Mail History of Scotland* (Glasgow, 1988-9). Kenneth White, ed., *Ecosse* (Paris, 1988).

F William Ashworth, *The History of the British Coal Industry, Vol. 5., 1946 – 82* (Oxford, 1986). John Butt and K. Ponting, eds., *Scottish Textile History* (Aberdeen, 1987). Neil K. Buxton, *Scotland in a Rapidly-Changing World* (Edinburgh, 1986). Robert Duncan, *Steelopolis: the Making of Motherwell, c.1750-1939* (Motherwell, 1991). John Foster and Charles Woolfson, *The Politics of the UCS Work-In* (London, 1986). Peter Payne, *The Hydro* (Aberdeen, 1988). Scottish Trades Union Congress, *Scotland: a Land Fit for People* (Glasgow, 1987). T.C. Smout, ed., *Scotland and the Sea* (Edinburgh, 1992). Angela Tuckett, *The STUC: The First Eighty Years, 1987-1977* (Edinburgh, 1986). Cordula und Lothar Ulsamer, *Schottland, das Nordseeöl und die britische Wirtschaft* (Schondorf, 1991).

G Tom Begg, *50 Special Years* (Glasgow, 1987). Callum Brown, *The Social History of Religion in Scotland* (London, 1987). R.A. Cage, ed., *The Working Class in Glasgow, 1750-1914* (Glasgow, 1987). Jenni Calder, ed., *The Enterprising Scot* (Edinburgh, 1986). Tom Gallagher and Graham Walker, eds., *Sermons and Battle Hymns* (Edinburgh, 1991). G. Gordon, ed., *Perspectives of the Scottish City* (Aberdeen, 1986). W.M. Humes, *The Leadership Class in Scottish Education* (Edinburgh, 1986). Billy Kay, *Scots: The Mither Tongue* (Edinburgh, 1986). Michael Keating, *The City that Refused to Die: Glasgow* (Aberdeen, 1988). Ian Levitt, *Poverty and Welfare in Scotland, 1890-1948* (Edinburgh, 1988). G. McLachlan, ed., *Improving the Common Weal: Scottish Health Services, 1900 – 84* (Edinburgh, 1987). Andrew MacPherson and Charles Raab, *Governing Education* (Edinburgh, 1988). William Storrar, *Scottish Identity: a Christian Vision* (Edinburgh, 1990). David Thomson, *Nairn in Darkness and Light* (London, 1987).

H-Ian Donnachie *et al.*, *Forward: 100 Years of Labour Politics in Scotland* (Edinburgh, 1988). Owen Dudley Edwards, ed., *A Claim of Right for Scotland* (Edinburgh, 1988). Michael Fry, *Patronage and Principle: A Political History of Modern Scotland* (Aberdeen, 1987). Tom Gallagher, ed., *Nationalism in the Nineties* (Edinburgh, 1991). John Holford, *Reshaping Labour: Organisation, Work and Politics in Edinburgh in the Great War and After* (Beckenham, 1987). William Knox, *James Maxton* (Manchester, 1987). Roger Levy, *Scottish Nationalism at the Crossroads* (Edinburgh, 1990). James Mitchell, *Conservatives and the Union* (Edinburgh, 1990). Austen Morgan, *Ramsay MacDonald* (Manchester, 1988). Graham Walker, *Thomas*

Johnston (Manchester, 1988). G. Warner, *History of the Scottish Conservative Party* (London, 1988). Iain S. Wood, *John Wheatley* (Manchester, 1990).

I Craig Beveridge and Ronald Turnbull, *The Eclipse of Scottish Culture* (Edinburgh, 1989). Alan Bold, *Hugh MacDiarmid* (London, 1988). George Bruce, *To Foster and Enrich: the Saltire Society, 1935-85* (Edinburgh, 1988). Moira Burgess, ed., *The Other Voice: Scottish Women's Writing Since 1808* (Edinburgh, 1987). Cairns Craig, ed., *The History of Scottish Literature*, Vol. 4, *Twentieth Century* (Aberdeen, 1987). Robert Crawford and Thom Nairn, eds., *The Arts of Alasdair Gray* (Edinburgh, 1991). George Davie, *The Crisis of the Democratic Intellect: The Problem of Generalism and Specialism in Twentieth Century Scotland* (Edinburgh, 1986). William Donaldson, *Popular Literature in Victorian Scotland: Language, Fiction and the Press*, (Aberdeen, 1986). Horst Drescher, ed., *Nationalism in Literature* (Frankfurt, 1989). Susanne Hagemann, *Die schottische Renaissance*, (Frankfurt, 1992). Christopher Harvie, *Cultural Weapons: Scotland and Survival in a New Europe* (Edinburgh, 1992). David Hewitt and Michael Spiller, *Literature of the North* (Aberdeen, 1983). Ian Lockerbie, ed., *Image and Identity: Theatre and Cinema in Scotland and Quebec* (Stirling, 1988). Duncan MacMillan, *Scottish Art, 1460-1990* (Edinburgh, 1990). C. Withers, *Gaelic Scotland: The Transformation of a Culture Region* (London, 1988).

Appendix: Chronological Table

Abbreviations E: election; S: Secretary for Scotland (after 1926 Secretary of State); PM: Prime Minister; RC: Royal Commission

1906   *E Jan*. Liberal landslide: Campbell-Bannerman PM, John Sinclair S.

1908   Asquith PM: Education (Scotland) Act.

1909   'People's Budget'; crisis with Lords; miners affiliate to Labour Party.

1910   *E Jan., Dec*. Liberals continue in power, Parliament Act.

1911   Scottish Exhibition, Glasgow; Agriculture (Scotland) Act.

1912   RC on Scottish Housing set up T.P. MacKinnon Wood S. Suffragette and Labour unrest; Scottish Unionist party formed from Conservatives and Liberal Unionists.

1914   Crisis over Irish home rule, outbreak of War (4 Aug).

1915   Coalition government (May); battle of Neuve Chapelle, Loos; Labour unrest on Clyde (autumn).

1916   End of 'Red Clyde' by April; battle of Somme, July–November; Lloyd George PM (6 December), R. Munro (Coalit, Lib.) S.

1917   Report of RC on housing; Bolshevik revolution in Russia (November).

1918   *E Dec*. Education (Scotland) Act; Battle of Amiens (August); sweeping 'Coalition' (mainly Conservative) majority.

1919   40 Hours Strike (end of Jan.)

1920   Major Labour gains in Glasgow municipal elections; Communist Party of Great Britain formed.

1921   Railways Act; 'Sankey' RC on Coal recommends nationalization; 'Triple Allaince' of miners, railway, and transport workers fails (Nov.).

1922   *E Nov*. Coalition ends; sweeping Labour gains; Unionist govt: Bonar Law PM.

1923   *E Dec*. 'Chamberlain' housing act; Baldwin PM, loses support through protectionist programme; 1st Labour government: MacDonald PM, William Adamson S; BBC begins broadcasting.

1924   *E Oct*. Wheatley housing act; Labour falls; Baldwin PM: Sir J. Gilmour S.

1926   General Strike (2–9 May); miners out until November; Secretary becomes Secretary of State.

1927   Union powers restricted; National Party of Scotland founded.

1928   Women over 21 get vote; Scottish Office reorganized; boards abolished.

1929   *E May*. Fusion of Church of Scotland and UF Church; Local Government (Scotland) Act: parish councils and eductional authorities abolished. Labour govt; Macdonald PM, Adamson S. Wall Street Crash (October)

1930   Scottish National Development Council formed.

1931	*E Oct*. Macdonald forms National Government, mainly Cons. (August): Sir Archibald Sinclair (Lib.) S. Comes off gold standard (Sept.). Crushes Labour.
1932	Liberals leave government over protection; Sir Geoffrey Collins S. ILP dis affiliates from Labour Party; 'Loyalists' form Scottish Socialist Party (SSP).
1933	Hitler in power (May); Labour takes Glasgow.
1934	Scottish National Party formed; Special Areas Act.
1935	*E Nov*. Rearmament started; National govt win. Baldwin PM.
1936	Walter Elliot (Un.) S; Scottish Economic Committee formed; Abdication Crisis; Spanish Civil War; St Andrew's House opened.
1937	Hillington industrial estate started; Chamberlain PM; Barlow Commission into distribution of industry set up.
1938	Empire Exhibition, Glasgow. Films of Scotland started; John Colville (Un.) S.
1939	3 Sept. war breaks out; evacuation.
1940	Barlow RC reports; Churchill PM (May): Ernest Brown (N. Lib.) S; SSP disbanded.
1941	Tom Johnston (Lab.) S (Feb.); Clydebank blitz (March); Council of State formed (October).
1942	Council of Industry formed (May); Cooper committee into Highland power. Beveridge Report (November).
1943	North of Scotland Hydro-Electric Board set up.
1945	*E July*. SNP win Motherwell; caretaker Unionist government; Lord Rosebery (N. Lib.) S; Labour's big majority; Attlee PM; Joe Westwood S.
1946	Bank of England, civil aviation nationalized; national insurance set up; severe winter brings emergency.
1947	Coal, cables nationalized; Arthur Woodburn S; peacetime conscription introduced; first new-town schemes.
1948	National health service set up; transport nationalized; pound devalued.
1950	Labour's majority reduced to 5 (Feb.); Hector McNeil S; Korean War breaks out.
1951	Conservatives win; Churchill PM; J. Stuart S. Festival of Britain.
1953	Korean War ends. RC on Scottish Affairs reports.
1955	*E May*. Eden PM; wins election (June); STV begins broadcasting.
1956	Suez; Russian invasion of Hungary (Oct.–Nov.); split in CPGB.
1957	Macmillan PM. John Maclay S.
1958	Slump in Scottish industry.
1959	*E Oct*. Macmillan wins, but Scottish voting against govt.
1960	Toothill inquiry begun.
1961	Toothill Report; Beeching Report. Government support for industry increased; steel strip mill and motor industry move to Scotland. Michael Noble S.
1962	Scottish Development Department set up.
1963	Sir Alec Dougals-Home PM; Buchanan Report.
1964	*E Oct*. Labour wins. Wilson PM: W. Ross S.
1965	Highland Development Board set up.
1966	*E March*. Labour majority increased. 'A Plan for Scotland'.
1967	Steel nationalized; Scottish Transport Group set up. SNP wins Hamilton; oil exploration begins. Social Work (Scotland) Act.
1968	SNP successes in local elections. Crowther, later Kilbrandon RC into

Constitution set up. Conservatives back devolution; Wheatley report on local government.

1970   *E.* Conservatives win. Heath PM, Gordon Campbell S; SNP support slumps.

1971   Upper Clyde Shipbuilders crisis.

1972   Scottish Economic Planning Department set up. Local Government (Scotland) Act sets up regions and districts.

1973   Miners' strike: three-day week; Yom Kippur war causes threefold rise in oil price. Kilbrandon Report. Britain joins EEC.

1974   *2E.* Labour wins narrowly, Wilson PM, Ross S. Big SNP gains. Labour promises devolution. Labour wins first regional election.

1975   Scottish Development Agency set up. Referendum confirms EEC membership.

1976   First devolution bill; Callaghan PM; Bruce Millan S.

1977   Bill fails; Lib.–Lab. pact enables new bill in autumn. SNP success in district elections.

1978   Scotland and Wales Act (subject to referendum).

1979   *E May.* Act fails to gain 40 per cent of electorate in referendum. Conservatives win. Thatcher PM: George Younger S. Slump in SNP support.

1980   Labour success in district elections; beginning of steel industry contraction.

1981   Closure of Chrysler car factory, Linwood, and Invergordon aluminum works. Social Democrats leave Labour pary.

1982   *March – June* Falklands War; *May* some Conservative success at regional elections.

1983   *E June* Alliance makes gains from Conservatives.

1984   *March* Miners' strike begins; *June* Conservatives lose 3 European Parliament seats; Labour gains in district elections include (for the first time) Edinburgh.

1985   *March* Miners' strike ends in defeat for NUM; peak year of oil production; shipyard crisis on Clyde.

1986   Gartcosh steelworks closed. Government reshuffle. Younger becomes M. of Defence. Malcolm Rifkind S.; *May* Heavy Conservative losses in regional elections. Replacement for rates announced. *July* Commonwealth Games in Edinburgh, largely boycotted.

1987   *E June* Conservative seats fall from 21 to 10.

1988   Poll tax enacted: *July* Piper Alpha oil platform blows up in North Sea, 167 killed; *November* Jim Sillars elected for SNP at Glasgow Govan; *December* Pan-Am Jumbo jet blown up over Lockerbie, 270 dead.

1989   *March* Constitutional Convention meets in Edinburgh; peaceful revolutions throughout Eastern Europe.

1990   *June* Conservatives lose last European seats; *November* Constitutional Convention reports; Mrs Thatcher overthrown; John Major PM; Malcolm Rifkind becomes M of Transport; Iain Lang S.

1991   *Jan-April*: Gulf War, much involvement of Scottish troops; electricity boards sold off; *September* Ravenscraig steelworks: complete closure announced for autumn 1992; *November* Liberal Democrats win Kincardine by-election.

1992   *April E* Conservatives slightly improve their position to 11 seats; sharp fall in Labour support at district elections; *July*: Ravenscraig closed; *December*, European summit in Edinburgh.

Index